The Civilian Conservation Corps in Alabama, 1933–1942

The Civilian Conservation Corps in Alabama, 1933–1942

A Great and Lasting Good

Robert Pasquill Jr.

THE UNIVERSITY OF ALABAMA PRESS
Tuscaloosa

The University of Alabama Press
Tuscaloosa, Alabama 35487-0380
uapress.ua.edu

Typeface: Garamond

Cover images: Bunker Tower, Cheaha State Park, built by Co. 468, 1934–1935.
Cover design: Todd Lape / Lape Designs

The information formerly on CD can now be found at the book's page on our website.
ISBN: 978-0-8173-5926-3

A previous edition of this book has been catalogued by the Library of Congress as follows:

Library of Congress Cataloging- in- Publication Data
Pasquill, Robert G.
The Civilian Conservation Corps in Alabama, 1933–1942 : a great and lasting good /
Robert Pasquill, Jr.
p. cm.
Includes bibliographical references and index.
ISBN 978-0-8173-1621-1 (cloth : alk. paper) — ISBN 978-0-8173-5495-4 (pbk. : alk. paper) — ISBN 978-0-8173-8114-1 (electronic) 1. Civilian Conservation Corps (U.S.)—Alabama—History. I. Title.
S932.A2P37 2008
333.76'1509761—dc22

2007049491

This book is dedicated to a remarkable group of gentlemen. Over the last five years, I have had the great pleasure and honor of meeting more than 100 former members of the Civilian Conservation Corps. They are humble in the telling of their story. There was neither boasting nor bravado in their stories, just a twinkling in their eyes and, on occasion, a mischievous grin, as they recalled fond memories from a long time ago. For many years, their stories were shared just among themselves at ever-growing smaller reunions at various state parks. As their numbers have declined, their concern was that their accomplishments might be forgotten. A Great and Lasting Good *is dedicated to these wonderful gentlemen. I hope it will serve as a record of their accomplishments for future generations. The accompanying CD contains the full interviews with these remarkable men.*

This book is also dedicated to my parents: my father, Robert Sr., who was born in 1929, just months before the Great Depression, and my mother, Emily, born in March 1933, just days before the birth of the Civilian Conservation Corps.

Contents

Preface and Acknowledgments ix

Introduction 1

1. Alabama, the Great Depression, and the New Deal 3

2. The Civilian Conservation Corps in Alabama 12

3. The CCC and the National Forests in Alabama 35

4. The CCC and the Soil Conservation Service 58

5. The CCC and the Tennessee Valley Authority 81

6. The CCC and the Alabama State Parks 114

7. The CCC and State Forests, Private Forests, and Others 181

8. Summary: A Great and Lasting Good Accomplished by the CCC 214

Appendix A. CCC Camps in Alabama 217

Appendix B. CCC Camps in Alabama by Enlistment Period 222

Appendix C. CCC Camp Newspapers in Alabama 228

Bibliography 231

Index of Names 237

Index of Places 239

Index of Topics 241

Illustrations follow page 103.

Preface and Acknowledgments

The Civilian Conservation Corps, the CCC, was one of the better known New Deal programs during the Great Depression. As a child of children of the Great Depression, I grew up hearing references to "hard times." As a youth playing in the woods of New Hampshire, I saw flood control dams and other projects constructed during this era. When I began my career with the U.S. Forest Service, first in South Carolina and now in Alabama, I began to get a better appreciation for the work of the CCC. I had a responsibility to record and protect their fire towers, bridges, administrative sites, and recreational structures. Twenty-five years later, that appreciation is still growing.

In the early 1990s, I went to the National Archives with my counterparts for the national forests in South Carolina and North Carolina, Robert Morgan and Rodney Snedeker. The purpose of "the CCC Posse" was to find out what records on the CCC were available at the National Archives and what records could be retrieved to give us the best picture of what the project work and camp living conditions were like. The "Camp Inspection Reports" were the basis of much of our work. They had been recorded almost quarterly, but only one report per year appeared to be archived for each camp. While lacking in some detail for individual projects, they gave a wonderful description of the progress of work projects and camp life.

In April 2001, I decided to begin a program of public education on the CCC. It had humble beginnings. I collected a CCC mess kit knife, a hat, some photographs, a few patches, and a few other pieces of memorabilia and began reading everything I could find on the subject. My initial idea was to tell as many people as I could about the work of the CCC in the National Forests in Alabama. I had a good bit of information on their work in the National Forests. However, as the programs progressed, I was invited to speak at various state parks, to assist in research projects, and to speak to other agencies. This modest project snowballed into a statewide research project covering all CCC projects in the state. I began to acquire records for other CCC camps from the National Archives. Other researchers shared their records with me. I found that many of the CCC camp newspapers had been archived at the Center for Research Libraries at the University of Chicago, and copies of them could be obtained on microfiche. I also began reading newspapers from around the State of Alabama. The popularity of the CCC was evident in the coverage that the local newspapers gave the program from 1933 to 1942.

Since April 5, 2001, there have been more than 60 programs given on the CCC. These programs have included talks in South Carolina, Georgia, and Mississippi, and I was even a speaker for the 2003 national reunion of the National Association for CCC Alumni in Sebring, Florida. All of these programs introduced me to more people connected with the CCC. I started interviewing former enrollees of the CCC. I met many of these wonderful gentlemen at CCC reunions but did the interviews over the telephone, in some cases, over several nights. My initial idea was to get ten or so interviews conducted to add to the research. After more than 100 interviews, I realized that the interviews could be a separate book, for condensing the lives of all these men into a single chapter would give only a sentence or two to their accomplishments. It was later decided to add the complete interviews on CD. With these various actions in motion, the relatively modest public education program began to take on larger dimensions. The research focused on the Camp Inspection Reports with various attached documents, camp newspapers, local newspapers, and interviews with former enrollees.

The idea of actually writing a book about the CCC in Alabama was not mine. After giving a program at Moundville during the University of Alabama's Museum of Natural History Summer Expedition in 2001, Dr. Douglas Jones and Dr. James Knight suggested the idea. Judith Knight of the University of Alabama Press nodded in consent. Who was I to argue? I am forever indebted to them for this initial spark. Over the past five years, I have tried to record all of the people who have contributed to this project. It is a long list, and if I have left anyone out, I apologize. Many of these people have moved on to other jobs since my initial contact with them, so I will acknowledge them where they were when they contributed. They have my enduring thanks.

In addition to Robert Morgan and Rodney Snedeker, several other Forest Service coworkers have made contributions. Jeffrey LeLande of Medford, Oregon, sent information on some of the Alabama companies that were sent to Oregon. Maria L. Schleidt shared information and set me up as a speaker for a CCC reunion in Mississippi. She later spent a short time working in Alabama and managed to oversee the restoration of the Open Pond Fire Tower in the Conecuh National Forest in Alabama. Tammy Truett, National Forests in Alabama, public affairs specialist, helped with early articles when my research began.

My friends at the National Association of CCC Alumni (NACCCA) have not only contributed information to me but also published articles in their *Journal* which were of great assistance. The late Bud Schertel, editor of the *NACCCA Journal*, arranged for me to speak at the 2003 NACCCA National Reunion. Harry Dallas, researcher, and Donna Broom have always been there for support and assistance.

Gene Morris, National Archives and Records Administration, has national renown for his knowledge on the CCC records and was an amazing resource to have. My friends at the Alabama Department of Archives and History assisted in the research of the state newspapers. They also allowed me to display CCC memorabilia two consecutive summers and lined up two programs. The Alabama State University students in the reference room have moved on, but they were great help for me every Saturday for nearly two years. Special thanks to Dr. Edwin C. Bridges, Leona Stemple, Sherrie Hamil, George Jennings, and Dr. Norwood Kerr.

Other researchers who shared information with me or allowed me to assist them in their research were my friend John E. Crooms, who I continued to work with on various projects concerning Oak Mountain State Park, and Jennifer Horn, who as a graduate student at Jacksonville State University did her thesis on the CCC at Cheaha State Park and the Talladega National Forest. Judy Hamilton, University of Alabama, allowed me access to the Walter B. Jones Photograph Collection. Dr. Alfred Cornebis, professor emeritus, University of Northern Colorado, shared information on the CCC artist Marshall Davis. Charles Foster, Gretna, Louisiana, shared his story of being an artist in Camp F-1 in the Alabama National Forest and also sent me a copy of the book he worked on later as a WPA photographer. Linda Eade, at the Yosemite Research Library at Yosemite National Park, sent CCC annual information on Alabama companies that were sent out to Yosemite National Park. Pat Bernard Ezzell shared information of the CCC and the Tennessee Valley Authority. Dwight Cooley, Wheeler National Wildlife Refuge, shared information on the CCC and the Biological Survey and the National Wildlife Service. My friend and counterpart with the Natural Resources Conservation Service (formerly Soil Conservation Service), Teresa Paglione, NRSC Auburn, shared history of the

SCS (and kudzu) and lined up several talks for the East Alabama Chapter of the Alabama Archaeological Society as well as a statewide program for all NRSC employees. Randy Hale, NRSC, Troy, Alabama, shared some wonderful photographs of CCC gully restoration work in Pike County. Patricia Whigham, of Geneva County, shared photographs of Company 2421 at Camp SP-1 at Hacoda from the private collection of Mrs. Henry O'Quinn, taken by her husband who was a foreman in the camp.

Many contributions have been made by my friends at the Alabama State Parks. I continue to work with Forrest Bailey, Alabama Department of Conservation and Resources, on CCC-related projects in the state parks. Connie Roberson at Cheaha State Park has been the wonderful hostess for the CCC reunions at the park and made me feel welcome when introducing me to the former enrollees. I continue to work with Park Ranger David Odom and his staff at Cheaha State Park. Talmadge Butler and Ken Thomas, DeSoto State Park, invited me to the park for a reunion and introduced me to many former enrollees. Patsy Dixon, Chickasaw State Park, invited me to be part of a plaque dedication at the park.

Many people have worked to set up the public education programs. These programs not only helped spread word of CCC accomplishments but also introduced me to additional former CCC enrollees. Rodney Johnson, Gadsden Civic Center, and Deirdre Coakley, of the *Gadsden Times*, gave me red-carpet treatment for two programs in Gadsden, including spots on local radio talk shows. My dear friends Charles and Wylene Ebert, of Foley, Alabama, set up a program at the Baldwin County Historical Society through Devida Hasty. Charles Ebert also shared information on the transient camp at Fort Morgan. Mike Bailey, historian at Fort Morgan, shared photographs of the transient work there. Dr. Harry Holstein and Dr. Phil Koerper, Jacksonville State University, have allowed me to give three different presentations to the Coosa Valley Chapter of the Alabama Archaeological Society. Eric Douglas of Andalusia, Alabama, has made arrangements for me to speak to both the Covington County Historical Society and the Alabama Trail Hiking Society. Other individuals have set up programs at various Alabama county historical societies. Forgive me if I left your name out. Please remember I'm always available to talk to county historical societies.

Several individuals have sent me pieces of CCC memorabilia connected with their families. Gary White, Double Springs, provided a photograph of CCC Camp F-5, which was located on land owned by his grandfather. The Carl Carlson Family gave me photographs of Camp F-2 and a 1935 Thanksgiving menu. Jay Hudson of Sylacauga sent me a photograph of Camp F-2 and a fantastic fall photograph of the CCC bridge at Hubbard Creek. John Wilson of Houston, Alabama, shared his story of his time at Camp F-3 as well as a photograph of the camp. Doug Pearson, of the *Jasper Mountain Eagle*, loaned me a copy of the 1936 District "D" annual until I could get my own copy.

Many more individuals shared their fathers and grandfathers with me. Those stories, too valuable to condense into a small chapter, are included as Appendix D on the accompanying CD. While only a fraction of those interviewed are mentioned in the text, all of the stories have contributed to a better understanding in the writing of this book.

Finally, I want to thank again and again the gentlemen who served in the Civilian Conservation Corps. When I enjoy the National Forests in Alabama, Alabama's state parks, the open waterways of north Alabama, the natural resources of the state, and the produce grown in its topsoil, I will always give thanks to the contributions of these men between 1933 and 1942. They have been referred to by many names, from "Roosevelt's Tree Army" to "The Forgotten Soldiers." Their work is still quite visible once you know where to look, whether in a terraced field, a stone structure in a state park, or a majestic fire tower standing tall over the pines. It is my sincere wish that their accomplishments, their "Great and Lasting Good," will not be forgotten.

Introduction

The Civilian Conservation Corps was one of many programs created by President Franklin Delano Roosevelt's New Deal. President Roosevelt addressed Congress on March 21, 1933, asking for a program to put men to work on natural resource projects. He proposed "to create a civilian conservation corps to be used in simple work, not interfering with normal employment, and confining itself to forestry, the preservation or soil erosion, flood control and similar projects." Roosevelt recognized that working for a wage was preferred to a handout. He could also take the unemployed out of unhealthy surroundings and improve their spiritual and physical health: "We can eliminate to some extent at least the threat that enforced idleness brings to spiritual and moral stability. It is not a panacea for all unemployed but it is an essential step in this emergency" (Watkins 1999:158).

On March 31, 1933, Congress passed the Emergency Conservation Work Act. President Roosevelt signed the executive order establishing the agency of Emergency Conservation Work on April 5; six weeks later, the Emergency Unemployment Relief Act was passed and $500 million was appropriated (Watkins 1999:159).

By the summer of 1933, the New Deal consisted of several new agencies. They were referred to as the "Alphabet Agencies" as they were reduced to acronyms. The confusion between the alphabet agencies is problematic today, as it was during the depression era. Many of the programs had overlapping responsibilities and served the same function from different funding sources. This overlap was part of Roosevelt's organizational style: "The very ambiguity of his scheme of organization—the overlapping jurisdictions and duplicated responsibilities—made flexibility easy. If things started to go bad, he could reshuffle people and functions with speed which would be impossible in a government of clear cut assignments and rigid chain of command" (Schlesinger 1958:531–32).

The Civilian Conservation Corps (CCC) was the popular name of the Emergency Conservation Work program. The Civilian Conservation Corps became official after the passing of the Civilian Conservation Act in April 1937 (Cohen 1980:6–7). It is often confused with similar programs, such as the Agricultural Adjustment Administration (AAA), the Public Works Administration (PWA), the Civil Works Administration (CWA), the Resettlement Administration (RA), the Works Progress Administration (WPA), and the National Youth Administration (NYA). In Alabama, all of these programs provided jobs to the unemployed. In some projects, the CCC enrollees worked alongside WPA laborers. The CCC was an independent agency from its creation in 1933 until July 1, 1939, when it was placed under the newly created Federal Security Agency (Lacy 1976:199). In November 1941, the CCC was consolidated with the National Youth Administration.

The Civilian Conservation Corps was officially ended on July 1, 1942. Between 1933 and 1942, Alabama averaged 30 camps. The CCC provided jobs for over 66,000 unemployed, including the enrollees and the technical and military personnel in the camps. The money sent home by the enrollees helped many Alabama families survive the Great Depression. It gave many young Alabamians opportunities to improve their education and to learn a trade. The CCC in Alabama built improvements at state parks, national forests, and parks on TVA land. They checked erosion on gullied land across the state and protected Alabama's forest resources.

1
Alabama, the Great Depression, and the New Deal

The Great Depression was the worst economic collapse of the twentieth century and, arguably, one of the worst in the history of the United States. Its causes can be found in the post–World War I markets and the prosperity of the 1920s. It has also been explained as a naturally occurring phenomenon, compared to the weather, with natural cycles (McElvaine 1993:26–29).

By 1932, unemployment was nearing 13 million people. One to two million were wandering across the country looking for work (Leuchtenburg 1963:1–2). A quarter of a million had lost their homes because of debt by 1932. During the first half of 1933, more than 1,000 homes were being foreclosed each day (Leuchtenburg 1963:53). By the end of the Hoover administration, more than 15 million workers had lost their jobs (Leuchtenburg 1963:19).

The State of Alabama was in financial trouble even before the country was feeling the effects of the Great Depression. The state budget was out of balance in 1927. The great flood of March 1929 in southern Alabama added to the financial disaster before the crash of the stock market on Wall Street. Between 1929 and 1931, a total of 63 banks failed in Alabama with a total loss of more than $16 million (WPA 2000:57). The *United States Census of 1930* recorded Alabama's population at over 2.6 million people. Robert D. Gunnels, in his master's thesis "The Civilian Conservation Corps in Alabama," wrote that there were just over 2 million persons ten years and older in Alabama in 1929. Of this number, 1.25 million were white and 750,000 were African-American. Only 51 percent of the entire Alabama population was employed full-time (Gunnels 1990:2). Based on the 1930 census, the number of wage earners in Alabama included 772,281 men, 254,014 women, and 89,920 children between the ages of ten and sixteen. Of a total 1.1 million wage earners in Alabama, approximately half were employed in agriculture (WPA 2000:73).

In Alabama in 1937, the two leading industries were woven cotton goods and blast furnace products (WPA 2000:58). Steel plants had fallen from 90 percent capacity in 1929 to only 26 percent in 1930 (Gunnels 1990:2). By the end of 1932, the steel industry nationwide was operating at only 12 percent of capacity, and there was no sign of any improvement (Leuchtenburg 1963:1).

Unemployment meant more than just the loss of income; it meant loss of pride and identity. For thousands there was little choice other than to go to the relief office. An Alabama lumberman was quoted as saying "It took me a month. I used to go down there every day or so and walk past the place again and again." An engineer from Birmingham was quoted as saying "I simply had to murder my pride" (Leuchtenburg 1963:120).

The situation in agriculture was no better. The net income of farmers across the nation in 1932 was less than one-third what it had been in 1929. Farm prices had fallen more than 50 percent (Schlesinger 1958:28). From 1910 to 1928, the mortgage debt on the plantations of the seven cotton states had nearly quadrupled. Increases in mortgage debt from 1920 to 1928 were proportionately higher in the South than in any other section of the country (WPA 1936:xxv).

The standard of living for Alabama's tenant farmers was low. Their houses were usually two-room shanties, poorly constructed of the lowest grade lumber. They rarely had sanitary facilities of any kind and almost never running water. The diet of the tenant farmer consisted of fat pork, beans, molasses, and cornbread, a monotonous diet deficient in both quality and quantity. "Pellegra [was] in effect, an occupational disease of the sharecropper and his family" (WPA 2000:82). In late 1936, Secretary of Agriculture Henry Wallace traveled through the southern cotton states. Upon his return, he wrote that the southern sharecropper lived in worse poverty than the peasantry of Europe and that the city people of the United States should be ashamed (Schlesinger 1958:376).

Cotton production dropped between 1915 and 1920 because of the presence of the boll weevil. While the effect was temporary, it created an exodus of workers. Between 1915 and 1929, hundreds of thousands of tenant farmers moved out of the cotton counties to industrial centers. The financial disorganization of 1928–29 forced hundreds more planters out of production and more tenants out of agriculture. The southern cotton growers recovered by the early 1930s but overproduced until the price of cotton fell to a point below the cost of production, forcing many marginal producers into bankruptcy (WPA 1936:38–40).

While Alabama's farmers survived the boll weevil, the severe erosion throughout the state was another matter. It was estimated in 1935 that nearly one million acres of farmland in Alabama were useless owing to erosion. Seventy-six percent of the state had suffered the effects of erosion. In one central region across the state, more than 500,000 acres of land, formerly under cultivation, had had its fertility destroyed. Individual landowners had begun a program of soil conservation under the advice of the U.S. Department of Agriculture and the Alabama Department of Agriculture. However, a 1931 study on erosion control by terracing reported that only 151,000 acres were being protected by this method (WPA 1936:24–25).

The southeastern cotton states had a relatively high rural relief rate in 1933 compared to other regions. After the beginning of the Agricultural Adjustment Administration, one of the early New Deal programs, the price of cotton increased and brought some relief to farmers still in cotton agriculture. This lowered the relief rate, but it was also lowered because plantation owners coerced their tenants not to apply for relief. The owners thought it was bad for morale. During 1934, plantation families with relief history received aid for only 3½ months (WPA 1936:xxx).

Between January 1, 1933, and June 30, 1935, one in every ten plantation families in the Muscles Shoals, Upper Piedmont, and two Black Belt cotton-growing regions of Alabama had been on relief (WPA 1936:161). Per capita expenditures for emergency relief were generally lower in the southern states than in other regions. Between January 1933 and September 1935, more than $287 million was expended for emergency relief in the seven southeastern cotton states. Alabama was on the low end, with an expenditure of only $7.25 per capita (WPA 1936:239).

The Alabama Relief Administration, established in 1932, had provided some relief to Alabama's poor, but its funds were limited. In addition, many rural southerners were too proud to apply for the limited relief offered. President Roosevelt's New Deal gave hope to the people of the nation. He referred to the South as "the nation's number one economic problem" in *The Report on Economic Conditions in the South* (Horn 2002:5). Alabama was $18 million in debt when the federal government called for states to create relief programs. "At a time when its citizens needed help the most, the state was least able to provide it" (Gunnels 1990:2). The *Florala News* reported on June 29, 1933, that after many questions by the state legislature and several audits, it was determined that as of October 1, 1932, Alabama was $19 million in debt.

The Alabama Relief Administration was created by official proclamation of the governor on December 31, 1932. In addition to having responsibility for direct relief cases, it was responsible for several projects, including rural rehabilitation of farms, transient relief, food preservation programs, distribution of surplus commodities, self-help cooperatives, college research projects, and receiving and handling of cattle from drought-stricken states. It would also be responsible for selecting youths eligible for the Civilian Conservation Corps (Alabama Relief Administration 1935:1–8). Thad Holt was the director of the program.

The Federal Emergency Relief Act was passed on May 12, 1933. The Federal Emergency Relief Administration (FERA) was initially appropriated $500 million, with half of this amount to be matched—one dollar of federal funds for every three dollars of state money spent during the three preceding months (Schlesinger 1958:267). Harry Hopkins was the director. The *Montgomery Advertiser* reported on July 4, 1933, that Alabama was to receive a grant of $588,142 based on the amount of expenditures over the previous three months. Alabama had previously received $522,962 in relief grants, thus having a total of over $1.1 million.

Between January 1933 and September 1935, obligations incurred in Alabama for emergency relief totaled $45.6 million. Of this figure, $43.3 million was from federal emergency funds. Only $163,742 came from state funds and another $2.1 million from local funds (WPA 1936:239).

The *Shelby County Democrat* reported on July 12, 1934, that Alabama was one of the states showing the greatest progress in rural rehabilitation work among destitute farm families. The state had 5,942 farm families under the rural rehabilitation program at that time. On December 21, 1934, the *Tuscaloosa News* reported that Thad Holt, the Alabama state relief director, had announced plans for taking the transients out of the cities and placing them on construction projects under conditions similar to those in the Civilian Conservation Corps camps. According to Holt, there were 2,000 transients drifting into Alabama each week, seeking meals and shelter at transient bureaus. Camps were established at Fort Morgan to work on the highway between the fort and Gulf Shores, near Centreville to work on the fish hatchery at Marion, and at Montgomery and Fort McClellan in Anniston.

On May 12, 1933, the Agricultural Adjustment Administration (AAA) was created under the Department of Agriculture (Watkins 1999:36). A cotton reduction program called for the withdrawal of more than 10 million acres from cultivation (Watkins 1999:380). The *Montgomery Advertiser* reported on July 4, 1933, that Alabama farmers were to destroy 988,000 acres of cotton. More than 60,000 Alabama cotton growers cooperated with the program.

Between 1933 and 1936, the AAA increased farm income in Alabama by $35.9 million in benefit payments. Thousands of farmers were able to reduce long-standing debts from 1929. The value of the farmland, however, depreciated from an average of $28 per acre to $19 per acre in 1935 (WPA 2000:82). The AAA was ruled unconstitutional by the Supreme Court in January 1936 (Leuchtenburg 1963:170). The program was criticized for indirectly displacing tenant and sharecropper families and not ensuring that the benefits reached these families.

The Public Works Administration (PWA) was established by Title II of the National Industrial Recovery Act on June 16, 1933, with Harold L. Ickes as its director. The PWA could initiate its own projects as a construction agency or make allotments to other federal agencies for construction projects. It could either loan or grant money to the states and other public entities for nonfederal construction projects. The object of the PWA, according to Ickes, was to "beautify the national estate through the honest building of durable public monuments" (Schlesinger 1958:282–84). The PWA built roads, highways, sewage systems, gas plants, electric power plants, schools and courthouses, jails, dams, and canals. It had begun to rebuild the navy and assisted in the modernization and mechanization of the army, until Congress forbade the use of PWA funds "for munitions, warships, or military or naval material" (Schlesinger 1958:287–88).

On October 19, 1933, the *Montgomery Advertiser* announced that Alabama had been assigned an allotment of $12 million for road construction projects under the PWA. *The Onlooker*, the weekly newspaper of Baldwin County, reported, however, on December 7, that the PWA relief for Alabama had failed to materialize. The causes for the delay were identified in part: $400 million had been taken from the PWA and given to the newly created Civil Works Administration, and there were not enough engineers in Montgomery for the projects.

On August 22, 1935, the *Ashland Progress* reported that the federal government would provide 45 percent of the total construction cost for several schools in Clay County. The money was to be borrowed at a low interest rate over 20 to 25 years. The *Florence Herald* announced on June 5, 1936, that the State Public Works Administration had approved construction of 43 cold storage units in the Tennessee Valley to be financed through the PWA or the Rural Electrification Administration. The total of PWA loans and grants was over $600,000.

By 1939, when the PWA was phased out and placed in the Federal Works Agency, there had been at least one PWA project in all but three counties across the nation. By 1935, the PWA claimed to be providing an average of 500,000 jobs per year. Harold Ickes figured the PWA had kept approximately 2 million people at productive work (Watkins 1999:244–245).

By late fall 1933, there were 1.9 million people on work-relief jobs through the Federal Emergency Relief Administration (FERA). In order to provide another 4 million people employment through the winter, President Roosevelt created the Civil Works Administration (CWA) by executive order on November 8, 1933 (Watkins 1999:178). With $400 million from the PWA, the CWA would be confined to "projects of a minor character." Participants would work up to 30 hours per week and be paid at the wage scale set up in the public works program (Ickes 1953:119–20).

On November 24, 1933, the *Gadsden Times* reported that 33,026 men and women in Alabama were to be switched from relief rolls to public construction payrolls and would be receiving their first paychecks from the CWA. Thad Holt, director of the CWA in Alabama, reported that the men and women were from 67 different counties. He hoped to assign people to the state's quota of 81,000 jobs before December 2.

The CWA helped the country get through the winter of 1933–34, but when the president saw the costs, he ended the program. He also feared the program was creating a class of workers that would never be able to get off the government payroll. He did not want the CWA to become a habit by continuing it through the summer. He told his advisors that nobody was going to starve in the warm weather (Leuchtenburg 1963:122).

The CWA ended on April 1, 1934. *The Onlooker* reported on April 5 that the CWA had brought more than $14 million into Alabama and employed approximately 175,000 people. Director Thad Holt stated that CWA checks had gone to "every place in the state where people live." At its peak, there were 119,722 men and 6,406 women on the payroll. Holt had received national recognition for the success of the CWA in Alabama, and Washington officials frequently pointed to Alabama as a model.

By January 1935, the depression was in its fifth year, and more people were being added to the relief rolls every day. In the State of the Union Message, Roosevelt announced plans to get rid of the Federal Emergency Relief Administration and reorganize the public works programs. The spring of 1935 witnessed the creation of another "cornucopia of alphabet agencies" (Leuchtenburg 1963:161–63). On April 8, 1935, Roosevelt signed the Emergency Relief Appropriation Act of 1935 (Watkins 1999:259). Executive orders created the Resettlement Administration and the Works Progress Administration.

The Resettlement Administration (RA) was created on April 30, 1935. Rex Tugwell, undersecretary of the Department of Agriculture, was its director. The RA's duties consisted of administering projects involving destitute or low-income families from rural and urban areas; initiating and administering a program of projects with respect to soil erosion, stream pollution, seacoast erosion, reforestation, and flood control; and making loans as authorized under the Emergency Relief Appropriation Act of 1935 (Resettlement Administration 1936:1).

The RA land development projects, dealing with erosion control and reforestation, were similar to those of the Civilian Conservation Corps, and often the two programs are confused. In Alabama, there were four land development projects: the Tuskegee Land Development Project (now the Tuskegee National Forest), the West Alabama Planned Development Project (now the western half of the Oakmulgee Division of the Talladega National Forest), the Pea River Planned Development Project (now part of Fort Rucker), and the Oak Mountain Planned Development Project (now part of Oak Mountain State Park). Congress passed the Bankhead-Jones Farm Tenancy Act in the summer of 1937. Secretary of Agriculture Henry Wallace terminated the Resettlement Administration and created the Farm Security Administration (FSA) to take over the same responsibilities. The programs never received enough funding and were never able to help more than a small percentage of sharecroppers and tenants. The strong political power of southern plantation owners was more than the administration or the Department of Agriculture could challenge (Watkins 1999:389).

The Works Progress Administration (WPA) was created on May 6, 1935. Harry Hopkins, former director of the Federal Emergency Relief Administration, headed the agency. WPA workers built or repaired highways, streets, roads, and culverts. They laid sidewalks, restored public libraries, schools, auditoriums, stadiums, and other public buildings and built playgrounds and athletic fields, parks, fairgrounds, and rodeo grounds. They built and repaired airports, dug municipal swimming pools, built and repaired sewage treatment plants, built bridges and viaducts over gullies, creeks, and rivers, and laid sewer lines. There was not a city or county in the United States that did not benefit from the WPA (Watkins 1999:262–63).

The *Shelby County Democrat* reported on September 26, 1935, that the first of four proposed camps for "idle women" had been established at Fairhope in Baldwin County. Mrs. Francis B. Stephenson, assistant director of women's projects for the WPA, stated that the camp was established for 70 young women between sixteen and twenty-two selected from relief rolls in Montgomery, Jefferson, Escambia, and Conecuh counties. It was to provide instructions in crafts and woodworking, recreation and health study, folk dancing, physical education, and other activities. The country club house was to serve as a dormitory. If the camp was successful, others were to follow.

The *Shelby County Democrat* reported on October 17, 1935, that Governor Bibb Graves had announced approval of another $2.5 million for WPA projects in Alabama. On April 16, 1936, it reported that an additional 1,000 men would be going to work at the new park at Oak Mountain being developed by the Park Service. They were to be selected by the National Reemployment Service from the WPA rolls.

By 1941, there were more than 30 airfields in Alabama, most of them constructed with federal work relief funds. The WPA spent more than $2 million on construction and improvements of existing airfields in Alabama (WPA 2000:93).

The National Youth Administration (NYA) was a subsidiary of the WPA, designed for people too young or otherwise unqualified for WPA programs (Watkins 1999:267). Its director was Aubrey Williams from Alabama, an aide to Harry Hopkins in FERA (Leuchtenburg 1963:129). Individuals on relief between eighteen and twenty-five who were out of school could work up to 75 hours and earn up to $25 a month. Ninety percent of these participants worked out of their homes. In rural areas, many participants lived in residence centers. They were placed in jobs with local businesses and in municipal and county offices and given vocational training. Participants in school could work three hours a day, seven hours on Saturday, and earn up to $6 a month. College students could work up to an eight-hour day but were limited to earning $20 per month. Graduate students could earn up to $40 per month. Students' work, usually clerical, was for government agencies and businesses. By March 1938, more than 480,000 young people were employed in NYA programs (Watkins 1999:270).

According to Eugene King of Haleyville, Alabama, by 1939 the NYA had become more popular than the CCC. The National Youth Administration placed a greater emphasis on education and offered more classes. Another factor favoring the NYA when Mr. King enrolled at the age of twenty was that the NYA was a coeducational program. He worked at the abandoned CCC camp at Kinlock learning carpentry (Eugene King interview, June 6, 2001; see the CD).

Earl Bray of Wing, Alabama, enrolled in the NYA in 1940 in Brewton, Alabama, at the age of fourteen or fifteen. His older brothers had been in the CCC in California and Mississippi in 1938. He worked two weeks and earned $12 a month at a woodworking shop at the Neal School in East Brewton. He was able to continue going to school while learning a trade (Earl Bray interview, March 25, 2004; see the CD).

Before its end in 1943, the NYA had employed an estimated two million people and maintained an excellent reputation throughout its existence. Unlike some of the New Deal programs, the NYA was never charged with racism. Aubrey Williams was committed to the pursuit of equal rights for African-Americans and had full support from Mrs. Roosevelt. Williams appointed Mary McLeod Bethune as the director of the NYA's Division of Negro Affairs (Watkins 1999:259–61).

In the fall of 1939, the president and Congress shifted their focus to the pending threat of war rather than the struggle to overcome the Great Depression (Watkins 1999:511). The *Dothan Eagle* reported on October 26, 1939, that the steel and iron mills in Birmingham were running at capacity and had hired an additional 15,000 employees. Because of the war in Europe, the mills had surpassed their World War I production. The *Dothan Eagle* reported on March 28, 1940, however, that there were still 9 to 12 million people unemployed.

While the economy was slow to respond to the orders for war matériel, the general public sensed by the end of 1940 that the war had put an end to the Great Depression (Leuchtenburg 1963:318–19). On October 3, 1940, the *Evergreen Courant* reported that during August 1940 many industrial improvements had been made in Alabama. The War Department had approved the location of a $6 million ammunitions plant in Gadsden-Attilla area. The plant would make machine shells for the army and employ 1,000 workers. A flour mill was to be built in Decatur. Investments were being made to increase production of the Aluminum Ore Company plant in Mobile, the Piedmont Brick Company near Maxwellborn, and the Republic Steel Corporation in Gadsden.

While the New Deal addressed many of the problems of the depression, it was not able to achieve prosperity in peacetime. There were still 6 million unemployed in 1941. It was not until 1943, two years after the United States entered the war, that the "army of jobless finally disappeared" (Leuchtenburg 1963:346–47). Mrs. Roosevelt, addressing the National Youth Congress in February 1939, stated that the New Deal could not solve the problems of the depression, saying that the New Deal and the federal government had helped but had not solved the fundamental problems. Mrs. Roosevelt said she never thought the federal government could solve the whole problem, but "it gave us time to think" (Leuchtenburg 1963:347–48).

2
The Civilian Conservation Corps in Alabama

On March 9, 1933, President Roosevelt met with the secretaries of war, interior, and agriculture; the director of the budget; the Solicitor of the Department of Interior; and the judge advocate general of the army. He proposed to put 500,000 men from cities and towns into the woods to plant trees, reduce fire hazards, clear streams, and check erosion. Each of the six men at the meeting had been chosen for specific reasons. The Departments of Interior and Agriculture were in charge of the national parks and national forests. The Department of War was the only organization that could enroll, feed, clothe, and transport men and supervise the camps. Money was needed, and a bill would have to be drafted, hence the need for the director of the budget, the solicitor of the Department of Interior, and the judge advocate of the army. In five hours, a bill was presented to the president. Changes were made, and one hour later the draft was retyped and presented to congressional leaders (Hoyt 1935:7–9). The speed with which the bill was drafted is important to keep in mind. Over the next nine years, many of the minor elements of the Civilian Conservation Corps would change.

On March 21, 1933, the *Gadsden Times* reported that a bill had been introduced to create a civilian conservation corps that would put 250,000 men to work by the summer. On March 23, the paper reported that the objections to the $30 per month wage had been addressed by Secretary of Labor Frances Perkins. She told the congressional committee that this was not an employment plan but a reforestation program to afford relief to the unemployed. Major R. Y. Stuart, chief of the Forest Service, asked for an amendment to the plan so that the work would be conducted on private as well as public land. On March 24, the paper reported that William Green, president of the American Federation of Labor, stated that the reforestation program "smacked of Fascism, Hitlerism and a form of Sovietism" when he appeared before a joint session of the House and Senate. He saw no need for military control, saying that the plan "violates the very spirit of volunteerism and freedom of personal action." General Douglas MacArthur, chief of staff of the army, had appeared, denying the bill was a "draft act" and that men would be picked off of the streets and forced into camps.

A second important amendment to the bill was proposed by Oscar De Priest, Republican congressman from Illinois and the only African-American member of Congress. He proposed that in the selection of the enrollees, there be no discrimination based on race, color, or creed (Lacy 1976:29).

Possibly in a move of conciliation to William Green, the president chose Robert Fechner, vice president of the International Association of Machinists, to be director of the reforestation program (Watkins 1999:161). Roosevelt appointed an advisory board of representatives from the Departments of Labor, War, Interior, and Agriculture. The board, with Fechner as its head, would work out the logistics of enrollment, supply, transportation, equipment, and discipline (Hoyt 1935:19–20)

The *Gadsden Times* reported on March 31 that the president had signed the Emergency Conservation Work Act. The enlistment of thousands of men from the jobless rolls in big cities had begun. The men would be paid $30 per month plus food and subsistence. Forest Service Chief R. Y. Stuart was meeting with state foresters and regional foresters of the U.S. Forest Service to plan projects, and he would also meet with private landowners. With the majority of the national forests in the West and most of the men in the East, the logistics of transporting men across the country had to be worked out. As there were only 6 million acres of national forest east of the Mississippi River, the cooperative projects on private land were critical.

On April 2, 1933, the *Montgomery Advertiser* reported that Colonel Page S. Bunker, the state forester, had submitted his reforestation plans to Washington. Projects in Alabama could employ an estimated 20,000 men and included construction of roads to Cheaha State Park on Cheaha Mountain, to the top of Flagg Mountain in Weogufka State Park, and one going into St. Stephens State Park; the development of Sumter State Park; and the construction of additional camping sites for tourists. Projects were proposed for all 13 state forests and 7 state parks

On April 6, the *Moulton Advertiser* reported that Representative Edward B. Almon from Lawrence County had discussed the reforestation program with the president. Representatives Almon and Bankhead had asked Forest Service Chief Stuart to establish camps in the Alabama National Forest for forestry and soil conservation.

The *Gadsden Times* reported on April 7 that, as the forestry conservation corps began their mobilization, the needs of the "Forest Corps" from hats to toothpaste would be met. Each man was to be issued army clothing while in the conditioning camp, consisting of an olive drab jacket and slacks (OD's), a work suit of denim, socks, shoes, a work hat, other miscellaneous clothing, and two blankets. Toiletries and mess kits were also supplied. Each recruit agreed to send $22 to $25 of the monthly allotment of $30 home to a dependent. According to Director Fechner, the remainder would be sufficient to meet the needs for spending money.

Each camp was to have approximately 200 men, housed in tents provided by the army. Work equipment was to be furnished by the Forest Service, the Park Service, the War Department, and the states in cases where the work was planned on state or private land. Transportation was provided by the army under the direction of the corps area commanders. The Red Cross, the YMCA, the Knights of Columbus, and other organizations planned to provide entertainment and welfare programs in the camps. The camps averaged 24 buildings, including kitchen and mess hall, recreation building, school building, infirmary, barracks for the enrollees, and quarters for the military and technical staff. In the beginning, most of the camps used army tents, with six men to a tent. Later, barracks were built, accommodating 40 to 50 men each. Meals were served outdoors in mess kits until mess halls were constructed (Cohen 1980:25–26).

The *Montgomery Advertiser* reported on April 10, 1933, that Thad Holt, director of the Alabama Relief Administration, had announced that the state had a quota of 5,000 recruits. "Junior" enrollees, unemployed, unmarried men between eighteen and twenty-five with family members on relief rolls, were selected first for emergency conservation work. The law required that the recruits be citizens, and they had to agree to send a substantial portion of their allowance to their families. A "relatively small number" of unemployed men of suitable age and experience were to be selected from relief rolls in the areas of the camps. These "local experienced men" (LEMs) would be "useful in the project and peculiarly entitled to share its advantages."

After selection, the men were sent to the nearest army recruiting station to receive medical examinations. Those found "apparently fit" were sent to an army camp to receive a final physical and be formally enrolled. Fort McClellan, District D headquarters, was selected in Alabama for this function. The men began earning their allowance after enrollment. The men spent ten days in a conditioning camp before being sent to the working camps. One of the most important aspects of the conditioning camp was to overcome any cases of malnutrition. According to Director Fechner, one of the chief objects of the conditioning camps was to "feed 'em up." Many of the enrollees had been without a balanced diet for some time.

The War Department had divided the country into nine corps areas. The Fourth Corps Area was nade up of southeastern states (Cohen 1980:25). On April 30, 1933, the *Montgomery Adviser* reported that 3,000 men were to arrive at the eight army posts in the Fourth Corps Area the following day. Men were arriving at the rate of 1,000 a day at Fort Barrancas, Florida; Fort McClellan, Alabama; Fort Bragg, North Carolina; Fort Screven, Georgia; Fort Benning, Georgia; Fort Oglethorpe, Georgia; Fort McPherson, Georgia (also Fourth Corps Area HQ); and Fort Moultrie, South Carolina. On May 18, 1933, *The Onlooker*, the weekly newspaper of Baldwin County, reported that the Fourth Corps Area had a quota of 38,000 recruits to be filled by June 7. The War Department had given authority to the corps area commanders to assign at least half of the U.S. Army's 12,000 regular officers to the reforestation program. Reserve officers would be assigned as medical officers and chaplains.

The *Montgomery Advertiser* reported on May 21 that Colonel Page Bunker, state forester, had received word that Alabama had been allocated four state forest projects consisting of 210,000 acres and creating jobs for 848 young men. Approximately 212 men were to be assigned to each camp, located in Mobile County near Oak Grove, Geneva State Park, along the Calhoun and Cleburne County line, and in Walker County near Jasper. It was too late in the season for tree planting. The work was to consist of road building, construction of firebreaks and of telephone lines, forest fire hazard reduction, fire prevention and suppression, and timber improvement. Army officers were to select the camp locations and oversee their construction. Three officers would run each camp. Colonel Bunker was in charge of the forest work.

Although the amendment had been added to ensure enrollees were selected without discrimination based on race, color, or creed, for the most part the camps were segregated, and the recruitment quotas were race specific. The *Montgomery Advertiser* reported on May 21, 1933, that the first group of African-American enrollees selected from Alabama had left Montgomery by train for Fort Benning. The 100 applicants were from Montgomery, Coosa, Tallapoosa, Marengo, Macon, Elmore, Dallas, Bullock, Covington, Lowndes, Chambers, Lee, and Russell counties. Additional examinations were scheduled the following week for both white and black applicants. Those accepted would be sent to conditioning camps by train each day.

On June 1, the *Moulton Advertiser* announced that the CCC companies had arrived in the Alabama National Forest. The people of Moulton were anxious to visit the camps. Newspapers and magazines had been collected for the camps, and local churches sent cars to the camps to bring the enrollees to Sunday services. Enrollees were invited to homes for Sunday dinner. Alabama was expected to fill its quota for the first enrollment period by June 5. Each enrollment period was six months, and enrollees were expected to work the full six months. By May 24, 1933, Alabama had sent 2,400 boys to the CCC camps. The payroll for Alabama had been $165,000. Out of this amount, $120,000 had been sent home to dependents of the enrollees.

On June 2, the *Montgomery Advertiser* announced that another eight state forestry camps had been approved for Alabama, creating jobs for another 1,696 men and covering another million acres in 10 counties. On June 9, the *Gadsden Times* reported that there were 5,299 young Alabamians at three army posts being conditioned for the 14 reforestation camps to be established in Alabama. Colonel Page Bunker planned to select 225 experienced foresters to assist 78 federal foresters at the camps. A captain and two lieutenants would be at each camp. There would also be 550 veterans in the camps to "assist in the routine of camp life." On June 8, 1933, *The Onlooker* reported that war veterans were to be given the chance to earn a dollar a day at the CCC camps. The veterans were to come from 67 counties. Seven percent of the veterans were to be those that served before the world war; the remaining 93 percent were to be veterans of the war.

On May 11, 1933, President Roosevelt had authorized by executive order inclusion of the veterans into the CCC, with a special enrollment of 25,000 veterans (Watkins 1999:162). Initially, Alabama's veterans from World War I and the Spanish-American War were selected to serve in the camps as role models in the junior camps. By mid-July 1933, three veteran companies were established: Company 2423 at Camp P-57 at Glencoe; Company 2420 at Camp P-60 at Chatom; and Company 2421 and Camp SP-1 at Hacoda.

Alabama's Camps Are Established

On June 22, 1933, the *Florala News* reported that State Forester Bunker's office was receiving hundreds of letters each day related to the president's reforestation program. Most of the letters regarded employment, but there were also requests for camps in various parts of the state and suggestions for projects and offers of assistance and cooperation from "numerous public spirited persons."

On June 29, the *Florala News* reported that the president had amended the regulations regarding the pay of the reforestation workers. Up to 5 percent of the authorized company strength was to be assigned as "leaders" earning $45 per month and 8 percent as "assistant leaders" earning $36. The company commander and project superintendent were to make the selections. A disciplinary system was also to be initiated; hearings would be held for offenses meriting attention by the rules of evidence. Records were to be kept on findings and penalties. Director Fechner thought the disciplinary system and increased wage scale allowances would be good for morale.

The *Florala News* also reported on June 29 that Thad Holt, director of the Alabama Relief Administration, had announced that the Reconstruction Finance Corporation was sending $2,000 each week to laundries and washerwomen to cover the cost of laundry of the men in Alabama's reforestation program. Feeding the CCC woodsmen cost $1,500 each day; if practical, all of the food was purchased within the state. Every six months, the parents and dependents of the enrollees were receiving $825,000. "This money does not miss a single crossroad." Another $165,000 was spent each month on the enrollees for housing, food, and clothing. The $5.00 an enrollee received each month was spent on "gum, cigarettes, and knickknacks, all of which he spends with the merchants of the nearby towns."

In the July 20, 1933, edition of the *Florala News*, State Forester Bunker clarified that the forestry program could work on private land if the work put the land into condition for increased and continuous timber production. This work included construction of firebreaks, observation towers, truck trails, telephone lines, emergency fire control, landing fields, and protective structures such as cabins and tool sheds. Reduction of fire hazards, control of insect epidemics, suppression of forest fires, and the control of erosion were also authorized. Private landowners could make applications at the CCC camps. The landowners were to use every effort to maintain and continue the work by the CCC.

The *Montgomery Advertiser* announced on August 20 that all of Alabama's forestry camps were in full operating condition with full quotas of men and were beginning project work. The housing, feeding, and sanitation needs of a 200-man camp were a tremendous challenge. Quarters had to be winterized for the colder months but also had to be comfortable during the summer. Mess halls had to be constructed. The water supply for drinking and bathing had to be carefully inspected. Wells would be needed for the drier months.

The camp establishment period was over, and the enrollment personnel were being turned over to their forestry supervisors for project work. Out of the 200 men, 25 would remain in camp for headquarters purposes. The men were enthusiastic in their work, and daily accomplishments were steadily increasing. The work was entirely new to to most enrollees, especially fire fighting. The progress reports coming into the state forester's office were encouraging. Not only was the work beneficial to the forestry of the state, but it was increasing enrollees' knowledge of the science and art of forestry.

As the first enrollment period ended, comfortable barracks for the winter became the priority. The *Gadsden Times* reported on September 28, 1933, that Robert Fechner had announced that 250 million board feet of lumber had been ordered for winter camps. This was the single largest government order for timber. It would stimulate the timber industry that employed a million men. In the South, the men would continue to live in tents.

On October 1, the *Montgomery Advertiser* announced that a proposal had been made to transfer the camps out of freezing weather. Some western camps were relocated to lower elevations; others would be transferred to southern states. The Alabama Commission of Forestry was expecting additional camps. On October 12, the *Montgomery Advertiser* reported that Alabama was getting three additional camps, to be established by companies from northern states.

On December 22, 1933, the *Gadsden Times* announced that the 315,000 CCC men across the nation would be having a real Christmas. Camps were decorating trees. A special radio program was to be broadcast by the National Broadcast Company with messages by Director Fechner and Secretary of Agriculture Wallace. The railroads were offering special rates to enrollees. Some 445,000 were to be served for Christmas dinners. The menu (which would be repeated each Christmas and Thanksgiving) consisted of oyster soup and crackers, fresh roast pork, young turkey and oyster dressing, sweet relish and cranberries, giblet gravy, lettuce salad, creamed mashed potatoes, southern-style sweet potatoes, cream peas, banana and apple pies, Boston cream pie and fruit cakes, ice cream, assorted nuts, candies, bread, coffee, cigars, and cigarettes.

An Educational Program Established

In December 1933, President Roosevelt approved the placing of an educational advisor in each camp (Lacy 1976:38). Company commanders and supervisors had been teaching courses to the enrollees up to this time. With the presence of a camp education advisor (CEA), the educational program became organized under trained educators. Military and technical personnel continued to teach, and many schoolteachers financed through the Federal Relief Administration (FERA) and other New Deal programs came to camps to teach. Based on the 1930 census, Alabama was ranked forty-fourth out of 48 states for illiteracy, with 16.6 percent of male adults illiterate (WPA 1936:233). Many CCC enrollees furthered their education while in camp.

On December 23, the *Gadsden Times* announced that Alabama would receive educators for its 28 camps. The Office of Education in the Department of Interior was to act in an advisory capacity, communicating directly to the secretary of war. Major General E. L. King, Fourth Corps Area commander, stated that the enrollees were from all classes. Some had high school education; some even had some college education. The purpose of the educational program was to "furnish some form of education for every member of the CCC during his leisure hours, with the ultimate aim of returning them to their homes better men and better citizens."

On March 15, 1934, the *Gadsden Times* reported that a six-day conference had begun in Montgomery for the camp educational advisors to broaden the educational opportunities of the 7,000 enrollees in Alabama's 28 CCC camps. Dr. Hobdy, director of the vocational education division of the State Department of Education, stated that a survey had shown that a few enrollees in camps between the ages of eighteen and twenty-one were without any schooling at all. A number were unable to read a newspaper or write a letter. Approximately half of the enrollees had left school before reaching the eighth grade, and 40 percent had not finished high school. There were only a few college graduates. The educational program was voluntary, but the CEAs were expected to encourage all enrollees to participate. Dr. Hobdy was quoted as saying that "We hope to assist the youths in finding their place in the economic scheme of things when the camps are disbanded."

In many camps, enrollees were selected to serve as "Assistant Camp Educational Advisors." B. H. Nunnelley, of Helena, Alabama, served as an assistant CEA at Camp SP-16 at Monte Sano State Park. He had earned his high school diploma before entering the CCC on October 15, 1937, at the age of eighteen. His selection resulted in his being promoted to "assistant leader" and earning $36 each month. His duties included keeping records for the CEA, lighting fires in the education building for morning classes, and organizing recreational trips and sports teams (B. H. Nunnelley interview, March 7, 2002; see the CD). In 1939, Joe Pershing Perry was planting honeysuckle bushes along the roadside at Camp F-5 in the Black Warrior National Forest when the camp's chicken project came down with the bloody flux.

Mr. Perry had taken agriculture courses in high school, and the CEA asked him if he could save the chickens. He treated the chicken coops successfully and was rewarded with a promotion to "assistant CEA." He assumed supervision of the agricultural projects. After his company transferred to Camp F-11, he taught classes three times each week. He recalled there were four WPA teachers in camp. His duties also included fingerprinting the new enrollees coming into camp and cleaning the library and classrooms (Joe Perry Pershing interview, March 1, 2002; see the CD). Ernest Hubbard was pulled from a field crew at Camp SCS-14 in Dothan in 1939 and promoted to "assistant CEA." He taught radio code, typing, and woodworking. He was then assigned to temporary duty at Camp F-9 at Open Pond on the Conecuh National Forest, where he taught Red Cross lifesaving and water safety to African-American enrollees during the summer of 1940 (Ernest Hubbard interview, January 8, 2004; see the CD).

The Second Year

The third enrollment period began on April 1, 1934. The *CCC Camp Directory for Alabama* recorded 30 camps in Alabama (see Appendix B). On May 13, 1934, the *Gadsden Times* reported that Raymond Foley, former assistant secretary of state, had said that the CCC had solved the nation's juvenile delinquency problem. The CCC was "the most original and enlightening of President Roosevelt's activities." In the CCC, 300,000 young men were taken from "the ranks of people and prepared properly by the government for life and society."

By the fall of 1934, many people were arguing to make the CCC a permanent agency. The Emergency Conservation Work Act was due to expire on March 31, 1935. The *Florala News* published an article on September 13 from *The Army and Navy Register* discussing military training in the CCC, a common debate throughout the life of the program. The CCC had survived early criticism by pacifists and subversives and had demonstrated its value. It had rescued thousands of young men from unemployment and had accomplished "splendid work" in the conservation of the national forests and timberlands. To secure the "maximum benefit," the CCC needed military training. It was not to interfere with project work and would prepare the men as reservists in cases of emergencies. It was hoped no emergency would occur, but it was also hoped the military training would be added to the continued CCC.

On September 30, 1934, the *Montgomery Advertiser* included Director Fechner's report to the president on the first 18 months of work. A total of 850,000 young men, war veterans, and Indians had been employed at a cost of $443 million. Enrollees had received $136 million in payments, $113 million of which had gone to their homes. The nation's forestry programs had been advanced 5 to 15 years.

On October 4, the *Florala News* reported that Director Fechner had praised the work accomplished in Alabama through the first two enrollment periods. The outstanding work included improvement of the state's forested lands, strengthening of the forest fire protection system, and development of the new state park lands. Enrollees in Alabama had planted more than a million trees, had spent more than 10,318 man-days on forest nursery work, had constructed 3,186 miles of firebreaks, 103 miles of telephone lines, and 603 miles of truck trails, had reduced fire hazards on 8,172 acres, and had expended 22,779 man-days fighting forest fires. They had constructed 5,329 check dams for erosion control and sloped and cleared 23,333 square yards of highway banks.

The CCC was gaining support in Alabama. *The Onlooker* reported on December 6, 1934, that the Alabama Commission of Forestry had stated that matériel as well as morale support was being given by various state departments, counties, and municipalities, as well as a large number of citizens. This cooperation had been extended to take full advantage of the president's program to develop the nation's resources.

Emergency Conservation Work Act Extended, 1935–1937

On April 1, 1935, the Emergency Conservation Work Act was extended for another two years. The president wanted to expand the enrollment to 600,000 men and extended the age for junior enrollees from 25 to 28 years. In September 1935, the CCC would reach its highest number of enrollees—502,000 (Cohen 1980:18). Alabama reached its highest number of camps—49—during the fifth period.

While the age limits were extended, the criterion that the juniors be unmarried remained. Enrollees who married during their enlistments were discharged after their six months or retained as local experienced men. Rumors of CCC camps for married men may have come from an article in the April 24 *Tuscaloosa News* titled "Young Married Men Placed in CCC Camps." Thad Holt, director of the Alabama Relief Administration, had reported that 150 young married men had been placed in "Alabama CCC Camps" in Coffee County to prepare government-owned land for relief worker homesteads. The *Marion-Times Standard* of March 28 had correctly reported that the program was being administered by the Rural Rehabilitation Administration of the Resettlement Administration, rather than the CCC.

On August 29, 1935, the *Democratic Reporter* in Marengo County reported that unlike many of the federal relief programs, the federal money being spent in Alabama on CCC projects did not have to be matched by the state. While Alabama had made a small financial outlay to acquire land for state parks, the federal government was devoting millions of dollars for the development of the land. This "free money" did have some complications, however, as reported in *The Onlooker* on December 26, 1935. The Alabama State Commission of Forestry had pointed out that work on state and private lands required long-term commitments that less wealthy states were finding difficult to meet. It was necessary to restrict their activities and facilities to only those involving the federal program. As a permanent CCC was being discussed in Washington, many states were discussing how best to take advantage of the federal program.

On May 28, 1936, the *Cleburne News* announced that over 1,600 boys between eighteen and twenty-five from Alabama had been selected for CCC camps. The new recruits filled the vacancies in the state's quota of 6,100 enrollees, and they would be sending $25 of their $30 monthly allotment home. According to the State Welfare Commission, Alabama families were receiving approximately $152,000 monthly, or $1,730,000 a year, from these allotments. By October 1936, the yearly allotment going to families had increased to $2 million, according to the *Moulton Advertiser*. On October 8, the paper reported that another 1,300 Alabama boys had been recruited to fill the state's quota of 6,300 enrollees.

On October 29, 1936, the *Cleburne News* announced that Director Fechner had released a report stating that between April 1933 and August 1936, the CCC had given employment to 31,247 men from Alabama. The CCC had brought $23,680,000 into the state in total obligations. Of the employed men, 27,914 had been enrollees and another 3,333 had been non-enrolled reserve officers and supervisory personnel. An estimated $5,475,000 had been paid to dependents by Alabama enrollees. Major accomplishments in Alabama included 87,024 acres treated for erosion control, 241,260 check dams constructed, 19,167 acres of forest timber stand improvement completed, and 64,414 man-days spent fighting forest fires.

The Civilian Conservation Act, 1937–1939

On April 1, 1937, *The Onlooker* reported that the president would ask Congress to make the CCC a permanent agency with an authorized strength of 300,000 men. Director Fechner announced that Alabama would have an enrollment quota for 2,477 men. Of this number, 2,318 were to be junior enrollees, 102 World War I veterans, and 57 local experienced men.

On April 5, the president's proposal for a permanent CCC was approved by the Senate but not by the House. The Civilian Conservation Corps Act would extend the CCC to 1940. The act increased the authority of the director, added to education and training opportunities, and lowered the age of enrollees to between seventeen and twenty-three years. It also dropped the relief requirement and set the authorized strength at 315,000 men (Cohen 1980:18). The new act officially established the name of the Civilian Conservation Corps, which up to this time was only its popular name (Cohen 1980:6–7).

On April 14, 1937, *Our Mountain Home* announced that the CCC was expanding its health program for enrollees to include dental services. A team of dental officers and two enrollees would visit each camp at least once every six months, spending two weeks at a time. The services would include examinations, fillings, and any emergency remedial treatments. Prior to this, only extractions of teeth and treatments for relief of pain had been authorized. The Office of Surgeon General had reported that occurrence of disease in the CCC camps had been kept to a "remarkably low figure." The death rate in camps during the last fiscal year was lower than that occurring among men of similar age groups throughout the country. Over 2,000 medical officers of the regular army and the reserves, plus civilian physicians, and over 300 nurses in addition to the Army Nurse Corps, were employed to look after the health of the enrollees. Healthy work in the outdoors, the regular planned routine of work, the recreation programs, as well as the wholesome food had contributed to the health of the men. A study conducted in the Fourth Corps Area during the previous fiscal year had shown that on average, enrollees had gained six pounds during their first two months in camp.

The daily ration developed by the army in 1932, considered to be the best ever given to an American soldier, was the same ration given to the CCC enrollee. The quartermaster was purchasing food for over 500,000 men, up from 118,750 before the CCC. Inspectors insured that all food purchased was produced and handled under sanitary conditions meeting War Department standards. The Veterinarian Corps inspected all meats and dairy products. Initially, nearly all of the cooks and bakers had been regular army, but CCC enrollees had been trained in the camps and had replaced them.

The Quartermaster Corps reported that the Fourth Corps Area, with 56,000 enlisted men, consumed 195 train carloads of beef, pork, sugar, flour, butter, beans, and other articles of food every 30 days. These carloads included 1.6 million eggs, 210,000 pounds of butter, over a million pounds of cereal, and 210,000 pounds of onions and other food products. The 30-day menu included 1,050,000 pounds of beef, 210,000 pounds of chicken, 420,000 pounds of pork, and 210,000 pounds of bacon.

On July 1, 1937, the Civilian Conservation Act took effect. It authorized a maximum enrollment of 300,000 men, with no more than 30,000 war veterans. There would be another 10,000 Indians and 5,000 men enrolled in the territories and insular possessions. Junior enrollees would be between seventeen and twenty-three. They did not need to be from a family on relief but in need of employment. The director had authority to exclude "such classes of persons as he may consider detrimental to the well-being or welfare of the Corps, except that no person shall be excluded on account of race, color or creed." The enrollment period was to be six months and not to exceed two years. Enrollees would earn $30 per month. Ten percent of the company could earn $36 per month as assistant leaders, and 6 percent could earn $45 as leaders (Merrill 1981:199).

On September 30, 1937, the *Cleburne News* reported that the comptroller general had clarified that any previous service in the CCC prior to the Civilian Conservation Act of June 28, 1937, did not count when computing the two-year maximum. This clarification allowed former enrollees with two years' experience to re-enroll. The corps wanted men with character and ambition. Men were to be selected that were "best able to contribute to, and profit by, the experience of camp life." "The success of the Corps depended clearly upon the quality of its enrolled personnel."

According to Robert Allen Ermentrout, a former CCC company commander, the act of June 28, 1937, signaled significant changes in the program. In 1933, "Congress passed the buck to the president." A far more confident Congress took more control of the 1937 act. The primary purpose of the 1933 Emergency Conservation Work Act was to employ citizens in useful public projects to relieve economic conditions. The 1937 act provided employment and training for youthful citizens through the performance of public work. It directed that there be at least 10 hours of general education and vocational training each week. Young men attending school could now enroll in the CCC during summer vacations (Ermentrout 1982:48–49).

On January 5, 1938, the *Haleyville Spotlight* reported that the CCC boys were ready to fight. Director Fechner had stated that there were 2.3 million youths in America trained in the CCC camps that were ready to act as a volunteer army in an emergency: "While CCC men are not militarized in the ordinary sense of the word, their training is such that they are about 85 percent prepared for military life." There were 300,000 boys in camp at the moment and another 2 million who had been in camps. These men "could be trained into first class fighting men at almost an instant's notice." Fechner also said that the military aspect of the CCC was unintentional, as the purpose of the CCC was to solve the unemployment problem.

On January 17, the *Montgomery Advertiser* reported that according to Director Fechner, a broad program of protection of farmlands and forests had been advanced in Alabama. The conservation activities of the CCC in Alabama included reforestation of wastelands to restore them to timber productivity; strengthening the forest fire protection system through the construction of trails and fire towers connected by telephone lines; advancement of erosion control programs in agricultural areas; and improvement of the state's recreational facilities. In Alabama during fiscal year 1937, CCC enrollees had constructed 289,000 check dams, seeded and sodded more than 1.5 million square feet of gullies and banks, planted more than 5.8 million seedlings in gullies, and planted more than 6 million seedlings for reforestation. They had spent more than 16,000 man-days fighting forest fires and more than 12,243 man-days on fire suppression. The enrollees constructed a permanent archaeological museum and other improvements in a number of state parks. An average of 37 camps opened during 1937 with a total of 14,204 young men and veterans enrolled in the program. War Department figures showed that the average enrollee spent nine months in the CCC before leaving to accept employment or for other reasons. Alabama enrollees had sent over $2 million to their families, and over $7.3 million had been made in total obligations in Alabama for fiscal year 1937. As of November 1, there were 9,119 men in the CCC in Alabama.

On December 23, 1938, the *Tuscaloosa News* reported that Loula Dunn, state welfare director, had announced that 1,057 Alabama youths would be enrolled in the CCC between January 9 and 19. These enrollees would be sent to Fourth Corps Area camps, having been chosen from Anniston, Fort Payne, Huntsville, Athens, Wilson Dam, Birmingham, Jasper, Tuscaloosa, Demopolis, Selma, Montgomery, Dothan, Andalusia, and Mobile.

On January 5, 1939, the *Cleburne News* carried an article titled "Forests Protected By 'Shock Troops' Of CCC." Four million man-days had been spent fighting forest fires during the five years of service. Many thousands of miles of firebreaks built across the southern states were of inestimable benefit in holding fire losses to a minimum. CCC enrollees had also waged a war against such silent killers as insects, disease, and fungi. The CCC had contributed to the forest wealth, especially in the southern states, where they worked in areas acquired by the national forests that had been previously logged and subjected to severe burning. CCC work in restoring these forests was dual in nature, rebuilding forests while also building men.

The *Cleburne News* also reported on January 5 on the vocational courses available in camps in District D (northern Mississippi and Alabama); poultry raising, gardening, woodcraft, carpentry, nursery operations, radio engineering, and cooking were being offered. The CCC had placed more cooks in private employment than in any other occupation. Approximately 5 percent of District D enrollees were illiterate. During the past year, 400 enrollees had been taught to read and write. Teaching the enrollees to be self-sustaining was the most important goal. R. D. Davis, the District D education advisor, wanted to see the enrollees able to support themselves without government aid when they left the CCC.

Creation of the Federal Security Agency

On July 1, 1939, Congress created the Federal Security Agency. The CCC, which had been an independent agency since its inception, was placed under the new agency (Lacy 1976:199). Director Fechner protested and submitted his resignation, which the president did not accept. Congress also passed an act assuring the continuation of the CCC until June 30, 1943 (Cohen 1980:144).

On July 17, the *Tuscaloosa News* reported that reserve officers in the U.S. Army would be given opportunities to fill staff assignments in the CCC. Officers on duty at the camps would be given preference, and vacancies would be filled from other eligible applicants. John S. Hassell, born in 1912 in Tuscaloosa County, had been commissioned a second lieutenant after completing the ROTC program at the University of Alabama. He had served in CCC camps in Mississippi, South Carolina, and Georgia during 1935 and 1936. In 1939, when the CCC was turned over to civil service employees who were reserve officers, Mr. Hassell became a subaltern or junior officer at camps in Tennessee. He was assigned as a subdistrict inspector in 1942, stationed at Talladega (John S. Hassell interview, January 28, 2002; see the CD).

By the fall of 1939, with the outbreak of hostilities in Europe, questions were being raised once again whether CCC enrollees would be pressed into service. *Our Mountain Home* carried an article on September 19 assuring mothers that the "CCC is not liable for service in [the] Army." With another 100,000 replacements about to be recruited, Director Fechner wanted every mother to know that her son would not be "put behind a gun." After December 31, the camps were to be commanded by civilian officers rather than reserve officers of the army. No CCC enrollee would have any military commitment; however, CCC life made youths more fit to serve in the military if war should come to the United States.

The *Tuscaloosa News* reported on December 24, 1939, that Alabama's quota of 1,401 enrollees would be filled by 1,307 white and 95 black youths. Most of the youths would be sent to the 28 camps in Alabama. Replacement of the enrollees occurred every three months to fill the places of those who had finished their enrollment, left the CCC to accept jobs, or left to return to school. Since April 1933, approximately 43,000 youths from Alabama had enrolled. More than $12 million had come to Alabama in the form of allotments to needy families, and the state was receiving monthly allotments of $150,000.

On December 29, the *Tuscaloosa News* reported that sixty-three-year-old CCC Director Robert Fechner was in serious condition at Walter Reed Hospital. He died two days later. On February 14, 1940, the *Tuscaloosa News* announced that James J. McEntee, Fechner's assistant, was to be the new director. His selection was taken as a sign that the CCC would remain a non-military organization. McEntee, like Fechner, was opposed to authorizing military training in the CCC.

Dropping the Relief Requirement and Contributing to National Defense

On June 20, 1940, the *Evergreen Courant* reported that the CCC would enroll 3,867 youths from Alabama during July. Of this number, 2,250 would be sent to West Coast camps; the remaining 1,617 would be stationed in Alabama and other southern states. There were 7,600 Alabama youths in the CCC at the time, sending $179,000 home to their families monthly. Since April 1933, Alabama's needy families had received more than $13 million from the approximately 50,000 youths who had enrolled.

On June 24, the *Tuscaloosa News* announced that the CCC had dropped the requirements making it necessary for enrollees' parents to be on relief. Better employment conditions had lowered applications for the CCC. The boys would now be selected if they were unemployed and needed jobs. Youths from families on relief would still receive preference.

The *Evergreen Courant* reported on June 27 that the Division of Selection in Washington had announced that while they were not advocating military training, "practically all work done in the CCC camps will contribute directly toward national defense." The CCC would help "by continuing its present operations in the conservation of human and natural resources and by emphasizing further technical training for enrollees for non-combatant duties such as mechanics, machine operators, cooks, road and bridge builders, radio operators, and other occupations which demand additional employees in times of emergency."

On July 5, the *Tuscaloosa Times* reported that Director McEntee had announced that the CCC had adopted "military calisthenics" as a supplement to the enrollees' health program. The exercises were similar to the army's except that rifles were not used. Each camp would have a 15-minute exercise period before breakfast. Prior to this, exercises had been voluntary. The new exercises had been approved by the War Department as part of the national defense program.

On July 31, the *Tuscaloosa News* carried an article by Stephen J. McDonough, AP science writer, who wrote that although the CCC was not a military organization, it had proved to be an excellent training ground. During its seven and a half years, more than 2.5 million youths had passed through the CCC. Their weight had increased, their general health improved, and their physical condition had gone from substandard to better than the standards for youths of the same age. The CCC had been forced to lower the weight requirements as 25 percent of the youths joining had been underweight. Another 45 percent, meeting all the requirements, were still below standard weight. Diet deficiencies were common among enrollees before joining. Thousands of youths who would not have passed the physical standards for military service were now able to pass "almost any examination." Further, the tuberculosis rate among CCC youth was about one-fifth that of the regular army. According to Director McEntee, one of the greatest contributions made by CCC youths was the voluntary testing of a new vaccine against pneumonia. Since its development in 1937, approximately 44 percent of the enrollees had volunteered to take the vaccine.

On August 11, the *Tuscaloosa News* reported that an army of 1,200 CCC youths was maneuvering through Alabama's private and state-owned woodlands on a mission of defending them against fire, erosion, and other dangers. Six of Alabama's 31 CCC camps were supervised by the Conservation Department's Division of Forestry. In the last 18 months, these camps had put in 8,841 man-days fighting forest fires, built three lookout towers and 29 bridges, constructed 258 miles of telephone lines and 1,688 rods of fences, erected 28 erosion control dams, constructed 87 miles of truck trails, and spent 4,983 man-days constructing firebreaks. They had gathered 2,000 bushels of pine seed and put in 1,090 man-days in the development of the state's new nursery at Autaugaville. Forestry Chief Brooks Toler estimated that the CCC had constructed $3 million worth of permanent improvements on private and state-owned lands in Alabama. Among the valuable assets, the CCC had assisted in mapping forest types in Washington, Butler, Mobile, and Escambia counties.

New Pay Regulations and a New Enrollment Schedule

On November 21, 1940, the *Moulton Advertiser* reported that the CCC had announced a new compulsory savings program. Enrollees would now place $7 out of their monthly $30 in a special savings account to be paid to them upon their discharge. Effective January 1, 1941, the enrollees would keep $8, $7 would go into the savings account, and $15 would be sent home to dependents.

On January 23, 1941, *The Onlooker* reported that Loula Dunn, state welfare director, had announced that 3,847 boys from Alabama would be enrolled in the CCC. Of this number, 1,247 would be selected to bring Alabama's 31 camps up to authorized strength (roughly 6,200). The remaining 2,600 youths would be sent to camps on the West Coast. On January 29, the *Tuscaloosa News* reported that Miss Dunn had announced that there would be eight enrollments during the year rather than the usual four. Regular quarterly enrollments would be conducted in January, April, July, and October. Intermediate enrollments, where the enrollees would be sent to only Fourth Corps Area camps, would be conducted in February, May, August, and November.

Prior to this, some of the enrollees were asked if they wanted to go to a western camp. Farris D. George of East Gadsden, Alabama, recalled that he was asked during his interview in September 1938 if he wanted to go to the West Coast. He requested to be placed in a western camp. After receiving his shots and conditioning at Fort McClellan, his company was sent by train to Camp P-219 at Triangle Lake, near Blakely, Oregon (Farris D. George interview, February 14, 2002; see the CD).

On February 13, 1941, *The Onlooker* reported on the new enrollment schedule. The intermediate enrollments were designed to stabilize the camps in the states where the youths had enrolled. Those applicants selected during the regular enrollments could be sent to camps in other army corps areas. By filling the camps eight times each year, unemployed men had to wait less time for enrollment, and with smaller requisitions the selection process could be more thorough. Camp morale would improve because of less influx and exodus of enrollees, and having less "green men" arriving in camp made project planning easier and improved safety conditions.

The Eighth Anniversary of the CCC

On April 5, 1941, the CCC observed its eighth anniversary. As was the tradition, camps across the nation celebrated the day with open houses, inviting the public to visit the camps and see the project work. On April 10, *The Onlooker* reported that the CCC was protecting Alabama's natural resources. The 5,400 enrollees in Alabama were developing parks, constructing fire towers and roads and a forest nursery, patrolling state and national forests, and assisting in erosion control. During the last eight years, the CCC had contributed millions of dollars to the state park system. Seven camps under the supervision of the National Park Service and the Division of State Parks had constructed 106 cabins, 5 lodges, 7 lakes, 4 bathhouses, and more than 100 miles of roads. For the first time in 1939, the people of Alabama were able to enjoy their state's recreational developments when five state parks opened and were visited by thousands of guests. Without the CCC and the National Park Service, Alabama would not have been able to develop its state park system.

Six camps under the supervision of the Department of Conservation's Division of Forestry were providing fire protection, developing a nursery, and providing other forestry products. The camps were located at Vredenburgh, Uriah, Brewton, Robertsdale, Dadeville, and Bessemer. The value of forest protection in Alabama was estimated at several million dollars.

Nine camps under the supervision of the Soil Conservation Service were working on prevention of soil erosion and on pasture development, tree planting, and terrace outlet construction. There were four camps in the national forests, working on fire fighting, construction of fire towers, and timber stand improvement. The Fish and Wildlife Service had a camp engaged in wildlife activities at the Joe Wheeler Reservation.

In addition to conservation work, the CCC was also engaged in national defense activities. The enrollees were being trained in auto mechanics, truck driving, blacksmithing, metal work, and other jobs that prepared them for private employment in defense industries. *The Onlooker* encouraged its readers to visit their local camps.

On May 15, 1941, the *Moulton Advertiser* reported that Lt. C. C. McCutchen, company commander at Camp F-11, had announced that high school and college students could enroll in the local CCC camp for work and national defense training during the summer. The students would receive honorable discharges to return to school in the fall. This new policy for the summer of 1941 would allow students to earn the $30 allotment and receive national defense training for three months rather than the full six-month enrollment. Bruce Mantel of Brewton, Alabama, enrolled at the CCC camp at Uriah on May 26, 1941, after finishing grade 11. He served at Camp P-77 at Uriah, Camp TVA-6 at Athens, Alabama, and Camp SCS-35 at Hickory, North Carolina. He was discharged on August 14, 1941, and returned to Brewton to finish grade 12 (Bruce Mantel interview, November 18, 2003; see the CD).

On June 25, 1941, the *Tuscaloosa News* reported that Director McEntee had announced that all of the approximately 5,000 enrollees in Alabama were receiving national defense training. There were 1,346 enrollees at two cooks' and bakers' schools and a central motor repair shop (in Talladega). The other Alabama enrollees were being trained in work directly or indirectly related to the defense program.

Consolidation with the National Youth Administration

On October 27, 1941, the *Tuscaloosa News* carried an Associated Press article reporting the president's plan to consolidate the CCC with the National Youth Administration (NYA). The plan would transfer all administrative duties from the War Department. The president had written to Paul V. McNutt, head of the Federal Security Agency, asking him to make the arrangements: "In view of current world conditions, I feel that the War Department should be removed from all activities which may interfere with its main objective—preparation for defense."

On December 1, the acting southern regional forester mailed a memorandum to all Forest Service personnel along with a November 24 letter from CCC director McEntee to the Department of Agriculture's representative on the CCC Advisory Council. With the publicity of the consolidation of the CCC and the NYA, and the withdrawal of the War Department from CCC affairs, Director McEntee wanted all field personnel connected with the CCC to be informed. Although there would be personnel changes, McEntee stated that the general operations of the CCC would continue. The regional forester instructed Forest Service employees to accept the decision and to remain neutral in any controversies (letter on file, Alabama Department of Conservation, Record Group RC2, Alabama Department of Archives and History).

Pearl Harbor and America's Entry into World War II

Immediately following the attack on Pearl Harbor and America's declaration of war, the CCC offered all of its camps to the army for work on military projects and offered assistance to the Red Cross for war emergencies. Except for fighting forest fires, all work off military reservations was canceled on January 1, 1942. Thousands of enrollees and camp administrators left the CCC to enter military service, creating a tremendous drain of manpower (Cohen 1980:145).

On January 14, 1942, *Our Mountain Home* announced that the CCC enrollment for Talladega County had been set. All interested boys were to inquire at the Welfare Department office. Only boys younger than the draft age would be accepted.

On February 6, Rezin E. Pidgeon, acting regional forester in Atlanta, wrote to all forest supervisors in the southern region regarding employment of custodians at abandoned CCC camps. They could have their families living with them but were not to leave the camp without permission of a superior officer. During low fire danger, they could leave camp for two hours to "secure his subsistence from nearby stores." The abandoned camps were to be inspected monthly by a "responsible officer" (letter on file, Alabama Department of Conservation, Record Group RC2, Alabama Department of Archives and History).

On March 25, *Our Mountain Home* reported that President Roosevelt was "strongly opposed" to any attempt to eliminate or hamper the NYA and the CCC, declaring that both programs were important to the war effort. Senator McKellar of Tennessee had presented a bill to abolish the two agencies. The president wrote to Paul McNutt, federal security administrator, stating the bill did not meet with his approval.

The Final Six Months and Liquidation of the Camps

The *CCC Camp Directory for Alabama* reported eight camps during the nineteenth period, which began April 1, 1942. The Forest Service had a camp at Munford, there was a private forestry camp at Vredenburgh, the TVA had a camp at Wilson Dam, and the Soil Conservation Service had camps at Clanton, Hamilton, and Talladega. The TVA camp at Huntsville had been converted to Camp AF-1 and was working at the Huntsville Arsenal. The SCS camp at Dothan was converted to Camp ASCS-1 and worked at Napier Field.

On April 28, A. W. Hartman, the regional CCC officer in Atlanta, sent a memo to the southern region forest supervisors advising them of a letter of April 21 in which "We have received instructions from Washington that all CCC surplus dynamite and explosives are to be transferred to the War Department immediately" (letter on file, Alabama Department of Conservation, Record Group RC2, Alabama Department of Archives and History).

Congress was pressured to abolish the CCC. President Roosevelt had asked for a budget of $49 million to continue the work with 150 camps. After debate, the House voted not to appropriate any funds after June 30, 1942. The Senate had voted to retain the CCC but rescinded after further debate. The CCC would receive no more funding after June 30, 1942. Eight million dollars were appropriated to liquidate the assets of the CCC (Cohen 1980:145).

On June 6, the *Montgomery Advertiser* reported that the House of Representatives had voted to deny funds to continue the CCC. The House had withstood strong pressure from the administration for a wartime continuance of the CCC on a semimilitary basis. If the Senate upheld the House's vote, the CCC would be finished, at least for the duration of the war. Since its creation in 1933, the CCC had cost $3 billion.

On July 1, *Our Mountain Home* reported that on June 30, the House of Representatives, standing firm in its opposition to the administration, had once again refused to vote funds to keep the CCC in existence. The Civilian Conservation Corps was officially ended.

In July 1942, A. W. Hartman, regional CCC officer, sent a memo to the state foresters and forest supervisors in the southern region regarding the disposal of CCC camp buildings. Based on an act of Congress approved on July 2, 1942, the director of the CCC was authorized during fiscal year 1943 to dispose of any camp buildings no longer needed by the CCC. The buildings were to be offered first to the War Department and the Navy Department. Most of the camp buildings in the Fourth Corps Area had already been transferred to the Army-CCC, who in turn transferred them to the engineers (letter on file, Alabama Department of Conservation, Record Group RC2, Alabama Department of Archives and History).

On August 22, 1942, Fred Morrell, assistant chief of the Forest Service, sent a memo to the regional foresters regarding surplus CCC property. Inventories were to be made of all property not yet turned over to the army. The property was to be divided into five categories. Serviceable automotive and heavy equipment was to be transferred to the Department of War or Navy, the Civil Air Authority, or the Forest Service. Small tools and supplies were to be designated in the same way. The fifth category was for unserviceable automotive and heavy equipment (letter on file, Alabama Department of Conservation, Record Group RC2, Alabama Department of Archives and History).

On December 17, A. W. Hartman, regional CCC officer, wrote a memo to the forest supervisors of the southern region regarding the disposition of the remaining CCC camps. Any camps that could not be disposed of through a state, county, municipality, or local organization were to be disposed of in the best interest of the government. Hartman was of the opinion that many of the remaining CCC camps could be sold at public auction, with the restoration of the camp area made part of the conditions of the sale (letter on file, Alabama Department of Conservation, Record Group RC2, Alabama Department of Archives and History).

William D. Sadler of Munford, Alabama, was working as a Forest Service squad foreman in 1942 after serving in three CCC companies between 1934 and 1940. His main responsibility in 1942 was the liquidation of CCC camps. He worked on the closing of camps in the Black Warrior, Conecuh, and Talladega National Forests (Camps F-11, F-9, F-10, and F-12) and the private camp at Vredenburgh (Camp P-76). He was constantly on the move. As soon as the equipment was made ready for auction, he would move on to the next camp (William D. Sadler interviews, April 27, May 8, 2001; see the CD).

3
The CCC and the National Forests in Alabama

In April 1933, the only national forest in Alabama was the Alabama National Forest in Winston and Lawrence counties; it had been proclaimed a national forest by President Woodrow Wilson on January 5, 1918.

On April 6, 1933, the *Moulton Advertiser* reported that Representative Edward B. Almon, from Moulton, and Representative William B. Bankhead, from Jasper, had asked Forest Service's Chief Stuart to establish CCC camps in the Alabama National Forest. On June 1, 1933, the *Moulton Advertiser* reported that three reforestation camps had been established there with a contingent of 11 officers and 572 men. The camps would be opened to the public on June 4, and the public was urged to make the boys feel at home. Arrangements had been made to send cars to the camps to bring enrollees to church and Sunday school, and many enrollees had been invited to dinner. The people of Moulton were asked to save newspapers and magazines that were to be delivered to the camps by Mrs. Gaines.

Company 463, Camp F-1, Moulton, Alabama

Company 463 was the first CCC company organized in the state of Alabama, at Fort McClellen on April 28–29, 1933. It consisted of junior enrollees from the counties of northern Alabama. While the company was being conditioned, 2nd Lt. Price C. McClemore was sent to Cheatham Knob with a detachment to establish Camp F-1. Although hampered by a lack of transportation and adequate water, the men began to arrange the campsite with a temporary kitchen and water storage tank. The camp was named "Camp Wheeler" to honor General Joe Wheeler from Moulton.

Camp F-1 was established on May 26, 1933. The work project consisted of the construction of roads, bridges, fire towers, firebreaks, and telephone lines, and stream improvement. The men were also conducting a timber survey across the forest, the only one of its type in Alabama at that time (1934 CCC District D Annual).

On November 23, 1933, the *Moulton Advertiser* reported that a fire in Camp F-1 had destroyed two barracks and damaged a third with several boys injured. The cause was unknown, but the fire had spread rapidly. Henry Bradfield, from Birmingham, went back into the burning barracks to rescue Bonnie Rivers from Hurtsboro. Bradfield was considered a hero. Three years later the CCC would establish a certificate of valor for exceptional courageous action. The *Moulton Advertiser* reported on April 30, 1936, that Bradfield had been among the first 11 enrollees and former enrollees to receive this award. He received the medal for valor, a Carnegie Medal, and $1,000. His act of bravery was included in the *CCC Enrollees Handbook* printed in 1935.

During the spring and summer of 1934, a young artist named Charles C. Foster was assigned to Camp F-1. Although he arrived in camp after the fire, he shed some light on the possible cause and quick rate of spread. He recalled that the boys frequently brought Coke bottles filled with gasoline into the barracks to kill bed bugs. He also stated that the barracks walls were covered with tarpaper that tended to peel from the walls (Charles C. Foster interview, June 4, 2001; see the CD).

A Camp Inspection Report dated April 16, 1934, recorded 161 enrollees under the command of Captain J. H. Palmer. It also recorded that Camp F-1 was plagued from the start by a lack of water. To make matters worse, Company 464 was also stationed at Cheatham Knob. The water problem was brought to the attention of Director Fechner, who wrote to the War Department on April 30, 1934, stating the source of water was a small mountain spring that dried up in the summer. The Forest Service was hauling water to the camp. The men were going to Moulton to bathe.

Camp F-1 was abandoned on October 27, 1934. The scarcity of water finally forced the camp to close in spite of its beautiful location. The *Moulton Advertiser* reported on October 18, 1934, that Company 463 was being relocated to Camp F-4, which had been established the year before. Company 463 had done a "fine service," and the people of Lawrence County regretted seeing them move even such a short distance away.

Camp F-1 remained abandoned through the following summer. The *Moulton Advertiser* reported on July 18, 1935, that the camp was to be used to host the Northern District of the Women's Missionary Union assembly. On September 12, 1935, it was reported that the American Legion was holding a fish fry for veterans at the camp.

Company 464, Camp F-2, Danville, Alabama

Company 464 was also organized on April 28–29, 1933. The majority of junior enrollees came from Birmingham. While conditioning at Fort McClellan, they received inoculations for smallpox and typhoid. Many of them reacted to the shots and became sick. Liberal doses of castor oil and "C.C.C. Pills" hastened their recovery. Company 464 left Fort McClellan by train to Decatur and traveled the remaining 30 miles to Cheatham Knob in hay trucks. After a month at Camp F-1, they moved 14 miles deeper into the national forest and established Camp F-2 near a spring and waterfall on June 23, 1933. The waterfall served as showers until the bathhouse could be built. The camp, named "Camp Nathan B. Forrest" after the Confederate general, was located near Hickory Grove. The post office was at Danville. The work project consisted of road construction, timber stand improvement, road and telephone line maintenance, and construction of a 100-foot fire tower, two bridges, and 26 miles of firebreaks. They were also running a rock crusher on a 24-hour shift. Company 464 had successful baseball and basketball teams plus a miniature golf course, a swimming pool, and a recreation center (1934 CCC District D Annual).

A Camp Inspection Report dated April 15, 1934, recorded 162 men under the command of Captain Robert A. Lewis. The camp education program offered 28 courses ranging from those for illiterates to college level, with I. J. Quinn as the camp educational advisor. The *Moulton Advertiser* reported on September 13, 1934, that Camp F-2 had its own two-page camp newsletter called "Forrest Leaves" produced by the educational classes and mimeographed in the office of the county superintendent of education.

In October 1934, Company 464 was transferred to Oxford, Mississippi. Enrollees arrived at Camp F-17 on October 11, taking everything with them except the actual structures (1934 CCC District D Annual).

Company 3475, Camp F-2, Danville, Alabama

Company 3475 arrived at Camp F-2 on May 1, 1935. A Camp Inspection Report dated December 12, 1935, recorded 195 junior enrollees from Alabama and Florida under the command of Captain Stanley Smith. The work project consisted of the construction and maintenance of truck trails over 120 square miles of national forest under the supervision of J. W. Montgomery.

Carl Carlson, from Thomasville, Alabama, served in Company 3475 in

1935. In addition to road construction, he also fought forest fires. He recalled that most of the fires were started by people burning off the woods to allow for free-range cattle (Carl Carlson interview, November 15, 2002; see the CD). Allen Edwards, also of Thomasville, was at Camp F-2 at the same time. He too worked on road construction crews and fought forest fires. Mr. Edwards recalled that Company 3475 was at Camp F-2 less than a year (Allen Edwards interview, October 22, 2002; see the CD).

Camp F-2 was abandoned sometime during the sixth enrollment period. Woodrow Biddle, from Fort Payne, Alabama, was transferred to Camp F-2 on October 23, 1935, after serving in Company 463. He transferred from Company 3475 on January 7, 1936, as Camp F-2 was closing (Woodrow Biddle interview, March 4, 2002; see the CD). The *Moulton Advertiser* reported on September 2, 1937, that Camp F-2, which had been vacant for two years, was to be given to the 4-H clubs of six northwest counties in Alabama. It was not known if the camp would remain in place or be relocated.

Company 1403, Camp F-3, Haleyville, Alabama

Company 1403 was organized at Fort Benning in May 1933 with junior enrollees from south Alabama. After their conditioning, a convoy of army trucks carrying 128 men headed to Mount Olive, Alabama, under the command of Captain J. G. Breckenridge. It was decided to establish the camp at the Kinlock Springs when they paused to rest by the beautiful spring. Camp F-3 was built in six weeks with the plantation house of David Hubbard serving as headquarters. Wooden barracks were constructed along orderly company streets, along with a wooden mess hall. By June 6, 1933, "Camp Hubbard" was complete and the project work began (1934 and 1936 CCC District D Annuals).

Company 1403 established Camp F-3 with 188 men. Based on five Camp Inspection Reports, company strength was recorded between 153 and 198 men, under the command of Captain J. G. Breckenridge, May 1933; Captain D. H. Hutchinson, April 23, 1934; Captain C. W. O'Leary, January 12, 1935; 1st Lt. George C. Waters, December 9, 1935; 1st Lt. K. M. Rand, November 4, 1936; and Captain James C. Pruitt, November 16, 1937. The work consisted of road construction and maintenance, truck trail and phone line construction, timber stand improvement, fighting forest fires, and stream improvement. Company 1403 also built two metal and concrete bridges. This work was done under the supervision of R. A. Scott, April 23, 1934; W. L. Gerrard, January 12, 1935; J. F. Martin, December 9, 1935; J.B.F. Rylant (Acting), November 4, 1936; and J. W. Montgomery, November 16, 1937. At the time of the November 17, 1937, inspection, the work project was nearing completion and no new work was being planned.

William Edward Roberson, from Greenville, Alabama, served in Company 1403 from the spring of 1933 to the fall of 1935. He worked on a crew that drove through the forest looking for rocks to be crushed for road surfacing. This often required blasting the rock with dynamite. CCC safety regulations required that the enrollees be a half mile from the rock before it was detonated, but he was struck in the hand with rock fragments when someone used too large a charge, and he had to return to camp. Mr. Roberson also worked on the timber stand improvement crew. As the crew walked through the woods checking the tops of the trees, they cut every tree within six feet of the healthy trees to remove competition. Mr. Roberson recalled fighting a forest fire that burned very close to a house. The family was so grateful that their home was protected from the fire that they invited the crew to join them for supper. The family of seven had very little food to spare. The crew went back to the camp and returned to the home with food from the mess hall—the best meal the family had eaten in a very long time (William Edward Roberson interview, November 30, 2001; see the CD).

Woodrow "Woody" Wilson Chilcoat was born and raised four miles north of Kinlock Springs. In May 1933, at the age of eighteen, he "hobo'd" down to Fort Benning just in time to join Company 1403 with Captain Breckinridge. The company was headed for Mount Olive, but Mr. Chilcoat informed them that Kinlock Springs was the best source for water in the area. The company lived in tents through the end of 1933 while wooden structures were built. The old Hubbard Plantation House was fixed up for the office. The two-story, four-room house had chimneys at both ends and fireplaces in all four rooms. The frame house had chinking of mud and horsehair between the lathing that had been smoothed and finished to look like a white wall.

Mr. Chilcoat had two older brothers who were employed by the Forest Service. Teddy Roosevelt Chilcoat, a heavy machine operator, and Roy Chilcoat took CCC crews out into the forest, although Woody never worked on his brothers' crews. He worked on road construction at first, then went up into the fire tower as a watchman. Woody Chilcoat also worked on chestnut blight eradication occasionally through 1938. He said it was thought that birds were spreading the blight, but because it was not practical to kill all the birds, they cut down and burned all the infected trees.

Woody Chilcoat was present the night the Hubbard Plantation burned in November 1935. He heard the alarm and with the other enrollees fell out with buckets. Nothing could be done to save the house as the fire spread quickly. The company lost a lot of equipment in the fire (Woodrow W. Chilcoat interview, January 22, 2002; see the CD).

John B. Wilson, of Moulton, Alabama, served in Company 1403 for 18 months from 1933 to 1935. He worked on a road construction crew on the Northwest Road. The work was done with shovels, picks, and wheelbarrows. There was one bulldozer assigned to the project, but they rarely used it. Mr. Wilson described the layout of the camp. David Hubbard's house, located on the left after entering the camp on the top of a small hill, served as headquarters and sickbay. The mess hall was the first building on the right after entering the camp. Four barracks were lined up behind the mess hall (John B. Wilson interview, August 24, 2001; see the CD).

By November 1937, Camp Hubbard was four years old and considered an old camp. A Camp Inspection Report dated November 16, 1937, stated that a number of buildings needed repair. With the work project nearly completed, plans had been made to abandon the camp, and Camp F-3 was abandoned on December 20, 1937 (*Historical Records of CCC Camp Buildings*). According to Forest Supervisor Frank Razor's letter of November 19, 1945, to Marie Owens Bankhead of the Alabama Department of Archives and History, soon after Camp F-3 was abandoned, the 4-H clubs of northwest Alabama began construction of a camp with the help of the National Youth Administration (NYA). The NYA furnished the labor and the Forest Service salvaged the materials. Eugene King, of Haleyville, Alabama, worked as an NYA carpenter. They rebuilt the barracks, tearing down the buildings on the company streets and rebuilding them in a horseshoe pattern on the edge of the camp (Eugene King interview, June 6, 2001; see the CD).

Company 258, Camp F-4, Moulton, Alabama

Company 258 was organized on May 17, 1933, at the Plattsburg Barracks, New York. The junior enrollees from New York and New Jersey were sent to Idaho, where they worked on a Forest Service project for blister rust control. Those who reenlisted for the second enrollment period were transferred to the South in the fall of 1933. They established Camp F-4 as a tent camp on October 29 and received 175 replacements from Fort Dix in the Second Corps Area on November 5, 1933. Local civilian labor constructed the camp by January 1, 1934. "Camp New Yorker" was located near Grayson, Alabama (1934 CCC District D Annual).

On January 11, 1934, the *Moulton Advertiser* reported that Camp F-4 had hosted a dance attended by people from Decatur, Haleyville, Double Springs, and Moulton. It was held in either the mess hall or one of the barracks, decorated and heated by an immense fireplace with pine knots and a large backlog. Company Commander Captain J. H. Donaldson welcomed all visitors, and the town of Moulton welcomed Captain Donaldson and all of the CCC boys.

A Camp Inspection Report dated April 18, 1934, recorded only 76 men in the company at the time. The work project consisted of construction of roads, two bridges, and telephone lines, and timber stand improvement, all under the supervision of Wayne Slaughter. The 1934 District D annual recorded that on April 2, the enlistments of 106 enrollees had expired and the boys returned to Fort Dix, New Jersey. On April 21, 124 replacements came from Fort Dix, and other enrollees from Alabama filled the ranks to increase the company's strength.

According to the 1934 annual, during the summer months of 1934, Company 258 led all camps in the Alabama, Cherokee, and Pisgah National Forests for work accomplished. On October 18, 1934, the *Moulton Advertiser* announced that Company 258 had transferred to a new camp in Mississippi.

Company 463, Camp F-4, Moulton, Alabama

On October 18, 1934, the *Moulton Advertiser* reported that Company 463 had moved from Camp F-1 to Camp F-4. Lack of water forced the company to move nine miles south, just above the Winston-Lawrence county line. The new camp was called "Camp Collier," and the enrollees were from Alabama, Georgia, and Tennessee.

A Camp Inspection Report dated January 5, 1934, recorded 159 enrollees present, with 19 home on leave for the holidays and one in the hospital. Captain Joe H. Palmer was also in the hospital, and Captain G. D. Miller was temporarily in command of the company.

Water supply problems continued to plague Company 463. There was water for bathing only three times during November and December. It was supplied from a well and spring, but there was not an adequate pumping system in the camp. Morale was below average, the camp needed repairs, and there was no recreation equipment.

By the summer of 1935, Camp F-4 was in proper order. On August 15, 1935, the *Moulton Advertiser* ran the first of six weekly articles entitled "CCC Camp F-4 News." The enrollees were enjoying a new pool table in the recreation hall and had recently held a checkers tournament. Company Commander Major Dumas had been complimented on the cleanup of the camp by officials after an inspection conducted on August 9. On September 22, the *Moulton Advertiser* reported that improvements had continued. Company streets and walkways had been covered with crushed rock to eliminate dust and mud, the library had been expanded, enrollees were building new furniture for the recreation hall, and a new camp educational advisor, W. E. Green, had arrived. According to Woody Biddle, Camp F-4 was abandoned on October 23, 1935.

Company 3476, Camp F-5, Double Springs, Alabama

On April 16, 1935, a cadre of enrollees from Company 463 was detached to begin construction of Camp F-5 under the command of Captain William S. Rockwell. The camp was completed on July 1, 1935, and on July 6, junior enrollees from Alabama and Georgia arrived to bring the company strength up to 216 men (1936 CCC District D Annual). "Camp Riverside" was located on the eastern shore of the Sipsey Fork, just south of present-day Highway 278.

A Camp Inspection Report dated December 9, 1935, recorded that the work project was scattered over 144 square miles and consisted mostly of road construction and maintenance under the supervision of R. A. Scott. The 1936 District D annual recorded that they had constructed the Cullman Road as well as telephone lines, including a line connecting the Central Tower to the Forest Service office in Double Springs. Their work also included the construction of fire towers and fire presuppression and suppression. There were 196 men under the command of Captain Rockwell.

On June 19, 1936, by proclamation of President Roosevelt, the Alabama National Forest was renamed the Black Warrior National Forest and expanded to the south, almost doubling in size. Surveying the new forest boundary was added to the project work, as noted in a Camp Inspection Report dated November 1, 1936. The work project was being supervised by John W. Montgomery. There were 165 enrollees from Alabama, Georgia, Mississippi, and Maryland under the command of 1st Lt. William C. Smith.

On April 7, 1937, the *Haleyville Spotlight* reported that the CCC was preparing to celebrate a fourth anniversary. Since its beginning, five camps had been established in the national forest. People were encouraged to drive the 160 miles of well-constructed roads built by the CCC and enjoy the scenery and the recreational areas. The success in suppressing forest fires was largely owing to the construction of fire towers and the 140 miles of telephone line connecting them to administrative points, a central dispatch, and an efficient fire-fighting organization at the CCC camps. Other achievements included timber stand improvement and inventory, bridge construction, collection of seeds, and nursery work.

On November 4, 1937, the *Moulton Advertiser* reported that there were three recreation projects under construction in the national forest. The Natural Bridge picnic grounds had been finished two months earlier, the first of its kind in the Black Warrior. The CCC boys had constructed a parking lot and picnicking facilities for small parties that might be attracted to the unusual rock formation. During the last two months, there had been over 2,500 visitors. A week earlier, construction on a dam had begun that would impound a 35-acre lake at Brushy Creek. Boating, bathing, and camping facilities were to be built for 1,500 visitors. The lake would be stocked with bass, bream, and other game fish. Work had also begun at the Sipsey River picnic grounds. A parking area, picnicking facility, picnic shelter, and bathhouse were under construction. This third recreation area was one of the most attractive locations in the state of Alabama, with numerous waterfalls and caves, according to the article.

On March 8, 1938, the *Moulton Advertiser* reported that the lake basin at Brushy Creek was nearly cleared. Excavation for the dam was under way, and the pouring of concrete was to begin soon. Plans were drawn for picnic shelters near the lake, and a softball field was to be laid out on a flat plain overlooking the creek. Individual fireplaces, barbeque pits, and picnic tables were also to be built.

On September 21, 1939, the *Moulton Advertiser* announced that Camp F-5 was to be moved to the old location of Camp F-4. On October 26, the paper reported that Company 3476 had begun moving to Camp F-11 at Grayson, Alabama. District Ranger Thomas A. Wilson stated that Camp F-5 had carried a heavy workload since 1935, completing all of the planned work in the Black Warrior National Forest. In addition to road and telephone line construction and maintenance, they had built a 100-foot fire tower and lookout fireman's dwelling, two picnic grounds, a 327-foot dam, and a 20-by-80-foot warehouse. They had also conducted timber stand improvement, planted trees, collected seed, and fought forest fires.

Company 3476, Camp F-11, Moulton, Alabama

On October 2, 1939, Company 3476 moved to Camp F-11 to be more centrally located for project work. According to the *Historical Records of CCC Camp Buildings*, the structures from Camp F-5 were relocated to the new camp by November 15. The new camp was called "Camp Collier," retaining the old Camp F-4 name.

A Camp Inspection Report dated October 17, 1939, recorded 196 men under the command of Stewart A. Martin, a civilian. The last two weeks in camp had been spent in improvements, and the project work under John W. Montgomery was about to begin. The project work consisted of road and bridge construction, surfacing roads, and development of a recreational area (Brushy Lake).

A Camp Inspection Report dated November 13, 1940, recorded 189 men under the command of Charles C. McCutchen. The forest ranger reported that the project work and working ability of the boys were good. The camp was in healthy condition, with the educational program functioning properly and recreational opportunities and amusement being provided for the enrollees.

The following year, a Camp Inspection Report dated November 26, 1941, recorded 190 men under the command of 2nd Lt. Edward L. Lindsey. Timber stand improvement, forest fire protection, a fire tower, and tower maintenance had been added to the work project. The company had acquired additional equipment for road construction.

James Hardin Garrison, of Haleyville, Alabama, arrived in Camp F-11 in early 1941 and began working in the rock quarry. He had a reaction to his typhoid inoculation, and his sledge hammer "got the best of him." After he recovered, he was assigned as a truck driver (James Hardin Garrison interview, May 22, 2001; see the CD).

Camp F-11 was abandoned sometime during the eighteenth period, likely in February 1942.

The Conecuh National Forest

On January 21, 1935, the National Forest Reserve Commission established the Conecuh Purchase Unit in Covington and Escambia counties. The Conecuh National Forest was created by presidential proclamation on July 17, 1936. It consisted of 54,177 acres of cutover and burned-over lands, mostly barren except for scattered trees that had been considered undesirable by logging operators.

Company 3474, Camp F-9, Andalusia, Alabama

Company 3476 was organized on August 24, 1935, at Fort McClellan. The African-American junior company remained at Fort McClellan until February 3, 1936, when it went to Andalusia, Alabama, to establish Camp F-9 (1936

CCC District G Annual). The *Andalusia Star* reported on February 6 that the company of 210 men had established their camp near Open Pond. According to the *Historical Records of CCC Camp Buildings*, the men initially lived in tents. Eventually, 40 structures would be built across the 16.5-acre camp.

On April 2, 1936, the *Andalusia Star* reported that the Open Pond CCC camp was a "beehive of activity." Ten buildings had been constructed. Open Pond was their source for water; it was pumped to a tank and then fed to the buildings by gravity flow. A quarantine placed on the camp for influenza was expected to be lifted the following day, and project work had begun on road and bridge construction. Enrollees were patrolling the forest with firefighting equipment.

On April 23, the *Andalusia Star* reported that in addition to roads and truck trails being constructed, fire towers were to be built and connected by a telephone system. This would reduce the time needed to report and take action on forest fires. The enrollees were also going to replant areas of the forest not likely to restock naturally.

In January 1937, Company 3474 began publishing the "Open Pond Breeze." This camp newspaper, printed by the journalism class and copied on a mimeograph machine, contained news of the camp, work projects, messages from the commanding officer, camp gossip, and articles written by the editorial staff. The camp educational advisor supervised the editorial staff. Three issues, January–March 1937, were archived at the Center of Research Libraries at the University of Chicago.

Also in January 1937, Company 3474 began planting a large plantation of pine trees. Sixty enrollees had planted 22,000 trees on the first day. The pine seedlings came from an Emergency Conservation Work nursery in New Augusta, Mississippi. Company 3474 had also made improvements to their camp. Grass had been planted with wire placed to protect the grass from sheep and hogs. The recreational hall was equipped with two pool tables, a radio, and tables for cards and checkers. Clifton C. Hodnett Patrick, CEA, had arrived in camp on May 17, 1936. The educational program offered 48 courses at the elementary and high school levels ("Open Pond Breeze," January 25, 1937).

By mid-February, the work project at the Blue Pond Plantation was completed, with 826,500 trees planted on 1,000 acres at 6-by-8-foot intervals. A total of 250,000 longleaf and 576,000 slash-pine seedlings had been planted, with 90 percent survival. The Blue Pond Plantation was the first large-scale planting project in the national forests in Alabama ("Open Pond Breeze," February 1937).

Company 3474 had a basketball team. It had defeated the CCC team at Chapman (Company 4434) but had been upset by the high school team at De Funiak Springs, Florida. The sportswriter for the "Open Pond Breeze" analyzed the game and offered three factors contributing to the loss: Company 3474 had not practiced because of recent forest fires; the team was "heavy on their feet" from the three good meals they received each day (the high school boys were lucky to have a light lunch if anything at all); and, most revealing, the people at the game were very friendly, and as a dance was scheduled after the game, the team "couldn't keep [their] eyes on the ball and on the ladies too" ("Open Pond Breeze," February 1937).

In March 1937, the fire season had become so severe that the enrollees were not allowed to leave camp, so their basketball season was cut short. Plans had been made to dig a well in the camp. With a well for water, Open Pond would be opened for fishing and bathing. The enrollees were looking forward to a cool dip in the pond in the summer ("Open Pond Breeze," March 1937).

On September 2, 1937, the *Covington News* reported that the Forest Service was developing plans for a recreation area at Open Pond for bathing and picnicking. A large picnic shelter and a bathhouse, with running water and lavatory facilities, were to be built, as were picnic benches, barbeque pits, and fireplaces. It was expected to be completed by the summer of 1938.

A Camp Inspection Report dated December 3, 1937, recorded 199 enrollees from Alabama, Florida, and Louisiana under the command of 1st Lt. E. G. Graveley. The work project consisted of road construction and maintenance, construction of fences, tree planting over an area of 3,000 acres, development of a recreational area at Open Pond, and construction of the Yellow River fire tower. G. C. Walker was the project supervisor.

On February 3, 1938, the *Andalusia Star* reported that the Forest Service had completed the planting of 2,500,000 pine trees. This project had begun on November 29, 1937, and required 2,800 man-days. The CCC enrollees planted on average 890 trees each six-hour day.

On June 23, 1938, the *Covington News* reported that the recreational area at Open Pond would be opened to the public by Labor Day; however, the public was invited to use the facilities at the present time. A beautiful log cabin bathhouse had been built on the eastern shore of the pond with dressing rooms and a shower room. There was also a combination concession and basket room with 440 baskets. The bathhouse was "built of large hewn timbers, its setting among the majestic pines portrays a beautiful and restful atmosphere to the surroundings." It was set on concrete piers with [lead] termite shields. A picnic shelter 17-by-40 feet with a 6-foot fireplace was also under construction. Carpet grass had been sodded around the buildings and between the beach and picnic grounds. There were 17 combination table and seats in the picnic area and 12 fireplaces, plus a barbeque pit.

In July 1938, Camp F-9 was selected to host the Fourth Corps Area training for Red Cross lifesaving. The *Andalusia Star* reported on July 14 that approximately 130 African-American enrollees, two from each camp in North Carolina, South Carolina, Tennessee, Alabama, Mississippi, and Louisiana, were to receive senior lifesaving certificates. The 36-hour training was held at Camp F-9 and at Blue Pond over six days. William Allen of Pensacola, Florida, was an enrollee in Company 4450 at Camp P-81 in Wewahitchka, Florida. He recalled attending the lifeguard training at Camp F-9 for a two-week period in the summer of 1939 (William Allen interview, March 6, 2001; see the CD). Ernest Hubbard, born near Perdido, Alabama, had been sent from his camp in Dothan, Alabama, to Camp F-9 at Lakemont, Georgia, to attend the Red Cross lifesaving and water safety course and become a qualified instructor. After his training, he was sent to Camp F-9 at Andalusia to train African-American enrollees in lifesaving and water safety during the summer of 1940 (Ernest Hubbard interview, January 8, 2004; see the CD).

A Camp Inspection Report dated October 5, 1938, recorded 176 enrollees under the command of Captain Lamar D. Gaston. The work project, under the supervision of William P. Moon, was spread over an area of 240,000 acres. A monthly camp educational report, prepared by CEA Clarence C. Walker Jr. reported that most of the men in the company had learning at the elementary school level. Literacy classes were offered and elementary classes for first through eighth grades. Twenty enrollees had learned to read and write since arriving in camp. The library and reading room contained 425 volumes, and the enrollees were reading 7 newspapers.

In September 1939, the company of 192 men was under the command of J. C. Pruitt, a civilian, according to a September 21 Camp Inspection Report. The work project continued under the supervision of Mr. Moon. Company 3471 had received an award for the best garden in District G for the spring and summer of 1939. Three men had received employment as a result of classes taught in camp. Ten enrollees had learned to read and write. CEA Walker was expecting good financial returns from a swine project that was doing well. A new library was under construction, and the camp had 600 volumes in the library, including reference, traveling, and permanent libraries.

A Camp Inspection Record dated November 10, 1941, recorded 187 men under the command of 1st Lt. William M. Anderson. The work project was now under the supervision of Glenn C. Walker. In 1941, Company 3474 had planted 3,335 acres of pine seedlings, conducted timber stand improvement on 6,600 acres, built 15,460 rods of fence, and spent 924 man-days fighting forest fires. The camp educational program had added courses in mechanics, metalworking, electricity, and woodworking as part of the national defense training program. Special emphasis had also been placed on classes for illiterates, which had 32 enrollees.

According to the *CCC Camp Directory for Alabama*, Camp F-9 was abandoned sometime during the eighteenth period, likely in February 1942.

The Talladega National Forest

On January 21, 1935, the National Forest Commission created the Talladega Purchase Unit. The Talladega National Forest was created by proclamation of President Roosevelt on July 17, 1936. The Talladega Division consisted of the Shoal Creek Ranger District, roughly Piedmont to Cheaha State Park, and the Talladega Ranger District, from Cheaha State Park to Sylacauga. Each district had a junior African-American company.

Company 3477, Camp F-6, Heflin, Alabama

The *Cleburne News* reported that a CCC camp was established in Helfin on May 16, 1935. Congressman Joe Starnes was largely responsible for getting the camp. When the paper reported on June 27 that the camp would be occupied by black enrollees, a strong protest ensued. Businessmen and merchants voted 51 to 2 in favor of having no camp over having a camp with black enrollees. The people of Heflin were assured that there would be no CCC camp in Heflin. The camp, however, would be established.

Company 3477 was organized at Heflin, on July 17, 1935, from an advanced cadre of men from Company 465 located at Camp SP-7 at Munford, with additional enrollees from Alabama, Florida, and Louisiana. On July 31, additional enrollees from Calhoun, Etowah, Marengo, Hale, Choctaw, and Sumter counties arrived, bringing the company's strength up to 190 men (1936 and 1938 CCC District D annuals).

The Historical Record of CCC Camp Buildings recorded that Camp F-6 was located on the south side of Heflin on 20 acres of leased land. The men were temporarily housed in tents until the buildings were completed. Water was provided by a well 220 feet deep and stored in a 5,400-gallon tank on a steel tower.

The work project was to be conducted across rough mountainous country that was accessible only by foot or horseback. Company 3477 was to make the forest more accessible, then to establish lookout towers connected by telephone lines to protect the forest (1936 CCC District D annual). The *Cleburne News* reported on August 1, 1935, that the Forest Service was to construct a 75-mile scenic road along the crest of the main ridge running through the newly acquired national forest. The scenic road, called the Skyway Motorway, was to connect Sylacauga to Borden Springs. The 1936 annual reported that 17 miles of the "Skyway Motor Way" had been located, opened, and graded. When the road was finished, it would be one of the most beautiful scenic routes in Alabama and the South.

Arthur Burton of Kellyton, Alabama, served in Company 3477 from July to December 1935 as a machine operator on road construction between Highway 78 and Cheaha State Park. He also taught the other enrollees how to use the machinery. He recalled that there were three caterpillars and another machine used on the road. During his six-month enrollment, he worked exclusively on road construction and was never taken from this job to fight forest fires. After his six-month enrollment ended, he was called back as a local experienced man to serve as driver for the project superintendent (Arthur Burton interview, August 27, 2001; see the CD).

A Camp Inspection Report dated December 19, 1935, recorded that Company 3477 had 189 men from Alabama, Tennessee, Mississippi, and West Virginia under the command of Captain G. R. Bridges. The project work was under the supervision of W. P. Moon. The camp educational advisor, Joseph M. Lawson, reported that the average enrollee had a fourth grade education. One-third of them could not read a newspaper or write a letter home. Two classes for illiterates had been organized. Several enrollees with college training were helping in the educational program, as well as army and Forest Service personnel.

Money had been appropriated for a camp newspaper, which was to be printed twice a month beginning in January 1936. Three issues of the "Carver Outlook" were archived at the University of Chicago—February 12, March 31, and November 23, 1936. Sentell Martin was the main editor with a staff of four or five editors who reported on camp activities. All enrollees were asked to contribute to the paper, and a box was placed in the recreation hall for jokes.

On February 19, 1936, *Our Mountain Home*, a weekly newspaper of Talladega County, reported that Company 3477 had sent a detachment of 60 men to the abandoned CCC camp at McElderry, formerly Camp SP-7. The purpose of the side camp was to rebuild the road from McElderry to Cheaha State Park that had been damaged by heavy rains and flooding.

A Camp Inspection Report dated November 14, 1936, recorded 148 enrollees from Alabama, Georgia, Florida, Mississippi, and Louisiana under the command of Captain H. M. Brock. The work project, under Supervisor Moon, had expanded to include fire suppression as well as construction of roads and telephone lines.

Beginning on August 27, 1937, the *Cleburne News* printed six weekly installments of "Life in a C.C.C. Camp" written by Samuel L. Younge, the CEA for Company 3477. The articles took the reader through the CCC enlistment process and "walked" them through the camp, explaining the function of each building. The reader was also "introduced" to the company commander, his staff, and the functions of the various programs in camp.

A Camp Inspection Report dated November 5, 1937, recorded 251 enrollees from Alabama, Florida, and Louisiana under the command of Captain T. L. Brown Jr. The camp was terribly overcrowded, with 60 enrollees in each barracks and others quartered in the infirmary, woodshop, and schoolroom. The company was fed in two shifts. While road construction was still the primary work, the work project also included construction of bridges, fire towers, and telephone lines. Forest stand improvement, landscaping, and campground development had also been added. It was estimated that the approved projects would be completed in six months; however, the work could be carried on indefinitely. It was also noted that motor transportation was no longer being furnished for recreation, by order of the company commander. Special Investigator J. C. Reddoch noted that the nearby town of Helfin was "inhabited largely with white people and because of this the colored company would like to be furnished recreational trips to centers that are inhabited by their own race."

Mr. Burton recalled that the relationship between the CCC enrollees and the people of Heflin was strained, and the citizens didn't care much for the CCCs. He remembered that an enrollee had been murdered in town, and that incident had not helped relations (Arthur Burton interview, August 27, 2001; see the CD). The *Cleburne News* reported on July 2, 1936, that an enrollee from Camp F-6 was found dead along the Bankhead Highway. Foul play was suspected, but there was not enough evidence for an arrest.

A Camp Inspection Report dated August 24, 1938, recorded 198 men under the command of Captain Sam H. Browne. The work project, under the supervision of G. C. Walker, now also included the construction of firemen's dwellings at the lookouts. No transportation was available for the baseball team to travel to other camps, and there were only two trips to Anniston each month. Special Investigator Reddoch noted that company morale would improve if the trips were made weekly.

According to a Camp Inspection Report dated September 9, 1939, there were 194 men under the command of Robert A. Lewis, civilian commander. The work project, under G. C. Walker, was suffering because of excessive time for transportation. A new camp was to be built closer to the work, and Camp F-6 was preparing for the move. The recreation hall, the educational building, and one of the barracks had been dismantled. The new camp, Camp F-12, was located 21 miles north of Camp F-6.

Company 3477, Camp F-12, Piedmont, Alabama

Camp Choccolocco, F-12, was established on October 1, 1939. By October 11, the structures from Camp F-6 had been transferred to the new camp located approximately 12 miles south of Piedmont. The camp was 16 acres in size, located in the Talladega National Forest near the community of Grantley.

It had been reported in the *Piedmont Journal* on September 22 that the camp at Heflin was moving. Piedmont wanted to be designated business headquarters of the camp. As such, the camp would do most of the needed purchasing in the town, which could be as much as $5,000 each month. Further, the enrollees would spend a portion of their allotment in town. Town officials, service clubs, and citizens were encouraged to make a concerted effort to make Piedmont the designated railhead. Company 3477's primary work project was constructing the scenic highway running from Cheaha State Park. They were presently working on the section between Grantley and Borden Springs. According to the *Piedmont Journal* of March 22, 1940, Piedmont had become the designated railhead for Camp F-12, and all supplies requisitioned by the government and all mail for the camp would come through the town. Incidental purchases for the camp and the enrollees' purchases would further boost the Piedmont economy.

A Camp Inspection Report dated August 29, 1940, recorded 199 enrollees under the command of Robert A. Lewis. The work project was progressing, but, because of poor roads leading to the camp, it was inaccessible. In spite of the isolation, the camp was in a satisfactory condition and company morale was high. On October 25, the *Piedmont Journal* reported that the gravel road over the mountain to the CCC camp was in good shape. Even though the road was narrow, it traversed a beautiful scenic route through the mountains, and numerous people were visiting the camp. Camp Commander Lt. William M. Anderson extended a cordial welcome to all visitors.

The *Piedmont Journal* reported on July 11, 1941, that Company 3477 was being transferred to south Alabama, as the War Department was consolidating camps. The "Sky Way Motor Way" was completed to a point about five miles from Bethel Church (less than a mile from Borden Springs). The road had been graded and cherted and was in fine condition. According to the NACCCA database, Company 3477 transferred to Camp P-77 at Uriah, Alabama, on July 11 to work on a private forestry project.

Company 3478, Camp F-7, Talladega, Alabama

Company 3478 was organized on July 17, 1935, at Camp F-7 at Chandler Springs, Alabama. The company of African-American junior enrollees was developed from a cadre of 25 men from Company 465 from Munford, 110 men from Birmingham, and 50 men from other locations in Alabama and Mississippi (1936 CCC District D annual).

The *Talladega Daily Home* reported on July 19 that a detachment of enrollees had arrived from Birmingham on their way to CCC Camp F-7. With a unit of 56 boys from Decatur, this brought the number of enrollees in camp to 126, and another 75 were expected. The camp would work on reforestation projects in the Talladega Reforestation Unit. On July 26, the *Talladega Daily Home* reported there were 183 enrollees at Camp F-7, with company strength eventually to exceed 200. Six engineers and construction engineers from the Forest Service were to arrive soon to serve as project supervisors on road construction. On July 29, the paper reported that a scenic road was to be constructed along the mountain crest, connecting Sylacauga and Borden Springs. Enrollees from CCC Camps F-7 and F-6 were to work on the project, with an additional 40 laborers from Talladega County and 20 laborers from Clay County hired through the Works Progress Administration (WPA). As the work progressed, WPA laborers would be hired from Cleburne and Calhoun counties. Other work projects included installing a system of fire towers and telephones to assist in fire protection.

On November 13, 1935, *Our Mountain Home* reported that Company 3478 had gone into action on their first forest fire, a 300-acre fire near the abandoned CCC camp at McElderry. Two 16-man crews fought the fire under the supervision of W. R. Silcocks, Talladega Unit forest ranger.

A Camp Inspection Report dated December 20, 1935, recorded 209 men from Alabama, Mississippi, and Tennessee under the command of Lt. Edwin

L. Olds, USNR. The work project consisted of construction of truck trails, bridges, and fire towers and fire suppression under the supervision of G. C. Walker.

The 1936 *Official Annual of District D* stated that the work project was in "full swing" by August 20, 1935. Seven miles of motorway had been cleared and graded between Sylacauga and Cheaha State Park with more than 200 steel and masonry culverts. Other projects included construction of telephone lines, a 200-foot concrete bridge, and a 100-foot steel tower. Recreational opportunities in camp included a choir, a chorus, and two quartets that specialized in singing traditional spirituals. The groups performed in local churches and theaters. Enrollee Sandy Witt had administered first aid for a rattlesnake bite to a young lady living in a nearby farmhouse when no doctor was available. During the winter of 1935, Witt had attended to three children suffering from burns.

On July 22, 1936, *Our Mountain Home* reported that construction on a 100-foot steel tower at Horn Mountain was completed, and two other towers were under construction near Hollins and Heflin. Three or four 35-foot steel towers were to be built to complete coverage of the forest. Telephone lines had been installed between Talladega, Camp F-7, and the Horn Mountain tower. Six additional radio receivers were to be used at the towers and CCC camps and in an emergency fire truck. The central radio station was at the Forest Service office at the city hall in Talladega.

On August 26, *Our Mountain Home* reported that Forest Supervisor Frank W. Rasor had visited the Talladega forest unit, and he said the Talladega National Forest had possibilities unsurpassed by any national forest in the southeastern United States. A third of the Skyway Motorway had been completed the previous year. Most of the work had been done by hand, but with heavy machinery now available, the work would progress more rapidly. The Forest Service had plans for two large parks and playground projects, which would include artificial lakes, bathhouses, and other shelters, and a game refuge that would be stocked with deer, turkey, and fish. Two lookout towers were completed, and the foundation for a third had been poured. Eventually 10 or 12 fire towers would be erected across the forest unit.

Harold E. Woodard of Munford, Alabama, recalled that his father, William T. Woodard, was hired by the Forest Service to assist in the supervision of the work projects at the CCC camp at Chandler Springs around this time. His father had previously worked in Lawrence County driving a road grader, and he would eventually work up to acting project superintendent in 1940 (Harold E. Woodard interview, February 20, 2006; see the CD). William

Woodard was listed with the Using Service for Company 3478 in the 1936 and 1938 District D annuals.

Our Mountain Home reported on November 4 that Regional Forester Joseph C. Kirchner had approved the plans for the Devil's Den Recreation Area one-half mile from the Munford–Cheaha Mountain Road. Construction of a small dam would impound a lake of 25 to 30 acres (Lake Chinnabee). A bathhouse, picnic shelters, open fireplaces, and other improvements for camping and picnicking would be built.

According to a Camp Inspection Report dated November 16, 1936, there were 147 enrollees from Alabama, Florida, Georgia, Mississippi, and Tennessee under the command of Lt. Edwin L. Olds. The work project was under the supervision of E. C. Bailey. Special Inspector James C. Reddoch noted that there was no traveling or permanent library in camp and the camp was in need of textbooks.

On February 10, 1937, *Our Mountain Home* reported that Camp F-7 was providing housing for 105 African-American flood refugees. The men, women, and children had been evacuated from Arkansas before the Mississippi River reached flood stage. The 1938 District D annual recorded that the refugees stayed in Camp F-7 through March 1937.

Our Mountain Home announced on March 31 that Camp F-7 was preparing for the fourth anniversary of the CCC and was going to host a celebration for the four years completed in restoring and conserving the nation's natural resources. The citizens of Talladega were invited to attend. Dr. Buell Gordon Gallagher, president of Talladega College, was to be the principal speaker on the formal program.

On April 7, *Our Mountain Home* summarized the accomplishments of the two CCC camps in the Talladega National Forest since the summer of 1935. They had extinguished more than 700 forest fires. Twenty-eight miles of new road had been built and five miles of old road rebuilt. Approximately 75 miles of old logging roads had been cleared and repaired, allowing better access for fighting forest fires. Three fire towers were completed and communications maintained over 51 miles of telephone lines. Construction had begun on recreational areas that would include picnic grounds and shelters at scenic spots and on a Forest Service Ranger headquarters at Talladega, and additional dwellings for fire watchmen were being built. Timber stand improvement had begun at the Heflin camp and would soon extend over the entire forest area.

On July 27, 1937, the *Tuscaloosa News* reported that enrollees from Camp F-7 had assisted in the search and rescue of a two-year-old girl who had been lost for a night. "Christine Argo was found alive and well on a mountainside nearly 24 hours after she wandered off while at play." Sheriff W. D. Mayo organized the search party, recruiting 150 enrollees from Camp F-7 and another 200 from Camp SCS-13 at Ashland.

A Camp Inspection Report dated November 17, 1937, recorded 194 men under the command of Captain William D. Van Arnam. The work project supervisor, J.F.B. Rylant, estimated that six years would be required to complete the approved work. It was also noted that the camp had an inadequate supply of only six trucks, so two trips were needed to take the enrollees to the work site, which in some cases was 25 miles from the camp. Lack of transportation was interfering with the progress of the work.

According to the 1938 District D annual, published on February 1, 1938, Company 3478 had won the "best all-round colored company" in District D three times in succession. The company chorus and quartet won second place in the district contest held in Heflin on July 19, 1937. The work project included the construction of a 20-foot four-span steel truss concrete bridge and the establishment of an experimental nursery.

A Camp Inspection Report dated August 26, 1938, recorded 183 men under the command of Captain Comer L. Vandiver. The work project was scattered over 136,000 acres. In addition to road and telephone line construction and maintenance, a Zone Central Repair Shop had been built in Talladega to maintain CCC vehicles. The development of a recreation area was continuing with the construction of a concrete dam 164 feet long and 22 feet high.

The Skyway Motorway, the primary work project, had proceeded far enough from camp that additional driving time was needed. It was decided to move Company 3478 to the abandoned CCC camp at Munford where it would be closer to the road construction project and the Devil's Den Recreation Area. Camp F-7 at Chandler Springs was abandoned on June 21, 1939, and Company 3478 moved to the camp at Munford. According to the *Historical Record of CCC Camp Buildings*, the structures at Camp F-7 were dismantled and moved to the new Camp SP-17 at Munford during May and June 1939.

Company 3478, Camp F-10, Munford, Alabama

Company 3478 established Camp F-10 at Munford in June 1939. The camp at Munford had been originally constructed as Camp SP-2 in October 1933 by Company 259. According to the *Historical Record of CCC Camp Buildings*,

Camp F-10 had 40 structures in 1939, 11 of them relatively new, having been built in November 1938. The camp had served as a home for Companies 465, 468, and 2420-V.

A Camp Inspection Report dated September 29, 1939, recorded 192 men under the command of Lt. David E. Rainey. The work project, under the supervision of J.F.B. Rylant, consisted of the construction of the Devil's Den Dam and Recreation Area, sections of the Skyway Motorway, and the ranger's residence at the Talladega administration site, and timber stand improvement. It also included construction of forest roads, motorways, and telephone lines across the forest. Latrines, tool houses, and woodsheds were constructed at two lookout towers, and the structures at another five lookout towers were being maintained. Work progress had been hampered by rain and other work details, including construction details in camp and the reconditioning of some of the other buildings in camp. Special Investigator Reddoch described the camp as "excellent in every way." The recreation hall was "very attractive" and well furnished with indoor games. The camp had a natural boxing ring in a "natural bowl setting."

Harold E. Woodard recalled that his father, William T. Woodard, spent most of his time working with crews fighting forest fires after Company 3478 transferred to the Munford camp (Harold E. Woodward interview, February 20, 2006; see the CD). William T. Woodard was listed with the "Technical Personnel" in the September 29, 1939, inspection report as a squad foreman.

On October 9, 1940, *Our Mountain Home* reported that the officers' quarters in camp had been destroyed by fire on the sixth. It had started while the men were at their midday meal and was discovered by a Forest Service fire lookout. The officers' personal belongings were lost in the fire. The cause was under investigation. According to the *Historical Record of CCC Camp Buildings*, the officers' quarters was replaced on January 31, 1941, with a building from Camp SCS-5 at Carrolton, Alabama.

A Camp Inspection Report dated November 19, 1940, recorded 205 men under the command of Clyde L.R. Powell. The work project was progressing satisfactorily under acting project superintendent William T. Woodard. The enrollees were sent to Talladega twice weekly for recreational purposes, and all of the enrollees were participating in the athletic program.

According to a Camp Inspection Report dated October 16, 1941, Company 3478 had 188 men under the command of Captain G. R. Bridges, inactive reserve. J.F.B. Rylant had returned as the project supervisor. The work project consisted of the construction and maintenance of roads, bridges, and telephone lines across the forest, timber stand improvement, and the construction of a ranger dwelling and three firemen's dwellings. Construction of the 164-foot dam at the Lake Chinnabee Recreation Area continued.

A Camp Inspection Report dated June 22, 1942, recorded 180 enrollees under the command of Gatewood R. Bridges. The Skyway Motorway was still the primary work project. All of the structures along the scenic road were completed, and the final grading and drainage were 25 percent completed. It was predicted that Coon Creek Bridge would be completed by July 1, 1942. The construction of 6.1 miles of telephone line between the Cheaha–McElderry Road and the Talladega Ranger Station was 20 percent completed. Ten miles of the Skyway Motorway was to be "sprigged" with Bermuda grass (spot planting of small sods of grass). A children's bathing pool was to be constructed at Lake Chinnabee. Concrete boxes were to be placed on the cisterns at the Horn Mountain, Horseblock, and Hollins fire towers.

It is uncertain if any of the work projects mentioned in the June 22 report were completed with CCC labor. The Civilian Conservation Corps officially ended on July 1, 1942.

4
The CCC and the Soil Conservation Service

By the 1920s, soil erosion had been recognized both nationally and in Alabama as a serious problem that needed attention. County agents and agricultural workers had begun working on terracing and soil erosion control. In 1929, Congress appropriated money for the Department of Agriculture to study the problem, and 10 experimental stations were developed across the country. On August 25, 1933, the Soil Erosion Service (SES) was created as a temporary division of the Department of Interior. In April 1934, the SES created the Buck and Sandy Creek projects, consisting of 117,000 acres in Tallapoosa and Chambers counties, to teach farmers erosion control techniques. The *Alabama Erosion Survey of 1934* reported that almost 83 percent, over 27 million acres, of Alabama's lands had been damaged by accelerated erosion (Medlock 1985:1–2).

In May 1934, CCC Camps were established at Gainesville and Dadeville, and in October, a third camp was established at Camp Hill. The SES used the CCC enrollees to demonstrate techniques of controlling erosion on farms in the project areas. Thousands of farmers and other landowners visited the projects.

On April 27, 1935, the Soil Erosion Service was transferred to the Department of Agriculture and became the Soil Conservation Service (SCS). State headquarters were established at Auburn (Medlock 1985:4). In July and August 1935, nine more CCC camps were established in Alabama.

On April 8, 1936, *Our Mountain Home* reported that about 2,000 boys were assigned to soil erosion work in Alabama in 11 camps under SCS supervision. The work was coordinated with farmers and extension workers on thousands of acres. Technicians from the camps conducted surveys, recording soil type, topography, and extent of erosion. The farmers and soil conservationists then planned the best use of the land. Crop rotation and the use of winter and summer legumes controlled sheet erosion. Farmers terraced the cultivated lands, and the CCC enrollees constructed the outlets and outlet channels. Steep and potentially erosive slopes were retired from cultivation and planted in trees, grass, and kudzu. Gullies were stabilized with check dams and vegetation.

Most of the work conducted for the Soil Conservation Service projects was similar from camp to camp, consisting of constructing terraces and water-control systems on farmers' fields, planting trees and other plants on marginal cropland, and building erosion control check dams in gullies. The CCC enrollees grew seedlings for conservation work, developed habitat for wildlife, and helped in sediment studies.

Critical to the coordination of this work was the SCS county agent. In most cases, it was the county agent who first informed local farmers of the importance of having a CCC camp in the county. The *Ashland Progress* reported on April 11, 1935, that Clay County Agent F. M. White had met with local farmers at the courthouse to explain the necessity of having a soil conservation program. He urged those attending to visit the work being done around Lake Martin. It was hoped that a CCC camp would be coming to Clay County soon.

On August 15, 1935, the *Democratic-Reporter*, the weekly newspaper of Marengo County, reported that Mr. Winch, the county agent, had announced that terracing of farmers' fields was to begin. The County Board of Revenue had purchased a diesel tractor for this purpose, and farmers were to sign up with the county agent to have their fields terraced. The CCC men would construct the outlet ditches and headings and perform other associated work. On August 15, as the SCS was establishing a CCC camp in Clay County, the county agent, F. M. White, wrote in his column in the *Ashland Progress* that Clay County would have to furnish terracing equipment. Those farmers wishing to have their fields terraced would give promissory notes on the machinery for the cost of the work, and the notes would come due upon its completion. After the terracing was completed, the CCC enrollees would complete the ends of the terraces and build the outlet ditches. The materials for the work was free, to be furnished by the federal government.

Company 476, Camps SES-1 and SCS-1, Gainesville, Alabama

Company 476 was a junior company of Alabama enrollees organized on May 23, 1933, at Fort McClellan. After two weeks of conditioning, they were sent to Morris Station, Georgia, and established Camp P-75, a private forestry project, on June 25. On May 19, 1934, they transferred to Gainesville to establish Camp SES-1 under the command of Lt. Lee Helms. By that July, they had completed construction of two barracks, a kitchen, and mess hall and had begun hauling gravel for the camp roads. Captain W. G. Campbell had taken command, and work began to improve camp conditions (1934 CCC District D annual).

The 1936 District D annual recorded that Camp SES-1 had been designated Camp SCS-1 and named "Camp John A. Rodgers" after Gainesville's state senator. The work relationship between the army personnel and the SCS staff had been pleasant and "mutually helpful, to the great advantage of all concerned." On January 1, 1936, B. G. Allen relieved D. W. Pittman as the project superintendent. The camp baseball team won the 1935 subdistrict championship and played at the District D World Series at Fort McClellan.

According to the *CCC Camp Directory for Alabama*, Camp SCS-1 was abandoned before the end of the tenth period, which ended June 30, 1937.

Company 1405, Camps SES-2 and SCS-2, Dadeville, Alabama

Company 1405 was organized on May 18, 1933, at Fort Benning, Georgia. The junior enrollees from Alabama and Georgia had a five-week conditioning period, during which "these lads had it tough" before being sent to Baxley, Georgia, to work on a private forestry project. After several weeks of construction, the camp was under quarantine for unrecorded reasons. On May 24, 1934, Company 1405 transferred to Dadeville to establish Camp SES-2 under the command of Captain Hubert T. Andrews. The camp was built four miles from Dadeville, and initially it had no water or electricity (1934 CCC District D annual).

By 1936, Camp SCS-2 was completed and had improved significantly, with electricity supplied from the Alabama Power Company. The camp had two tennis courts, a large athletic field, and an observation tower of logs at the entrance. Company 1405 had a camp newspaper (issues of the "Bullard Bombshell" from 1936 to 1938 were archived at the University of Chicago). The work project was soil conservation in the gullied red hills of Tallapoosa County and consisted of terracing fields, controlling runoff, and reducing erosion. The enrollees from Alabama, Georgia, Mississippi, and Florida were under the command of Captain Harvey Price (1936 CCC District D annual).

Charlie R. Cauthen of Lapine, Alabama, enrolled in Company 1405 in April 1939. He worked for a while on the soil conservation project but decided to try to find work in the kitchen. He was first assigned to the KP (kitchen police) but eventually began cooking and serving breakfast for the camp officers. He was promoted to second cook, earning $36 a month. Mr. Cauthen was with Company 1405 when Camp SCS-2 was transferred to Camp SCS-17 at Hamilton, Alabama, on October 2, 1939 (Charlie R. Cauthen interview, October 28, 2002; see the CD).

Company 444, Camps SES-3 and SCS-3, Camp Hill, Alabama

Company 444 was organized on June 2, 1933, with junior enrollees from Alabama and Georgia. After two and one-half weeks of conditioning at Fort McClellan, they were sent to Commerce, Georgia, and on June 14, 1934, they were transferred to Glencoe, Alabama, where they established Camp P-57. On October 18, 1934, Company 444 transferred to Camp Hill. Their work project consisted of soil conservation and forestry and "filling up all of the gullies." On October 24, 1935, Company 444 was transferred to Camp SP-10 near Selma (1936 CCC District D annual).

Company 4435, Camp SCS-4, Brundidge and Troy, Alabama

According to the 1936 District G annual, Company 4435 was organized on July 20, 1935, and consisted of junior African-American enrollees under the command of Captain H. T. Hancock. On April 23, 1935, Captain Clarence L. Newton replaced Captain Hancock. On July 20, A. A. Shepard was assigned as the project superintendent, "ably assisted by a group of hard-working men." Initially, the camp lacked facilities for an educational program, but on August 27, J. T. Flournoy was assigned as the camp educational advisor, and he immediately organized vocational and academic classes. By September, the enrollees had built a swimming pool, and on December 22, a journalism class was created and began publishing a twice-monthly camp newspaper called the "Flash." It was "read with interest by both white and colored citizens of Brundidge" and was credited with creating a friendly relationship between the camp and local community (issues from 1936 to 1938 were archived at the University of Chicago).

On June 22, 1938, Company 4435 moved ten miles from Brundidge to Troy, retaining the designation as Camp SCS-4. On September 20, 1938, the company transferred to Camp P-76 at Vredenburgh, Alabama (NACCCA database).

Company 3479, Camp SCS-5, Carrollton, Alabama

On May 26, 1935, the *Tuscaloosa News* reported that the mayor of Carrollton, W. W. Curry, had received orders to begin construction of a camp for CCC soil erosion work. It was to be located on the Ellis McGee farm, adjacent to Federal Highway No. 17.

Company 3479 was created from a cadre of 25 men from Company 476 at Gainesville, Alabama, on May 27, 1935, under the command of Captain James H. Fike. The company was officially formed on August 16, receiving 175 junior enrollees from the procurement service at Jackson, Mississippi, from Alabama, Mississippi, Florida, and Georgia. Lt. Thomas A. Bradley was the company commander, Dr. Charles B. Gamble the CEA, and J. C. Haynie the project superintendent. Camp construction was completed on August 26 (1936 CCC District D annual).

Under Dr. Gamble, Company 3479 had an excellent education program. A manual training school was developed with a woodworking shop, and the 1936 annual reported that the shop made over 600 pieces of furniture and other camp equipment. The 1938 District D annual reported that the program had been so successful it was designated as a district training center, so enrollees in District D with an aptitude for woodworking could be transferred to Camp SCS-5. Over several months, enrollees made over 1,000 pieces of furniture and sold them for $2,000, according to the annual report. The 1938 annual recorded that over 1,000 pieces of furniture had been made.

The project work was of great value not only to the local farmers but also to the enrollees when they returned to their own farms. They were learning how to construct and maintain terraces and how to control erosion. The camp motto "Be Friendly" was followed, and the men were proud of the relationship between the camp and local neighbors. They took an active part in the community. Enrollee Walter Cook, who had completed lifesaving training, rescued a fellow enrollee after a rowboat overturned in a swollen stream (1938 CCC District D annual).

On October 30, 1939, the *Dothan Eagle* reported that 54 farmers in Pickens County had agreements with Camp SCS-5 to grow clover patches during the fall to help build soil over the winter.

Samuel D. Williams of Eatonon, Georgia, enrolled in the CCC in Barnwell, South Carolina, and was sent to Company 3479 on April 5, 1940, after his conditioning at Fort McPherson. He worked on a crew of 11 men unloading two carloads of coal for the camp. He was with Company 3479 when they transferred to Camp SCS-19 at Talladega on June 3 (Samuel D. Williams interview, August 27, 2001; see the CD).

Company 3480, Camp SCS-6, Greensboro, Alabama

Company 3480 was created from an advance cadre of 25 men from Company 465 at Munford, Alabama, on July 1, 1935. On August 2, another 185 enrollees arrived at the camp, located one mile west of Greensboro. The junior African-American enrollees from Alabama and Florida were under the command of Captain Frank A. Courtenay. Brooks Connell was the project superintendent. The Florida enrollees were enjoying themselves until snow began to fall, and by the time of the 1936 annual, all but two had returned to Florida (1936 CCC District D annual).

Dr. H. H. Bennett, chief of the SCS in Washington, was the guest of honor for Company 3480's annual field day and barbeque on July 13, 1937. He complimented the project work, which covered 450,000 acres, of which 35,517 acres were under agreement. Carl C. Morgan was the project superintendent at this time. Approximately 8,000 local persons attended the tours and lectures conducted by the SCS staff. The educational program had been a major objective in which 46 enrollees had been taught to read and write during 1937. Several enrollees had qualified for Civil Service jobs. Twenty percent of the enrollees left to accept employment outside of the CCC (1938 District D annual).

Company 3480 transferred to Monroeville, Alabama to establish Camp SCS-16 on October 3, 1939 (NACCCA database).

Company 3481, Camp SCS-7, Clanton, Alabama

On May 9, 1935, the *Union Banner*, a weekly newspaper of Clanton, reported that 12 acres had been leased to the U.S. government for a CCC camp to be located on the Selma Highway in West Clanton. Its purpose was to be soil conservation. Mr. Fant, the county agent, was pleased, as the camp would help him in the terracing program already in place.

The *Union Banner* reported on May 30 that a detachment of 25 men under the supervision of army officers had arrived from Bessemer to begin construction of the camp. Tents were erected, and there were plans to build wooden barracks for 200 men. City employees were laying water mains to supply water to the camp from Clanton.

On June 20, the *Union Banner* reported that word had been received that the CCC camp would be occupied by African-American enrollees. The town council passed a resolution stating that the town would prefer no CCC camp at all to having a "negro camp within the city limits." Whether or not the local protest was a factor, white junior enrollees were sent to the camp in August 1935.

Company 3481 was created from a cadre of 25 men from Company 487 at Bessemer on May 25, 1935. Construction of "Camp Clanchilala" began under the command of Captain Freeman Martin and Lt. Strickland ("Clanchilala was from "Clanton," "Chilton," and "Alabama"). The SCS supervisory personnel arrived on July 20. James H. Wood was the project superintendent. On August 11, enrollees from Florida, Alabama, Georgia, and Mississippi arrived in camp. The work project was throughout Chilton County (1936 District D annual).

On September 5, 1935, the *Union Banner* reported that camp construction was finished, with a rock-lined driveway, a boxing ring, a tennis court, and 16 buildings. The enrollees had received smallpox and typhoid shots, and project work would soon begin. A large portion of the company was from Key West and West Palm Beach, Florida, and many of the enrollees spoke only Spanish. CEA P. J. Benrimo was developing the educational program with instructors in woodworking and similar subjects.

On October 23, enrollees assisted in the search for an elderly man lost in a marsh near the camp. He was located within 15 minutes, given first aid in the camp, and carried on a stretcher to his home, where he soon recovered (1936 CCC District D annual). The relationship between Camp SCS-7 and the people of Clanton was good. The 1938 District D annual stated that the local people held the enrollees and camp staff in high esteem. Local businessmen visited the camp, and enrollees took part in the community activities. The *Union Banner* reported on March 24 and 31, 1938, that hundreds of parents from all over the state were expected to visit the camp for the fifth anniversary celebration planned for April 1.

Camp SCS-7 operated through the final work period in the summer of 1942.

Company 3482, Camp SCS-8, Alexandria, Alabama

Company 3482 was organized from a cadre of 25 enrollees from Company 475. An additional 175 junior African-American enrollees arrived on July 18, 1935, from Bibb, Jefferson, Sumter, Tuscaloosa, and Walker counties. The enrollees underwent conditioning in camp. Initially, all work was confined to the camp until the farmers had harvested the crops. The project work began in September under the supervision of Joe D. Tucker (1936 CCC District D annual).

Columbus Dothard of Ohatchee, Alabama, joined the CCC in 1936 and transferred to Company 3482 after six months in North Carolina. At Camp SCS-8, the crews were planting trees and kudzu for erosion control. Mr. Dothard's job was to keep all of the hand tools sharp and loaded on the trucks. He recalled that the men also fought forest fires (Columbus Dothard interview, February 15, 2002; see the CD).

The 1938 District D annual reported that the camp educational program was offering 33 courses and that 82 enrollees had been taught to read and write. The company quartet won first place in the district singing contest in June 1937, and the glee club took second place. The work project crews had planted 2,160,000 trees over seven square miles with ten-foot spacing. The monetary value of the planting and other soil conservation work could not be estimated in dollars and cents, as it would be showing returns for the next ten to twenty years.

The *CCC Camp Directory for Alabama* recorded that Camp SCS-8 was closed after the thirteenth period, which ended September 30, 1939.

Company 4447, Camp SCS-9, Auburn, Alabama

Camp SCS-9 or "Camp Sanford" was located one mile from Auburn. It was in District H, which was headquartered at Fort Benning, Georgia. The camp was occupied in late July or early August 1935. A Camp Inspection Report dated January 2, 1936, recorded 182 junior enrollees from Florida, Alabama, and Georgia under the command of Captain William G. Moses. The project work was under the supervision of M. A. Barnes. The educational program, under CEA Royal Mattice, offered 21 classes, including elementary, high school, and college courses, vocational courses, and courses on general subjects. Dr. Duncan, president of Alabama Polytechnic Institute, loaned a movie projector to be used by both Company 4447 and Company 4448 (at Camp SP-12, Chewacla State Park). API also provided four National Youth Administration teachers in each camp. Coach Meagher of the API athletic department donated a football and gave the enrollees use of the Auburn high school gym. Enrollees were given discount rates at sporting events and the Opelika Theatre, and monthly dances were held in camp.

A Camp Inspection Report dated September 28, 1938, recorded that the camp had 154 cooperative agreements throughout Lee County, totaling 35,652 acres. The education program continued under CEA Graves H. McDowall. Films were shown twice a month. The company had two traveling libraries containing 180 books, a reference library with 120 books, and reading and writing rooms.

Leonard L. Donald of Atmore, Alabama, enrolled in Company 4447 in April 1939. He was sent to Camp SCS-9 to go to the woodworking school. Since he had finished high school, he hoped he might also get to go to school at the university. He got homesick, however, and transferred to Camp P-77 at Uriah after three months (Leonard L. Donald interview, October 27, 2003; see the CD). Ernest Hubbard, born near Perdido, Alabama, also enrolled in Company 4447 in April 1939. He worked for four months with the crews clearing fields, planting kudzu, and constructing terraced farm fields. In the summer of 1939, he was sent to Dothan, Alabama, with a detachment to begin construction of a Camp SCS-14 (Ernest Hubbard interview, January 8, 2004; see the CD).

By September 1939 the work project was nearing completion. A Camp Inspection Report dated September 12, 1939, recorded 177 enrollees under the command of Lt. Edwin B. Cooper. They were working on highway erosion control and pasture improvement. The terrace outlet work was to be completed by October 1. A detachment of enrollees were at Dothan constructing a new camp.

On October 1, 1939, Company 4447 transferred to Camp SCS-14 at Dothan.

Company 4436, Camp SCS-10, Greenville, Alabama

Company 4436 was initially formed from two trucks of enrollees from the CCC camp at Bay Minette (Camp P-81, Company 484). On June 22, 1935, the trucks, under the command of Captain J. E. Mills, arrived at the campsite about a mile from Greenville. An additional 175 junior enrollees arrived from the railroad station on August 12 (1936 CCC District G annual).

John H. Guinn of Jasper, Alabama, was with the first two trucks of enrollees from Company 484, rated as an assistant leader. He had worked at Camp P-61 with the civil engineer and knew how to use a transit. When the trucks arrived at Greenville, he was given the task of laying out the camp in an open field. Mr. Guinn served at Camp SCS-10 for five years; as a rated man, he was not restricted to the two-year limit. He served as the supply sergeant for the first two and one-half years and was then promoted to "first sergeant" or "leader." As the first sergeant, he was responsible for the younger enrollees. He felt the people of Greenville appreciated the CCC boys. He had a good working relationship with the chief of police and the deputy sheriff. If an enrollee got into trouble, Mr. Guinn always tried to have the punishment take place at the camp rather than having the boy arrested (John H. Guinn interview, November 18, 2002; see the CD).

Company 4436's camp newspaper was called "The Advocate" and "The Mess Kit" in 1936, and "The Mail Bag" and "S.C.S. Sentinel" in 1938, and the paper was archived at the University of Chicago. On April 15, 1936, "The Mess Kit" recorded that Charles N. Kearley was the project superintendent and that he met regularly with two soil conservation groups to discuss their work. The paper related on July 1 that the work project included trimming and thinning a small pine forest. The cut brush was used in the construction of check dams in gullies. After the brush dams had caught fertile soil, the enrollees would plant trees in the soil. Terracing would follow, making the field more productive. Mr. Kearley wanted the enrollees to know that their work would create fertile soil for the next generation.

The January 15, 1937, issue of "The Mess Kit" reported that enrollee Lester Green had won an award for most improvement. He had entered camp at 122 pounds and within a year had gained 20 pounds of "robust muscles." He had also entered camp with little education and by year's end was in charge of a class studying practical arithmetic. He was awarded a handmade leather billfold.

January was tree-planting time. "The Mess Kit" announced that soon the enrollees would "follow the knotted line" (a knotted cord maintaining the planting interval). Thousands of trees would be planted, each doing its part in the war on erosion and floods, and later would provide timber for future generations. Camp SCS-10 was scheduled to receive 600,000 pine seedlings, 90,000 black locusts, 2,500 catalpa, and 400,000 kudzu crowns. The total of 1,092,500 plants worked out to about 8,500 per enrollee.

Thomas L. Sharpe of Montgomery, Alabama, transferred to Camp SCS-10 in January 1937 after serving at Camp TVA-11 in Moulton for six months. He worked in the auto shop as a blacksmith and did maintenance on the trucks as an assistant leader. He knew how to cut hair; he did so for the enrollees in camp, and many people from Greenville came to camp to get their hair cut. Mr. Sharpe played on the baseball team while at Camp SCS-10 and was even given a tryout with a semi-pro team in Andalusia. After playing baseball for a month, he decided to return to the camp (Thomas Lomax Sharpe interview, October 30, 2002; see the CD). Billy West of Greenville also played on the baseball team. He had joined the CCC in early 1938 at the age of fourteen. He taught himself how to throw a knuckleball, and the slow movement of the pitch confused batters. He worked on a crew planting kudzu and centipede sod in gullies (Billy West interview, December 18, 2002; see the CD).

"The Mail Bag" reported in August 1938 that in three years, Camp SCS-10 had worked on 34,094 acres on 157 farms under agreement. Company 4437 had been scheduled to be disbanded in September 1937, but the people of Greenville had been successful in keeping the company at the Greenville camp.

Company 4436 was transferred to Camp SCS-20 at Evergreen on June 1, 1940.

Company 4437, Camp SCS-11, Linden, Alabama

Camp SCS-11 was established in July 1935 from a cadre of 25 men from Company 1483 from Meridian, Mississippi. Company 4437 was organized on August 15, 1935, under the command of Captain M. G. Bonner. An additional 169 junior enrollees arrived the next day from Tampa, Florida, and more arrived October 22 from Jackson, Tennessee, and on November 12 from Foley, Alabama. Louis R. Smith was assigned project superintendent on July 5, 1935. The work project consisted of erosion control in gullies, terrace construction, planting fields in grasses, collecting seeds, planting trees, and fighting forest fires (1936 CCC District G annual).

A Camp Inspection Report dated January 8, 1936, recorded 184 enrollees at "Camp Boykin" from Alabama, Mississippi, Florida, Louisiana, and Tennessee. The work project, scattered over 853 square miles, consisted of constructing brush, earthen, wire, and rock dams and terrace outlets with concrete check and spreader dams. Eroded areas were reforested in pines and black locusts, and kudzu was planted.

In March 1936, Company 4437 published the first edition of "The Dope." The March and April issues were archived at the University of Chicago. The paper asked the enrollees for poetry, short stories, essays, jokes, novels, and plays. The March issue reminded the men that baseball season was approaching. A field meet was scheduled for April 5 with the public invited. Literary and athletic events would be held.

The April 1936 issue reminded the enrollees that the "world's best literature" could be found in camp. Many of the boys were improving themselves by reading. Camp dances were a favorite form of recreation, and a taxidermy class had begun. Rifles and shotguns were borrowed, and class members were stalking birds. A large woodpecker was the first taxidermy project by CEA Quinton T. Crowson.

On October 7, 1937, the *Democratic-Reporter* announced that Company 4437 had been disbanded the previous week, the enrollees to be transferred to other companies. An African-American company was to be sent to Camp Boykin under the command of Captain Earl Dewitt Dickey. The military and SCS staff were to remain.

Company 2451, Camp SCS-11, Linden, Alabama

Company 2451 was organized on October 3, 1937, with a cadre from Company 2423 at Corinth, Mississippi, under the command of Captain Gatewood R. Bridges. The African-American veterans were from all of the states of the Fourth Corps Area (1938 CCC District D annual).

A Camp Inspection Report dated November 23, 1937, recorded that Company 2451 was continuing the work began by Company 4437. Agreements were held on 22,507 acres for soil work across Marengo County. Louis R. Smith was the project supervisor. The camp had no educational program for the 218 men, but by the writing of the 1938 annual, Joseph A. Ross had been assigned as the CEA, and the men were enrolled in reading, writing, first aid, citizenship, auto mechanics, cooking, health, and safety classes. A glee club had also been organized.

Joseph A. Ross, born in Montgomery, Alabama, had earned an undergraduate degree from Morehouse College in Atlanta with a dual major in biology and chemistry and a master's degree in economics from Atlanta University in 1933. He was the camp education advisor at Camp F-13 in Morton, Mississippi, in 1936 and 1937 (Ms. Lettie Ross interview, September 20, 2002; see the CD).

Letters from local farmers praising the CCC work were published in the *Democratic-Reporter* on March 24 and April 14, 1938. A. L. Null wrote that he had always thought it best to have water run off his fields as quickly as possible, but after he terraced his field in 1935, he increased his corn yield by 40 percent. M. S. Bradford wrote that his farm had been a limestone patch not capable of growing broom-sage but that his fields had become productive after terracing. Ruby R. Lewis wrote that after a long wait, he finally got his turn with the county terracing machine, the first farmer in his community to do so. The CCC enrollees had sodded the outlets and built check dams in his gullies, and he concluded, "All glory to the Soil Conservation Service and the CCC now and forever."

On December 15, 1938, the *Democratic-Reporter* notified its readers that the CCC enrollees at Camp Boykin were available for fighting woods or grass fires. People were to contact A. A. Shepard, the project superintendent, if they wished assistance.

According to a Camp Inspection Report dated October 15, 1939, there were 157 men under the command of Captain Leonard P. Daniels. The work project, now under the supervision of Carl Morgan, continued throughout Marengo County. The educational program, now under CEA H. A. Wilson, had expanded, with vocational classes in agriculture, care of tools, carpentry, and music and vocals. The men showed interest in the woodshop, making furniture for the company and for personal use.

According to the *CCC Camp Directory for Alabama*, Camp SCS-11 was abandoned prior to the beginning of the fifteenth period, which began April 1, 1940.

Company 1432, Camp SCS-12, Clayton, Alabama

Company 1432 was organized on May 29, 1933, at Fort Benning, Georgia. The junior African-American enrollees were sent to Clayton, Alabama, that July to work on an erosion control project on the lands of A. B. Robertson (Camp PE-58). In July 1935, Company 1432 was rated as one of the two best companies in District H (1936 CCC District G annual). According to the *CCC Camp Directory for Alabama*, the SCS took over the project during the fifth period, which began on April 1, 1935, and designated it Camp SCS-12. On January 15, 1936, Company 1432, consisting of 210 men, was transferred to Camp SP-3 at Uriah, Alabama (1936 CCC District G annual).

Company 4488, Camp SCS-13, Ashland, Alabama

The *Ashland Progress* announced on June 27, 1935, that a CCC camp was to be built on the old fair grounds in the northern part of the city. The men were to work in soil conservation, using a large number of large terracing outfits. Twenty men were expected soon to begin building the camp, which would have 14 buildings. It would create a market for local produce, firewood, and other items.

On July 18, the paper reported that the first 30 enrollees had arrived on the fifteenth under the command of Lt. (Henry Collins) Urquhart. This initial cadre of African-American enrollees cleared an area for the camp and set up tents at the Clay County Fairgrounds. The camp was expected to be ready for a company of 300 men in 60 days.

The paper reported on August 8 that the initial cadre had been transferred and that 30 carpenters would have the camp ready in 10 days. It was to be occupied by white enrollees. Lt. Uquhart was still to be the commanding officer. Carl C. Morgan, the project superintendent, had arrived on August 7.

County Agent F. M. White's column "Farm Letters" appearing in the August 15 edition of the *Ashland Progress* reported that the CCC camp was nearly complete. The change from African-American to white enrollees had been made because of the objections of some of citizens living near the camp.

On August 22, 1935, Roy H. Ladd, the assistant CEA, began a series of articles that appeared regularly in the *Ashland Progress* titled "CCC Activities in Company 4488." He reported that the camp was nearly completed, and more than 100 recruits were expected from Florida by the end of the week.

On October 24, Ladd reported that Camp SCS-13 was preparing for its formal dedication. Hundreds of people were expected to attend the dedication of "Camp Hobbs," named after the Honorable Sam F. Hobbs, congressman of the district, who had supported the camps in Clay County. Colonel Baltzell, commanding officer of District D from Fort McClellan, Dr. Duncan from Auburn, and R. Y. Bailey of Dadeville, who was the regional director of the Soil Conservation Service, were also to attend.

The winter of 1935–36 was unusually cold. The *Ashland Progress* reported on January 30, 1936, that Clay County had received about a million trees and kudzu plants for the CCC boys to plant when the snow melted and the ground thawed. On February 6, the paper carried an article titled "Florida Boys See Snow." The Alabama boys of Company 4488 were telling tall tales of cold weather for the benefit of the Florida enrollees: Fires built out in the open had frozen, and the flames had been broken off and taken to the kitchen to be used as red pepper. The Florida boys took some ribbing when they checked out extra blankets, but they soon discovered the Alabama boys all had on their "long handles."

James Robert Priester was one of the "Florida boys." He joined the CCC in Orlando, Florida, and was sent to Camp SCS-13 on August 26, 1935. He worked on a survey crew and built terraces and rock spill dams. He was discharged from the CCC on March 31, 1936 (James R. Priester interview, April 23 and May 2, 2001; see the CD).

A Camp Inspection Report dated November 18, 1937, recorded that Company 4488 had 186 enrollees from Alabama, Georgia, Mississippi, and Florida under the command of Lt. James S. Moncrief Jr., the sixth commander in 12 months. Brooks Connell was the new project supervisor. The project work was scattered over Clay County, with agreements covering 20,379 acres for soil conservation.

Floyd T. Johnson served in Company 4488 from April 19, 1937, to March

31, 1939. He recalled Captain Goodyear as one of the company commanders. Captain Goodyear referred to the enrollees as "men." They weren't men yet, but they were going to be fed like men, worked like men, and they were soon going to be men. Mr. Johnson worked at many jobs in camp. He served as an officer's orderly, drove a truck and the company ambulance, and was assigned to "permanent KP." To be the ambulance driver, Mr. Johnson earned his first aid card, and he also taught first aid. He recalled that CEA Albert S. Johnson's education program taught many enrollees how to read and write (Floyd T. Johnson interview, June 8, 2001; see the CD).

William J. Jones from Delta, Alabama, transferred to Company 4488 in the spring of 1939 from Camp TVA-10. He built roads and planted kudzu. He recalled taking a bee culture class while at Camp SCS-12 as well as learning to drive a truck (William J. Jones interview, November 14, 2001; see the CD).

Camp Hobbs continued to have a high turnover of commanders. Inspection reports recorded the camp declining in repairs and maintenance until improvements appeared in September 1939. A Camp Inspection Report dated September 14 noted that Captain Oblivious C. Martin Jr. was the new commanding officer. The project superintendent, Brooks Connell, with six years of CCC experience, told the inspector that Captain Martin had improved the camp buildings, uniforms, mess, and canteen, and company morale had increased greatly. The work project had 241 agreements covering 27,831 acres. A detail of 50 enrollees were constructing a new camp at Cullman, and the men had recently built a 20-by-30-foot addition to the central repair shop at Talladega.

On April 10, 1940, the *Roanoke Leader* reported that a 25-man detail had begun construction on Camp SCS-21 at Roanoke. The people of Randolph County hoped Company 4488 would be as successful there as it had been in Clay County. In five years, Company 4488 had worked on 284 farms covering 32,490 acres, had run 979 miles of terrace line, had built 57,412 brush dams for gully control, and had planted 302,270 black locust and 1,234,660 loblolly and slash pine trees.

On June 12, the paper reprinted an article from the June 6 edition of the *Ashland Progress* reporting that Camp SCS-13 had closed. The camp had meant much to the farmers of Clay County. The official personnel of the camp had made "splendid citizens of the town, and it is with great regret that their duties force them and their families to remove from our midst." Many of the camp buildings were moved to other camps. A caretaker had been hired to watch the remaining structures. It was hoped the NYA or a similar project would make use of the remaining structures.

Company 4447, Camp SCS-14, Dothan, Alabama

The *Dothan Eagle* reported on August 14, 1939, that ten acres had been leased for a CCC camp on the Dothan-Headland Highway to do soil conservation work. On August 21, the paper reported that members of a veterans' CCC company had begun construction of the camp. The buildings were portable, and it was expected that 175 to 200 junior enrollees would be housed at the camp. On September 10, the *Dothan Eagle* announced that Houston County farmers wanting CCC work done on their farms were to submit their applications to County Agent C. M. Ling. The SCS staff had arrived at the camp, and work was to begin on October 1.

On October 1, Company 4477 transferred from Camp SCS-9. The *Dothan Eagle* reported that only 77 enrollees had arrived as the enlistments of many enrollees had expired. Lt. Edwin B. Cooper was the company commander, and there were nine SCS "officers" to supervise the project work, which would begin by the end of October. The paper announced on October 26 that farmers with approved terracing plans were to meet at the auditorium at the Houston County Courthouse.

The progress of the work project was reported in the local newspaper during the winter of 1939–40, but by March 1940, the camp faced condemnation by the State Health Department. The *Dothan Eagle* reported on March 5, 1940, that the camp septic system was not adequate. To keep the camp, the City of Dothan and Houston County ordered 3,000 feet of piping to connect the camp with Dothan's sanitation system.

A Camp Inspection Report dated September 19, 1940, recorded that the camp's sanitation, connected to Dothan's water and sewer systems, was rated excellent. Eleven desertions during August were owing to the men having to work on Saturdays to install the sewage system. An additional 600 man-days between May and August to install the system had interfered with the educational, recreational, and sports programs, but the project work had not suffered and was proceeding.

On October 30, 1941, the *Dothan Eagle* reported that "Camp Grover C. Hall" in Dothan was to be disbanded, as the CCC was reducing the number of white camps. Company 4447 was to be replaced with an African-American company if there were no objections. The County Board of Revenue was to discuss the matter. Probate Judge Saxon P. Poyner stated that the "farmers in the county would not object to the colored company since the CCC work programs have been especially beneficial to them in the past." The paper reported on November 2, however, that the residents living next to the camp had drawn up a petition protesting the change. Judge Poyner switched his position, stating that "he would go on record as opposing establishment of the Negro company here." While he disliked the prospects of losing the CCC camp, "he was not willing to put a Negro company in a white community just to retain it."

On November 5, the *Dothan Eagle* reported that the Board of Revenue had approved the change. While some of the locals protested, Charles Adams of Dothan had pointed out that according to information from the Alabama State Department of Welfare, there had not been a single complaint from an African-American CCC camp in Alabama. Mr. Ling, Houston County agent, had pointed out the importance of the CCC's work. W. D. Thomason, the Dale County agent, asserted, "if Houston County didn't have a place for the CCC camp with Negroes, Dale County was ready to take it."

On November 14, the *Dothan Eagle* reported that Company 4447 was to be disbanded the following day. Some enrollees were being sent to the West Coast, some to Tennessee, others to camps in Alabama. Ten enrollees were retained to straighten up the camp and put the buildings in order.

Company 3477, Camp SCS-14, Dothan, Alabama

On November 16, 1941, the *Dothan Eagle* reported that an advance party of ten trucks and an undetermined number of men had arrived the previous night from Uriah, and another 200 men from Company 3477 were expected later in the day. A. A. Shepard, the project supervisor, had stayed in camp with his SCS staff. He assured everyone there would be a continuation of the project work without interruption. The camp officers at Uriah were transferring with Company 3477 to run the camp. On November 18, the paper that reported the rest of the company had arrived and the work project would be "in full swing by the end of the week." The *Dothan Eagle* reported on November 23 that the crews had begun their soil conservation work. Mr. Shepard's SCS staff had increased to 14 with another foreman and project clerk. The work project was expanded to include Houston, eastern Geneva, and the southern halves of Dale and Henry counties.

A Camp Inspection Report dated January 9, 1942, recorded 183 men under the command of 2nd Lt. Lamar H. Nelson. The work project consisted of farm planning, pasture sodding, terrace construction, and the planting of trees and kudzu. The educational program under CEA William J. Clemons would be adding National Defense courses to the academic and vocational courses offered as soon as the camp received approval from the state authorities. Approximately 86 percent of the enrollees were enrolled in the educational classes.

According to the *CCC Camp Directory for Alabama*, Camp SCS-14 was abandoned during the eighteenth period, which ended March 31, 1942. During the nineteenth and last period, Camp ASCS-1 operated at the former Camp SCS-14, attached to Napier Field as a National Defense camp. Napier Field was the headquarters for the Army Corps Advanced Flying School.

Company 4472, Camp SCS-15, Cullman, Alabama

Company 4472 established Camp SCS-15 on September 20, 1939. A Camp Inspection Report dated November 15, 1940, recorded 200 junior enrollees under the command of Kenan M. Rand. The work project, under the supervision of Davis W. Pittman, consisted of terracing fields, constructing check dams, and planting trees and other plants on eroded lands. A detail had also been sent to dismantle Camp TVA-8. The camp education program, under CEA Robert R. Carothers, offered courses for beginners and at the elementary school and high school levels, as well as vocational classes. There were approximately 1,000 books in the camp libraries.

According to the *CCC Camp Directory for Alabama*, Camp SCS-15 was abandoned during the seventeenth period, which ended September 30, 1941.

Company 3480, Camp SCS-16, Monroeville, Alabama

On October 8, 1939, Company 3480, consisting of junior African-American enrollees, transferred from Camp SCS-6 at Greensboro and established Camp SCS-16. According to the *CCC Camp Directory for Alabama*, Camp SCS-16 was abandoned during the seventeenth period, which ended September 30, 1941.

Company 1405, Camp SCS-17, Hamilton, Alabama

On October 2, 1939, Company 1405 consisting of junior enrollees, transferred from Camp SCS-2 at Dadeville and established Camp SCS-17. The camp was shown in operation for the nineteenth period in the *CCC Camp Directory for Alabama*. The CCC officially ended after the nineteenth period, on June 30, 1942.

Company 2451, Camp SCS-18, Eutaw, Alabama

On June 3, 1940, Company 2451, consisting of African-American World War I veterans, transferred from Camp SCS-11 at Linden and established Camp SCS-18. A Camp Inspection Record dated October 17, 1940, recorded 197 enrollees under the command of Captain Roland E. Simms. Carl C. Morgan was the project supervisor. Special Investigator J. S. Billups noted that the condition of the camp was about the best of the recently established camps. Captain Simms had taken the initiative to improve the camp, and company morale had risen. The cooperation between the army and the technical personnel was excellent, and the work project was progressing satisfactorily.

The educational program under CEA A. H. Wilson offered elementary level courses and vocational classes. Many of the men had come to camp unable to sign their names for the payroll. Those men who had learned to read and write in camp helped demonstrate to the other men that they were not too old to learn.

A Camp Inspection Report dated October 17, 1941, recorded that the work project consisted of soil conservation done through agreements in Greene and part of Sumter counties. The education program continued to focus on the beginners. Daily attendance in the academic classes was only 38 out of 181 enrollees and only slightly higher in the vocational classes. CEA Wilson reported that it was difficult holding World War I veterans in class, but there was interest in the vocational projects such as beekeeping, gardening, and poultry raising.

According to the *CCC Camp Directory for Alabama*, Camp SCS-18 closed after the eighteenth period, which ended March 31, 1942.

Company 3479, Camp SCS-19, Talladega, Alabama

On March 13, 1940, *Our Mountain Home* announced that an army officer was coming to Talladega to select a site for a Soil Conservation Service CCC camp. County Agent O. V. Hill was reported as saying that Talladega County had been trying to get a soil conservation camp since the beginning of the CCC. The camp was to be near the town of Talladega but would serve the entire county, the work "serving as a practical remedy for erosion ills and as a lasting demonstration to farmers of what can be accomplished by proper methods."

Camp SCS-19 was established on June 3, 1940, located on the east side of Talladega in a field north of Highway 77. *Our Mountain Home* reported on June 12 that the full personnel of 200 boys had arrived and crews were already on project work, two in Winterboro and another at Estaboga. The 40-man crews were clearing bushes from pastures, digging the underbrush out by the roots to ensure that the pastures would remain clear.

Samuel D. Williams of Eatonton, Georgia, was in Company 3479 when it transferred from Camp SCS-5 at Carrollton on June 3, 1940. He planted trees in the vicinities of Lincoln and Sylacauga and recalled planting a lot of kudzu on eroded farmland. On July 18, he transferred to a company headed to the western camps (Samuel D. Williams interview, August 27, 2001; see the CD).

William T. Bell of Ashland transferred to Company 3479 in December 1940. He worked on a crew conducting topographic surveys for farmers, driving stakes along the contour lines to lay out terraces. He also cleared pastures for plowing and planting. He recalled that the SCS county agent planned all of the work. By the time Mr. Bell arrived at Camp SCS-19 at Talladega, he was anxious to get out of the CCC and get a job. As textile workers found better paying jobs in ammunition plants and other factories producing war matériel, textile jobs in Talladega became available. He spent most of his free time looking for a job in Talladega (William T. Bell interview, June 4, 2001; see the CD).

A Camp Inspection Report dated October 14, 1941, recorded 175 men under the command of Clifford McClure. The project work, under the supervision of Foster M. Patton, was conducted on 156 farms over 34,781 acres in Talladega County, west of the national forest and the Anniston army depot.

A Camp Inspection Report dated March 27, 1942, recorded that there was only 135 men in camp. The work project on 69 farms, consisting of 19,372 acres, had been completed. Work being conducted on the Anniston army depot included pine beetle control, fire hazard reduction, and tree planting. The lack of sufficient enrollment was having an effect on the project work.

According to a Camp Inspection Report dated June 19, 1942, there were only 67 enrollees in camp. By now, enlistments in the military were also affecting CCC enrollment. The work project had progressed very little since the March 27 report. CEA Memnon C. Scales reported that the aims of the educational program were not being met because of the constant and rapid turnover of the company.

Camps SCS-19 closed with the official ending of the CCC on June 30, 1942.

Company 4436, Camp SCS-20, Evergreen, Alabama

Company 4436, consisting of junior enrollees, established Camp SCS-20 on June 1, 1940. The *Evergreen Courant* reported on June 20 that Camp Superintendent George W. Huey was asking local farmers to contact the camp technical personnel to develop plans for their farms.

On September 26, the paper began a weekly column titled "C.C.C. News" written by the group leaders of Company 4436. It served as the camp newsletter and also informed the people of Conecuh County of the work being accomplished. The camp had made excellent progress. There were agreements on 91 farms for soil conservation. The camp had tennis courts and athletic fields, and the enrollees also went into town for additional recreation.

On October 3, "The C.C.C. News" pointed out the importance of the educational program. Five percent of the enrollees coming into camp could not read or write. It was not possible to return nineteen-year-old enrollees to school with pupils six or eight years old. The CCC offered courses in reading and writing where the enrollees learned with others of the same age, greatly reducing embarrassment. Mrs. Stain and Mrs. Brantley, WPA teachers in charge of illiteracy courses, had more than 40 boys enrolled.

The "C.C.C. News" continued to report on the project work, camp improvements, and activities through April 17, 1941. The *Evergreen Courant* reported on March 13 that the SCS camp at Evergreen had planted 450,000 kudzu plants in Conecuh County during the spring, covering most of the eroded land in the county. The kudzu was growing so well that a local citizen was heard to say, "Give the Soil Conservation five more years and they will have so much kudzu in the Country that Hitler can't possibly get in."

On January 8, 1942, the *Evergreen Courant* reported that Company 4436 was being sent to Fort Oglethorpe, Georgia, along with the army personnel. The SCS staff would remain in camp, and a company of African-American enrollees from Camp P-78 at Brewton would be transferred to Evergreen. George Huey, the project superintendent, stated that the new company would continue the work with a minimum of interruption. The new company's strength was approximately 200 enrollees.

Company 4434, Camp SCS-20, Evergreen, Alabama

Company 4434 transferred to Camp SCS-20 on January 20, 1942. The junior African-American enrollees continued the soil conservation work in Conecuh County for the next several months. On March 12, the *Evergreen Cou-*

rant announced that the CCC camp at Evergreen was to be closed on April 1. A nationwide policy called for all camps not directly connected with the construction of army camps, airports, or similar projects connected with the war effort to be closed. Camp officials were trying to complete as much of the project work as possible. The camp was to have been closed on March 15, but Congressman George Grant had been able to secure an extension.

Company 4488, Camp SCS-21, Roanoke, Alabama

On March 13, 1940, the *Roanoke Leader* announced that a Soil Conservation Service CCC camp was coming by the first of June. The people of Randolph County had been trying for some time to secure a camp. The camp was to be located on "the Roanoke Guano Company land on Highway 37 between Randolph County Training School and the Central of Georgia and A.B. & C. railroad crossing at mud cut." The 200 enrollees would work on soil conservation projects within a 25-mile radius of the camp.

On April 3, the *Roanoke Leader* reported that 25 boys from the CCC camp at Ashland had completed erecting portable barracks at the new campsite. Olin Blackwell of Gadsden was with this initial cadre, and he recalled that the camp was built with local labor and the CCC enrollees (Olin Blackwell interview, February 20, 2003; see the CD).

On June 5, the *Roanoke Leader* announced that the new camp had reached its full strength of 200 boys with the arrival of the enrollees from Ashland. The camp preparation was completed, and the company was ready to begin its project work.

On April 23, 1941, the *Roanoke Leader* reported that Company 4488 had received 54 new enrollees from the enrollment center at Anniston. Upon arrival, they were read the rules and regulations, clothed, given their shots, and instructed about calisthenics and other routine procedures. Nineteen of the recruits volunteered to join Company 5461 at Timber, Oregon. They were put on a Pullman coach at Birmingham for their trip to the West Coast. The planting season had just concluded at Camp SCS-21. Company 4488 had planted 700 Arizona cypress trees along with black locusts, loblolly, and slash pines, 755,406 kudzu crowns on farms in Chambers and Randolph counties, and 7,000 one-acre wildlife plots for farmers.

On October 29, 1941, the *Roanoke Leader* announced that Company 4488 was being disbanded. The enrollees were to be moved to other CCC camps in Robertsdale, Evergreen, Dothan, and Clanton. Company 4488 was to be replaced by Company 3480 from Camp SCS-16 at Monroeville. The army personnel would be transferred, but the SCS personnel and Project Superintendent Brooks Connell would remain in camp.

Company 3480, Camp SCS-21, Roanoke, Alabama

On November 3, 1941, Company 3480 transferred to Camp SCS-21. The junior African-American enrollees continued the soil conservation work projects begun by Company 4488 in Randolph and Chambers counties. Simon J. Turmon, born and raised in Eutaw, Alabama, had joined Company 3480 in April 1940. He had been promoted to assistant leader by April 1941, and transferred with the company to Camp SCS-21. In February 1942, he made the rank of leader, earning $45 each month. He enjoyed shooting pool in the recreation hall and playing for the baseball team. He remembered the educational program being rather informal, with the enrollees getting opportunities to "play" with typewriters and learning Morse code on the radio. Mr. Turmon also recalled working closely with an army officer sent to the camp for an inspection. Lt. John Hassell had overhead a cook threatening an enrollee, and the two men had worked together to discharge the cook before he could make good on his threat (Simon J. Turmon interview, March 2, 2004; see the CD).

John Hassell was born and raised in Tuscaloosa County. As a second lieutenant in the U.S. Army, he had served in three CCC camps in 1935 and 1936. He returned to the CCC in 1939 as a reserve officer with civilian status and was sent to Camp SCS-21 on an inspection in February 1942. He recalled that the enrollees were ill equipped for winter weather, with no "long handles" and only one blanket on their beds. even though the weather had been in the twenties. Although the mess sergeant had a menu written, there were not enough food supplies in the camp to make a meal. Mr. Hassell called his district headquarters at Fort Oglethorpe to get the proper food and clothing delivered to the camp and stayed at the camp until the conditions improved. The relationship between the camp and the local people had been strained, but once the basic needs of the enrollees were met, that relationship greatly improved (John Hassell interview, January 28, 2002; see the CD).

On May 6, 1942, the *Roanoke Leader* reported that Company 3480 was being disbanded.

5
The CCC and the Tennessee Valley Authority

On May 18, 1933, President Roosevelt signed the Tennessee Valley Authority Act, creating one of the most innovative programs in the New Deal. The TVA had a broad mission of power production, navigation, flood control, malaria prevention, reforestation, and erosion control (www.tva.gov 4/12/02).

In addition to the construction of dams, the TVA began reforestation projects, soil erosion control projects, and construction of recreational facilities along the waterways. The CCC provided labor for these projects. The TVA camps were either for reforestation and erosion control or for the construction of parks. On October 13, 1933, the *Sheffield Standard* reported that 1,000 CCC enrollees were being transferred from camps in the Northwest to the Muscle Shoals area. The projects outlined were construction of a park on the banks of the Tennessee River at Nitrate Plant No. 2; construction of an ornamental nursery and planting at Nitrate Plant No. 1; a highway beautification, improvement, and maintenance program of government property at Nitrate Plant No. 2; planting around the Wilson Dam power house, village, and grounds; general development and maintenance work on the government reservation at Nitrate Plant No. 1; and the possible establishment of a game breeding refuge.

On October 14, 1933, the *Gadsden Times* reported that the first CCC units had arrived at Florence, and 140 men had been quartered in the old officers' quarters at Plant No. 2. This was Company 2426, a World War I veteran company that had transferred from Tennessee, and more companies were expected soon. They would carry out a program of landscaping, soil erosion prevention, and reforestation on the government reservation at Muscle Shoals.

Bob O'Connell enrolled in CCC Company 286 at Fort Dix, New Jersey, and spent the summer of 1933 in Idaho. In October, he was sent to Muscle Shoals, Alabama. Four companies—251, 283, 285, and 286—set up their camps at Nitrate Plant No. 2, like spokes of a wheel around a large building that served as the recreation hall and education building. Mr. O'Connell worked on a crew that was restoring headstones at a cemetery (Bob O'Connell interview, March 29, 2002; see the CD).

On January 26, 1934, the *Sheffield Standard* reported that the CCC boys at Nitrate Plant No. 2 would be there for at least six months. The large recreation hall, 220 by 110 feet, was used by the four junior companies. The enrollees were engaged in road construction, landscaping, and erosion control and were building bridges and a nursery at Nitrate Plant No. 2. Each of the four companies had its own commander: Company 251, Captain W. Mansfield; Company 283, Captain A. Schaefer; Company 285, Captain J. J. Bausch; and Company 286, Captain R. Ward. Captain J. J. Bausch was overall camp commander.

Company 285, Camp TVA-2, Nitrate Plant, Alabama

Company 285 was organized at Camp Dix, New Jersey, on May 20, 1933. The junior enrollees were recruited from the larger cities of New York and New Jersey. They spent the summer in Halcomb, Idaho, working on a Forest Service project. On October 1, 1933, those enrollees who did not want to reenlist were returned to Camp Dix. The remaining 67 men were sent to Sheffield, Alabama, on October 16.

They were sent to Nitrate Plant No. 2, where they lived in tents until their barracks were completed on November 24, 1933. In early November, another 122 men arrived from Fort Dix to bring the company strength back to its authorized level. The work project consisted of beautifying the area, building soil erosion control dams, and planting and cultivating a nursery. On March 10, 1934, Leonard T. Wagnon was assigned as the camp education advisor and immediately began educational and recreational programs. During the summer of 1934, Company 285 had a very successful baseball team, playing other CCC teams and teams from nearby towns. Recreational trips were taken to local areas of interest. The enrollees produced a radio program that was broadcast over the local radio station each week (1934 CCC District D annual).

The *Florence Herald* reported in November 1934 that the Florence Civitan Club on the twenty-fourth and the Florence Chamber of Commerce on the thirtieth had been dinner guests of Company 285. Old-fashioned army dinners were served in mess kits, and musical entertainment was provided by the enrollees.

On August 3, 1935, most of Company 285 was transferred to Fort Bragg, North Carolina. A small cadre remained at Nitrate Plant No. 2 and formed CCC Company 4499 (1936 CCC District D annual).

Company 4499, Camp TVA-2, Camp TVA-13, Wilson Dam, Alabama

Company 4499 was formed from a cadre of men from Company 285 and another 200 men from Florida on August 3, 1935 (1936 CCC District D annual). Two days later, a severe wind destroyed several camp buildings, and the company moved into the area formerly occupied by Company 283 (1938 CCC District D annual).

The camp was officially designated as "Camp Ala. TVA Project No. 2 of the U.S. Forest Service," indicating that the technical supervision was provided by the Forest Service. The first task for company commander Captain Chester H. Knowles and Lt. Troy A. Baker was to get the camp area in shape. The work project consisted of working at the 100-acre Wilson Dam Nursery under the supervision of James D. Hays. In 1935, the enrollees shipped out 6 million pine and black locust seedlings to 33 CCC Soil Erosion Service camps in the Tennessee Valley. They also worked on soil erosion projects on farms in Colbert and Lauderdale counties (1936 CCC District D annual).

The 1936 annual recorded that the Company 4499 basketball team won the subdistrict championship in 1935 and went to the district finals at Fort McClellan. Captain Knowles, a former boxer, directed the company boxing team. In January 1936, the camp educational program began a newsletter called the "Wilson Dam Spillway." Issues from January 18 and March 20 were archived at the University of Chicago.

In 1937, Camp TVA-2 was redesignated Camp TVA-13. Company 4499 continued to work at the nursery, now 85 acres in size, expecting to produce 180 million pine and black locust seedlings to be planted throughout the Tennessee Valley. The also continued the soil erosion projects on private land (1938 CCC District D annual).

Camp TVA-13 at Wilson Dam was listed in the *CCC Camp Directory for Alabama* as having been approved for a "temporary continuance" for the nineteenth period in March 1942. Walter S. "Buddy" McGee of Pontotoc, Mississippi, joined Company 4499 on April 11, 1942. He was assigned to the company as senior leader and company clerk by the army officials at Fort McClellan to assist in closing the camp. Company 4499 was down to only a few enrollees, and most of the project work had come to a stop. The cooks' and bakers' school at the camp was also closing. It took several days for Mr. McGee to do the necessary paperwork. He stayed in the camp until the army came to collect the army-owned equipment. He was discharged from the CCC on July 18, 1942 (Walter S. McGee interview, March 19, 2007; see the CD).

Company 2426, Camp TVA-3, Town Creek; Camp TVA-P-5, Joe Wheeler Dam; Camp TVA-P-3, Wilson Dam, Alabama

Company 2426 was organized on June 29, 1933, at Fort Oglethorpe, Georgia. After three weeks of conditioning, the World War I veteran company was sent by train to Hohenwald, Tennessee, and then trucked to Meriwether Lewis Memorial Monument where they removed fire hazards and built bridle and footpaths. They transferred to the No. 2 Nitrate Plant on October 13 (1936 District D annual).

The *Florence Herald* reported on October 20, 1933, that 160 World War I veterans had arrived, and another 60 were expected to be recruited in Tennessee. The company was under the command of Captain T. C. Brown. The 1936 District D annual recorded that on December 13, 1933, the company moved their camp to Nitrate Plant No. 1 but continued to work at Nitrate Plant No. 2. On February 7, 1934, they moved to Joe Wheeler Dam where barracks had been built. On April 1, they were transferred from the technical supervision of the U.S. Forest Service to the technical supervision of the National Park Service, and the construction of a park for the TVA began.

Between August 3, 1934, and April 26, 1935, the *Florence Herald* featured a column written by W. T. Ward, the camp educational advisor. Titled at various times "Wheeler Dam News," "Wheeler News," and "Wheeler Dam," the column appeared every two weeks or so, serving as a camp newsletter for the enrollees and local people. On September 14, 1934, the "Wheeler Dam News" announced that Company 2426 was preparing for another "cheerful" dance in camp that was to be open to the public. Company 2426 had been working for months in "abandoned cotton fields, digging, filling up gullies, cutting down trees, covering the worn out ground with a coat of new soil." The park was being covered with Bermuda grass. Benches, tables, and fireplaces had been scattered across the park. Local citizens were visiting the park while it was still under construction. The shelter house was being built rapidly. W. T. Ward referred to the shelter as "a poem in stone." The rock for the shelter had been quarried in Russellville, Alabama, then cut to size at the park. "The masons of Medieval Europe did not work more faithfully in their task upon the great cathedrals." A foot trail with rock platforms or buttresses was built along the banks of the river to allow visitors a better view. W. T. Ward hoped the work of the veterans would be remembered.

On November 23, 1934, the "Wheeler News" recorded President and Mrs. Roosevelt's visit to Wheeler Dam Park. The veterans lined up on one side of the road outside of camp with their wives and children on the other. Returning from the dam, the president saw the veterans and with them a little girl holding a bouquet of large, beautiful chrysanthemums. A Secret Service man took the flowers from the little girl and presented them to the president. President Roosevelt shouted, "What good are the flowers without the girl, bring them both to me." Captain Harris, the company commander, presented the little girl to the president. The president passed the flowers to Mrs. Roosevelt and thanked the girl, accepting the gift from Company 2426. The girl was the daughter of Captain Harris, and the flowers had been grown in the garden of Mrs. W. C. Williams of Tuscumbia, Alabama.

On January 4, 1935, the "Wheeler Dam" gave a description of the average veteran in Company 2426. "He was born somewhere in the hinterland of Alabama, off the dirt road which connects X and Y, Alabama." The average veteran in Company 2426 had lived 16 years with his parents in a modest cabin, experiencing all the privations and inconveniences of a tenant farmer, then left home to make room for the "newcomers." At sixteen, feeling like a man, he got a job in the railroad yards. Not satisfied, he took a job in the coal mines, which paid more money, but he returned to the railroad yards when working underground became unbearable. When the war began, "the spirit of his fathers leaped within him. He would serve his country." He went to France serving in the Fifty-second Division. He was lucky not to be wounded or gassed. When he came home, he returned to the railroad yard to discover that his job had been filled while he was at war, and there was no place for him. He returned to the farm. He had married before joining the army; his children had grown and needed to be cared for. "The opportunity which had been denied him as a child was here for his children as the state had opened rural schools. They must take advantage of the schools, so to school he sent them. But his embarrassment was great when they discovered he could neither read nor write. He wanted to learn, but how could he do it, and where?"

W. T. Ward's article continued, "The Depression got him. He was a ruined man. When gloom was deepest the New Deal broke upon the nation. He was sent to Veterans Company 2426, Town Creek, Alabama." At the CCC camp, he joined a class organized by Mrs. Sam Morrison of Town Creek. He worked hard, never missed a class, and was able to write a simple letter home to his wife, the first love letter his wife ever received from him. The veteran wondered what his daughter, who would be graduating from high school soon, thought of the letter.

The "Wheeler Dam" column of April 19, 1935, summarized the accomplishments of Company 2426 at Joe Wheeler Dam Park. The park contained 1,200 acres. Since February 1934, Company 2426 had cleared over 300 acres, constructed a mile of good roads between the main roads and the shelter houses on both sides of the dam, and constructed over a mile and a half of trails. A lookout house had been built at the mouth of Big Nance Creek, constructed of colored sandstone quarried and dressed by the veterans. The shelter house east of the dam was built out of rock, with two rest rooms and two fireplaces. The second shelter, west of the dam near the mouth of Big Nance Creek, was frame construction with two fireplaces. Over 5,700 feet of pipes connected these two shelters with the main water system in the park. Thirteen stone open-air ovens had been built along the riverfront, along with 25 tables and seats. Two tennis courts were already seeing action from the people of Wheeler Dam Village. Thirty thousand trees and shrubs had been sent to the park; 9,000 had been planted, and the other 21,000 were in the nursery for later planting. A dam had been built to create a lily pond. A cascading spillway was built out of rock from the bottom of the Tennessee River for the pond's overflow. A footbridge was built over the spillway. Lilies, shrubbery, moss, and flowers had been planted around the pond.

On November 1, 1935, the *Florence Herald* announced that Company 2426 was being transferred to the Norris Dam in Tennessee to work on the Big Ridge Park. The work at Norris Dam was similar to that at Wheeler Dam. On January 11, 1936, Company 2426 returned to Alabama and Camp TVA-P-3 at Wilson Dam. The work project, under the supervision of J. T. DeJarnette, was similar to that at Joe Wheeler Dam Park (1936 CCC District D annual).

In June 1936, the Muscle Shoals Park was dedicated. The *Florence Herald* reported on June 5 that the 400-acre tract was ready for public recreation. The park, located below Wilson Dam, was the product of two years of work by the CCC under the cooperative supervision of the TVA and the National Park Service. On June 12, the paper reported that approximately 500 people attended the dedication ceremony for the TVA–Muscle Shoals Park, located on the south bank of Tennessee River, adjoining Sheffield on the Nitrate

Plant No. 2 reservation. James T. DeJarnette, project superintendent, and H. J. Wallace of the TVA were praised for their work.

According to the *CCC Camp Directory for Alabama*, Camp TVA-P-3 was closed after the end of the eighth period, which ended March 31, 1937.

Company 251, Camp TVA-P-4, Nitrate Plant, Alabama

Company 251 was organized at Camp Dix, New Jersey, on May 20, 1933, with junior enrollees from the metropolitan areas of New York and New Jersey. They spent the summer in Lowman, Idaho, working on a Forest Service project. On October 1, 1933, those boys not reenlisting were sent back to Camp Dix. The remaining boys were sent to Sheffield, Alabama, by train on October 16, 1933, where they were trucked to Nitrate Plant No. 2. They lived in tents until barracks could be built; another 120 replacements arrived from Camp Dix on November 6, 1933. Their work project, under the supervision of the TVA, consisted of beautifying the area, building erosion control dams, and clearing ground for a nursery. During the fall and winter months, the company's recreation consisted of playing football and basketball; dances were held at the camp, and the company produced radio programs (1934 CCC District D annual).

On May 24, 1934, the *Sheffield Standard* announced that Company 251 was holding an open house, and the commanding officer, Lt. C. E. Donnigan, was inviting the people of the Muscle Shoals area to inspect the camp. The open house was being held in recognition of Company 251's receiving the award for the best all-around CCC camp in District D. Much of the credit was due to James DeJarnette, project superintendent, under whose supervision the CCC at Nitrate Plant No. 2 had turned "a jungle" into "a most beautiful naturalistic park" at Muscle Shoals.

In April 1935, Company 251 produced a camp newspaper called "See See See" from Wilson Dam. The April 30 edition was archived at the University of Chicago.

Company 251 was likely disbanded in the late summer or fall of 1935 when the other Second Corps Area companies were reorganized into Fourth Corps Area companies or sent back to camps in the western states.

Company 283, Camp TVA-P-5, Nitrate Plant, Alabama

Company 283 was organized at Camp Dix on May 18, 1933, with junior enrollees from New York and New Jersey. After two weeks of conditioning, they were sent to Placerville, Idaho. Their first night in Idaho under the pine trees seemed a paradise compared to the dirty city streets they had come from. In October 1933, those enrollees wishing to reenlist were sent to Sheffield, Alabama, and Nitrate Plant No. 2. The project work, under the supervision of C. M. Terry, initially consisted of ripping up the railroad tracks and concrete at Nitrate Plant No. 2. The 16-pound sledgehammers made their marks with sore backs and blisters, but they were soon gone as muscle and flesh began to cover thin bodies (1934 CCC District D annual).

The large recreation hall built for the four CCC companies was the center of activity. It contained a poolroom, a canteen, a barbershop, a library, ping-pong tables, and a room for the educational program. One large room served as a basketball court, dance hall, and movie theatre. Dances were held every Friday night. A basketball league was formed, and Company 283 won the league championship. Tiny gold basketballs were worn on watch chains and shown to all the southern belles who attended the dances.

On April 19, 1934, enrollees arrived from Camp Dix to replace the boys who had not reenlisted. Soon after, the supervision of the project work shifted from the Forest Service to the Park Service. Company 283 began work on constructing roads and sloping and sodding banks. The National Park Service drew plans for cabins, tennis courts, baseball diamonds, horseshoe courts, a pool, fire towers, bridges, picnic grounds, and trails. The boys were soon working as carpenters, plumbers, and masons (1934 CCC District D annual). Company 283 transferred to Camp F-109 in Riggins, Idaho, on July 20, 1935 (NACCCA database).

Company 286, Camp TVA-6, Athens, Alabama

Company 286 was organized at Camp Dix on May 17, 1933, with junior enrollees from New Jersey. After two weeks of training, they established Camp S-230 at Centreville, Idaho, where they worked on a state forestry project. At the end of the first enrollment period, the 38 men who reenrolled were sent to Sheffield, Alabama. Replacements arrived from Camp Dix on November 5, 1933, bringing the company strength to 236 men. On December 10, they moved into new barracks at Nitrate Plant No. 2. During the winter, the men worked under the supervision of the TVA, working at the plant, building roads, and beautifying the plant area.

On May 28, 1934, Company 286 was transferred to Athens, Alabama, and established Camp TVA-6. The work project consisted of soil erosion control and soil reclamation. The men lived in tents for two months. On August 25, the company moved across the street into new portable barracks, which were considered comfortable and an ideal campsite (1934 CCC District D annual).

On June 1, 1935, a cadre of men from Company 286 organized Company 3483. On July 1, Company 3483 moved to Huntsville, Alabama, and established Camp TVA-7 at the base of Monte Sano Mountain. Company 286 had an infantile paralysis quarantine for two weeks in July 1935 . As soon as it was lifted, the company left for California. A small cadre of enrollees and local experienced men remained at Athens to assist with the establishment of Company 5401 (1936 CCC District D annual).

Company 5401, Camp TVA-6, Athens, Alabama

Company 5401 was organized on August 3, 1935, at "Camp Huston" at Athens, Alabama. The cadre of juniors from Company 286 was joined by local experienced men and enrollees from Camp Foster at Jacksonville, Florida. The project work began on August 19 after two weeks of conditioning. The camp was a U.S. Forest Service Soil Erosion Camp under the supervision of the TVA. The project work was centered in Limestone County, along the northern side of the Tennessee River, and consisted of constructing erosion control dams and terraces and planting trees. TVA engineers had determined that there were 120,000 acres of land in Limestone County in need of erosion work. By 1936, Company 5401 had worked on over 37,000 acres and planted over a half million black locusts and pine trees (1936 CCC District D annual).

Between August 1935 and February 1936, Company 5401 was twice awarded the distinction of best company in their subdistrict. In March 1936, Camp TVA-6 was the training site for the champion boxers of District D as they prepared for the Southern AAU Championships in Memphis. The educational program, under CEA Leonard Roth, was both varied and thorough, and the men had taken to it with great enthusiasm. The project superintendent was O. L. Bradford. The enrollees, under the command of 1st Lt. Joe Wilson, were from Florida, Alabama, Tennessee, and Mississippi (1936 CCC District D annual).

By February 1938, Company 5401 had begun construction on a large fish hatchery on the Elk River where it flows into the Tennessee River. The hatchery was the largest in the world, according to the 1938 annual. Fish from the hatchery were to be sent to all parts of the country to stock streams and ponds. Company 5401 was enjoying baseball, basketball, track, and boxing. The educational program had expanded, with courses offered at the

College at Athens, taught by young lady students, and a WPA teacher offered courses in camp (1938 CCC District D annual).

According to the *CCC Camp Directory for Alabama*, Camp TVA-6 was abandoned after the sixteenth period, which ended March 31, 1941.

Company 3483, Camp TVA-7, Huntsville, Alabama

Company 3483 was organized at Camp TVA-6 from a cadre of men from Company 286 on June 1, 1935. Additional men from Company 444 at Camp Hill joined on July 1 at the new camp located outside the city limits of Huntsville on McClung Street at the foot of Monte Sano Mountain. The men lived in tents while barracks were being constructed. On August 21, another 174 enrollees arrived from central Mississippi. While the men went through their conditioning period, improvements were made to the camp (1938 CCC District D annual).

On September 6, 1936, the work project began, consisting of erosion control under the supervision of the Department of Agriculture. Company 3483 worked on more than 30 farms in Madison County, constructing terrace dams, digging drainage ditches, planting trees in barren areas, and paving badly eroded areas with brush and straw, while also taking an active part in fighting forest fires. T. E. Norris was the project supervisor (1936 CCC District D annual).

By 1938, Company 3483 had worked on over 100 farms. In addition to the soil conservation work, they also assisted in wildlife control work in the Wheeler and Guntersville areas, collected pine cones, and fought forest fires. At the time of the 1938 annual, Camp TVA-7 had received a new coat of paint, the walks had been paved with small pebbles, and shrubbery had been planted in the camp area. Company 3483 had done well in intercamp sports, winning most of their games. There were tennis courts in the camp, adding to the recreation program. Company 3483 was proud that over 60 of their men had found work outside the CCC (1938 CCC District D annual).

Company 3483 was replaced by Company 2449-V on September 30, 1938 (NACCCA database).

Company 2449-V, Camp TVA-7, Huntsville, Alabama

Company 2449 was organized on October 10, 1937, at Camp TVA-11 at Moulton, Alabama. The World War I veterans transferred to Camp TVA-7 on September 30, 1938.

On September 23, 1939, the *Decatur Daily* reported that the men were under the supervision of the TVA Forestry Relations Department, engaged in soil conservation on TVA and private land. The work allowed on private land was limited to gully control and tree planting on eroded land. Landowners provided the materials to construct temporary check dams. Terrace outlet construction was conducted if the landowner provided the seed and fertilizer in return for the labor and technical assistance. Local farmers could secure CCC assistance through the county agent in Huntsville. The article also reported that a detachment of 50 men were to move to a new CCC camp near Somerville in Morgan County (likely a side camp).

According to the *CCC Camp Directory for Alabama*, Camp TVA-7 continued as a Forest Service project doing soil conservation work until the end of the eighteenth period on March 31, 1942. During the nineteenth period, Camp TVA-7 operated as a national defense project, designated "Camp AF-1, the Huntsville Arsenal."

Company 5432, Camp TVA-8, Guntersville, Alabama

According to the *CCC Camp Directory for Alabama*, Camp TVA-8 was established during the fifth period as a soil conservation project supervised by the Forest Service. The camp was closed at the end of the fifth period, at the end of September 1935. A month later, the camp at Guntersville was reoccupied as a side camp of Camp TVA-10 with Lt. J. N. Franklin in command of 75 enrollees (1936 District D annual).

According to the *CCC Camp Directory for Alabama*, Camp TVA-8 was reestablished for the fourteenth period, which began October 1, 1939. Wade Gladden of Gadsden, Alabama, enrolled in the CCC at Gadsden on October 3, 1939. After getting his shots and conditioning at Fort McClellan, he and other enrollees were sent to Company 5432. The work project consisted of planting trees along the backwaters of Guntersville Lake and on the farmlands overlooking the lake. The men built erosion control dams, cutting limbs from the woods and staking them down in the ditches across the eroded slopes, under the supervision of Forest Service employees. Mr. Gladden enjoyed playing ping-pong and shooting pool in the recreation hall when not working. He remembered there was a ball field in camp where they played pick-up games rather than playing against other CCC camps. He was detailed to Stevenson to work on the construction of Camp TVA-14 on August 16, 1940 (Wade Gladden interview, February 8, 2002; see the CD).

Company 5432 was transferred to Camp TVA-14 at Stevenson, Alabama, on August 15, 1940 (NACCCA database).

Company 3403, Camp TVA-9 (BS-1 and FWS-1), Hartsville, Alabama

According to the *CCC Camp Directory for Alabama*, Camp TVA-9 operated during the fifth period, which began October 1, 1935, as a soil conservation project supervised by the Forest Service. It was reopened on October 1, 1939, designated as Camp BS-1 during the fourteenth period, working on a biological survey project at the Wheeler Pool Migratory Waterfowl Refuge. The NACCCA database shows Company 3403 establishing Camp BS-1 at Hartselle, Alabama, on October 1, 1939.

On October 19, the *Decatur Daily* reported that the Hartselle CCC camp had reopened with the arrival of 99 men, three administrative personnel, and eight technical personnel from North Carolina. Another 100 men had arrived from Wilson Dam, and 15 more were expected. The work project, under the supervision of the Biological Survey, Department of Interior, consisted of the development of a 41,000-acre migratory waterfowl refuge in Morgan, Lawrence, and Limestone counties. Because the camp had been abandoned for four years, camp improvements were the first priority.

According to the *CCC Camp Directory for Alabama*, Camp BS-1 was designated Camp FWS-1 on October 1, 1940 (about the time the Biological Survey changed to the Fish and Wildlife Service) and operated until the end of the eighteenth period.

Company 5432, Camp TVA-10, Scottsboro, Alabama

On April 4, 1935, the *Progressive Age*, a local weekly newspaper, reported that Captain John F. Hanley of Camp McClellen, J. W. Nicholson of the TVA forestry and soil department, and Carl T. Jones, representing the "U.S. Forestry division," had come to Scottsboro to make arrangements for a CCC camp. The site was located on Wood's Cove Road just outside the city limits. It was the first CCC camp in Jackson County.

In June, a cadre of 25 men from Company 472 at Fort Payne arrived in Scottsboro and began construction of the camp in a half-acre cotton patch. A month later, this cadre was swapped with a cadre of veterans from Monte Sano. By July 25, work had begun on the headquarters building, and the camp was expected to be ready in a month. On August 25, orders were received that the camp was to be for junior enrollees. The veterans, except for the mess stewards and cooks, were sent to Town Creek (Camp TVA-3) . On August 28, 69 junior enrollees from Montgomery and another 81 from Mobile arrived in camp. Another 50 enrollees arrived from Birmingham on August 30. After two weeks of conditioning, the enrollees were turned over to the "Using Service" to be taught soil erosion work. V. L. Scharnagel was the project superintendent. CEA David L. Darden reported for duty on September 18, 1935 (1936 CCC District D annual).

The relationship between the camp and the people of Scottsboro was reflected in the *Progressive Age* on July 23, 1936. A CCC truck had overturned, killing one enrollee and injuring two others. The article described the funeral service of enrollee Joe S. McQuaid and stated, "the sad death of this young man had caused genuine sorrow and regret among the people of Scottsboro. He was very popular among his comrades and officers and also made friends among the people of the town."

During 1937, Company 5432 worked on the Higginbottom Project near Scottsboro where they constructed 455 temporary brush dams. The soil conservation work, under the supervision of Mr. Scharnagel, operated over 800 square miles in Jackson and Marshall counties. The enrollees had constructed hundreds of terrace outlets, planted trees by the thousands, collected bushels of seed, and collected posts from the area of the TVA reservoir basin. In addition to the actual soil erosion work, the project taught the local farmers how to conserve their soil resources and how to fight erosion (1938 CCC District D annual).

On October 11, 1938, Floyd Tudor, who was born and raised in Sheffield, Alabama, enrolled in the CCC and joined Company 5432 at Camp TVA-10 right after graduating from high school at the age of seventeen. When he first arrived in Scottsboro, he was put on a crew planting trees. He was soon sent to a side camp at Guntersville with about 40 enrollees. The side camp was under the supervision of Mr. Blanchard, a junior forester with the U.S. Forest Service. Mr. Tudor was promoted to assistant leader and took the job of Forest Service clerk and first-aid attendant.

Mr. Tudor went to Fort McClellan in December 1938 for radio school for several weeks but returned to Guntersville upon completing the training. When the rest of Company 5432 moved to Guntersville in October 1939, he was given the job of company clerk. He retained the job of first-aid attendant, and one of his duties was the regular inspection for venereal disease, which was prevalent at that time. Any enrollees who contracted venereal diseases were discharged from the CCC. Mr. Tudor also swapped jobs with the first sergeant of the company on occasion and when approved by the company commander, Lt. Jesse B. Dubois. He enjoyed the change of pace with the different duties.

Mr. Tudor enjoyed going into Guntersville in his free time. He recalled that the people of Guntersville liked the CCC enrollees and appreciated the business that the camp brought to the town. The enrollees were very well behaved in town and would be invited to attend parties and other social gatherings. At one party, Mr. Tudor met the lady he would later marry (Floyd Tudor interview, February 15, 2002; see the CD).

The people of Scottsboro were also fond of the CCC enrollees. When they heard that Company 5432 might be moving to Guntersville, they protested the move. The *Progressive Age* published a letter from Congressman Sparkman on August 17, 1939. He had contacted the Forest Service, who had jurisdiction over the camp. The Scottsboro camp would not be moved; it would be kept as a service unit, possibly to be reoccupied later, but Company 5432 would be sent to Guntersville to do project work in the vicinity of the dam. According to the *CCC Camp Directory for Alabama*, Camp TVA-10 was not reoccupied after the thirteenth period, which ended September 30, 1939.

Company 3487, Camp TVA-11, Moulton, Alabama

On May 9, 1935, the *Moulton Advertiser* announced that Lt. Rice had arrived with 20 men from Camp F-4 and was erecting tents in Masterson's pasture on the west side of Moulton. On June 5, the paper reported that Captain Mark J. Roy had arrived in Moulton to take command of the detachment. It reported on June 27 that the camp was nearly completed, then on September 12 that the men of Company 3487 were hard at work making improvements to "Camp Roddy" under the command of Captain Roy.

A Camp Inspection Report dated December 11, 1935, recorded 183 junior enrollees from Alabama and Mississippi under the command of Captain Arthur S. McCollum. The work project, under the supervision of the Forest Service, consisted of soil erosion work over 600 square miles. Joe W. Burleson was the project superintendent. The camp education program, under CEA Robert W. Peacock, offered courses at the elementary and high school level, with woodworking, typing, bookkeeping, first aid, and forestry taught as vocational classes.

On April 9, 1936, the *Moulton Advertiser* reported that since the early summer of 1935, more than 200 men from Alabama and Mississippi had been working under the supervision of the Forest Service and TVA, systematically controlling erosion in Lawrence County. The cooperation with local farmers was excellent. Farmers wanting the enrollees to do terrace work applied through the county agent. Many farmers provided rock and sand for terrace projects, even those who did not ask for CCC help. The County Board of Revenue purchased an air compressor to be used by the CCC camp. Since August 1935, the enrollees had worked on 3,000 acres of farmland and planted 350,000 trees on 270 acres of eroded land.

During the very dry summer and fall of 1935, Company 3487 had assisted the Alabama National Forest in forest fire protection. In March 1936, Company 3487 planted 1,030,000 trees in the Tennessee River Basin. The local people, pleasant and cooperative neighbors, showed their appreciation. The men went into Moulton and Decatur for recreation. Captain Bertram Kaufman was the company commander in early 1936 (1936 CCC District D annual).

On July 7, 1936, Thomas L. Sharpe enrolled in the CCC at the courthouse in Montgomery and was sent to Camp TVA-11 in Moulton. He did his conditioning at the camp and received shots for typhoid and smallpox. Soon after his arrival, the camp was quarantined because of an outbreak of polio. He recalled that the enrollees were given an experimental vaccination for polio. He worked on a crew that dug and lined drainage ditches, and he also worked in the auto mechanics shop. He knew how to cut hair and had brought his barbering equipment from home when he enrolled. He became the company barber, charging 20 cents for a haircut. A small portion of this money was turned back to the company fund. Hair tonic could be purchased at the company canteen (Thomas L. Sharpe interview, October 30, 2002; see the CD).

A Camp Inspection Report dated September 25, 1936, recorded that 1st Lt. James B. Miller took command on July 19, 1936. When he arrived in camp, he found the company mess insolvent for more than $200. The men had also written to CCC Director Fechner complaining about the food and blaming the mess steward. The enrollees were being sent back to camp from the work project because of hunger. On September 24, Project Supervisor Joe W. Burleson had written to Special Investigator Neil McL. Coney Jr. about the food. The situation had greatly improved since the arrival of Lt. Miller. Burleson admitted he was overstepping his authority in the matter, but the state of the mess was having an effect on company morale and project work. Lt. Miller also wrote to Special Investigator Coney on September 24. He was trying to pay the bills but would not allow the men to go hungry. The enrollees did not like the mess steward because of his age and personality, but he was competent and therefore was not replaced. Lt. Miller was training a new man to be the mess steward.

Special Investigator Coney reported his findings on September 26. The mess steward was a former member of a veterans' company and easy to irritate. Some of the complaints had been made just to anger him. The menu needed to have more variety, better preparation, and larger servings. Corn beef hash and cabbage had been served too frequently, as were starchy foods and beans. There was a total lack of baked goods and hot breads. The complaint of "wormy pudding" as reported to Director Fechner was not substantiated. The medical officer was of the opinion that the food was wholesome. The situation had greatly improved with the arrival of Lt. Miller and would be corrected once the mess fund was solvent and the kitchen personnel better trained.

When the camp was inspected on November 6, 1936, by J. C. Reddoch, he reported a "wonderful improvement" in the food. The men were still eating out of mess kits, which was a frequent complaint found in Reddoch's inspection reports. Lt. Miller planned to buy china in the following months if the mess funds permitted. At the time of the inspection, there were 167 men from Alabama, Mississippi, and Florida. The work project, under Joe W. Burleson, consisted of the construction of terrace outlets, gully control with brush dams and vegetative planting, and gathering seeds.

On September 30, 1937, the *Moulton Advertiser* announced that Company 3487 was being disbanded. The enrollees were being transferred to camps at Athens, Munford, and Huntsville and were being replaced with a veteran company. The Army and Forest Service personnel would remain and continue working with the veterans. The men of Company 3487 had formed social ties with the people of Moulton, who regretted losing them but wished for their happiness in the future.

Company 2449-V, Camp TVA-11, Moulton, Alabama

Company 2449 occupied Camp TVA-11 on October 10, 1937. A Camp Inspection Report dated November 12 recorded 181 World War I veterans from Alabama, Georgia, and Mississippi under the command of Captain Alfred W. Goodyear. Joe W. Burleson was the project superintendent. Camp TVA-11 had agreements on 2,007 acres scattered over Franklin, Lawrence, and Morgan counties. It was expected that another six months would be needed to complete the planned work.

Camp Education Advisor R. R. Caruther's educational report for October 1937 recorded that there was only one class of reading and writing offered for illiterates, and less than 5 percent of the men were participating in the education program.

The men, however, many of whom had come from farms, were eager to learn as much as possible about soil conservation. The local farmers also appreciated the program and showed interest in the project. The men of Company 2449 were enjoying exploring the Black Warrior National Forest, paying particular attention to plants and wildlife. Although they had not yet been called to fight a forest fire, fighting fires and treating erosion were far more to their liking than fighting in a war. They were proud of their 15-man crew who planted 3,500 trees in a single day and of enrollee Lester D. Beasley, who had driven 110,000 miles without an accident (1938 CCC District D annual).

A Camp Inspection Report dated September 10, 1938, noted that the project was nearly finished and the camp was expected to be abandoned by October 1. Although the camp had been without an educational advisor since December 17, 1937, the technical personnel were teaching classes five nights a week. Reading, writing, and arithmetic were offered at the elementary school level, a course in accounting was offered, and related educational work was done in carpentry, radio, mechanics, first aid, safety, and health. Job training was given in dam and terrace outlet construction and truck driving. The company had two permanent libraries of 99 books and a reference library of 52 books. The camp received several newspapers and magazines.

Camp TVA-11 was abandoned at the end of the eleventh period, which ended September 30, 1938, according to the *CCC Camp Directory for Alabama*. Company 2449 transferred to Camp TVA-7 at Huntsville on that date.

Company 3488, Camp TVA-12, Russellville, Alabama

According to a Camp Inspection Report dated December 10, 1935, Company 3488 occupied Camp TVA-12 on August 8, 1935. There were 187 junior enrollees from Mississippi, Florida, and Alabama under the command of 1st Lt. Benjamin Antin. The work project, under the supervision of N. T. Norris, consisted of construction of masonry dams for terrace outlets, excavation of diversion and drainage ditches, seeding and sodding eroded areas, and paving eroded areas with loose rock and brush over 150 square miles in Franklin County.

CEA Edgar C. Merritt's educational report for November 1935 recorded that courses were offered at elementary and high school levels. Vocational classes were offered in woodworking, leather working, typing, soil erosion, truck driving, surveying, wireless telegraphy, and applied electricity. On-the-job instruction was offered in soil erosion, truck driving, surveying, cooking, and clerking. Half the company was participating in the educational program. The woodworking classes, working on Saturdays and rainy days, had built the furniture for the welfare building. Company 3488 did not have a library at the time.

The *CCC Camp Directory for Alabama* listed Camp TVA-12 as a new camp for the fifth period, and it showed as an approved camp for the sixth period, October 1935–March 1936. Camp TVA-12 was not included in the 1936 District D annual, suggesting that the camp was abandoned sometime prior to March 31, 1936.

Company 5402, Camp TVA-P-12, Huntsville, Alabama

Company 5402 was organized from a cadre of men from Wilson Dam in June 1935. On August 19, 1935, another 198 boys arrived from Mississippi. After conditioning, they were turned over to the Park Service on September 6 to begin construction of Monte Sano Park. K. L. Haggard was the project superintendent and Captain Harry Villiard the company commander. Monte Sano Park was located five miles east of Huntsville on 2,000 acres purchased by Madison County and later turned over to the TVA. By the time of the 1936 annual, lodges, trailside shelters, overnight cabins, overlooks, and log seats had been constructed (1936 CCC District D annual).

In May 1936, Company 5402 began publishing a camp newspaper called the "Monte Sano Broadcast." The May–August 1936 and February 1937 issues were archived at the University of Chicago. The May 20 issue reported that 21 new enrollees from Miami and Palm Beach, Florida, had arrived in camp; arriving at three o'clock in the morning, they found their bunks "short-sheeted." They were assigned tasks such as "tending to the mules" and "slopping the hogs" for the first several days. There being neither mules nor hogs in camp, the new enrollees took these pranks in stride, showing that they could "take it."

Since the start of the work project on September 6, 1936, the men had constructed a 30-by-90-foot garage to house the Park Service trucks. Twenty combination tables and benches had been built along the bluff lines and down the mountainsides. They had quarried approximately 3,000 cubic yards of sandstone and carried it to construction sites. They had fought forest fires within the park. A 38-by-62-foot public lodge, built of sandstone and wood, was about 60 percent complete. It was to have restrooms, a commissary, a kitchen, and a large assembly room and would be "equipped with the facilities for the conveniences of large groups of park guests." Two of the four overnight cabins were nearly completed. The cabins were "planned for simplicity of service with ruggedness in construction and will fit into the landscape." They were built of solid stone and would "no doubt last for two or three centuries." Stonewalls were constructed around the bluff lines in the park. Road construction in the park was nearly completed, and this system tied into the road being built up the mountain by Camp TVA-P-13.

The July 31, 1936, issue of the "Monte Sano Broadcast" reported that District Commander Colonel Baltzell had placed the camp under quarantine as cases of infantile paralysis had increased in the local community. The boys were making the best of their time shooting pool, playing ping-pong, and pitching horseshoes.

A geological survey of Monte Sano Mountain by a student geologist, H. G. Stokes, was under way. A natural well in a cave had been located at the base of the mountain. Dr. Walter B. Jones, state geologist, had explored the cave, descending by rope ladder to a ledge 186 feet below the surface. The well was being considered as an attraction for park guests. Elsewhere in the park, the roads were being surfaced with crushed rock, and 12 additional camp stoves had been approved for the picnic area, as the large number of visitors from Huntsville had shown the need.

Roy Hill of Talladega, Alabama, served in Company 5402 during 1936. He recalled working on a road construction crew and had also picked cedar seeds for a nursery. When Camp TVA-12 was abandoned in 1937, he transferred to Company 5401 at Camp TVA-6 (Roy Hill interview, May 23, 2001; see the CD).

The February 1937 issue of the "Monte Sano Broadcast" reported that four overnight cabins were completed, three more under construction, and four waiting for approval for construction. Based on public visitations to the park, the enrollees could not build enough overnight cabins for the visitors. The public lodge was completed. Additional work at the picnic area was planned, including a guardrail, a stone overlook, and a parking area. Foreman Jones and a crew of eight enrollees were exploring the natural well. The only way to enter the well was by means of a steel cable and wench lowering the explorers to the ledge. A tunnel had been discovered running from the ledge to a large room, 70 to 80 feet long with walls over 100 feet high. If the well could be developed for visitors, it would be the most interesting feature of the park.

According to the *CCC Camp Directory for Alabama*, Camp TVA-P-12 was disbanded after the eighth period, which ended March 31, 1937.

Company 3486, Camp TVA-P-13, Huntsville, Alabama

Camp TVA-P-13 was the "sister camp" to Camp TVA-P-12, which was located across the street. On July 8, 1935, a cadre of men from Company 472 under the command of Captain Jack Haynie arrived at Monte Sano Mountain to erect the camp. Monte Sano Mountain rises 1,000 feet above the surrounding valley. On August 19, enrollees from southern Mississippi arrived, and another 46 from northern Mississippi arrived in March 1936.

In March 1936, Company 3486 began publishing a camp newspaper called the "Camp Clay Crier." Issues of March–October 1936 and January 26, 1937, were archived at the University of Chicago. The March 14 issue reported that Camp TVA-P-13 was named after Clement C. Clay, a nineteenth-century Madison County delegate to the State Convention, a circuit court judge, state representative, and U.S. congressman from the Huntsville district. Through the *Huntsville Times*, the people of Huntsville and Madison County had suggested the name for the camp.

By March 14, 1936, 2.5 miles of the road leading down the mountain to Huntsville had been completed, and another 7.4 miles of foot trails had been completed leading to "points of interest." The park was keeping its natural appearance, with the exception of the addition of a few "conveniences" such as picnic tables and several camp ovens in the picnic areas. Plans had been submitted for a horse barn, a superintendent's lodge, a service building, and picnic and parking areas. Plans for wayside shelters, a swimming pool, and overlooks were also being proposed.

The "Camp Clay Crier" reported on May 23, 1936, that Company 3486 had received 29 new enrollees from Miami and Arcadia, Florida. Work on the park road, the superintendent's house, and the horse barn was nearly completed. The education program had added a course in trigonometry in preparation for classes being taught in transit work. The woodworking class was making tables for the reading room. Camps TVA-P-12 and TVA-P-13 shared a 35mm movie projector. Most CCC camps had 16mm projectors, but the 35mm projector showed newer and better movies.

The June 17 "Camp Clay Crier" announced that Mr. Conover, the NPS foreman at Camp TVA-P-12, had taken over the work project. It was also announced that the "Opening Dance" would be held that Friday in the pavilion. The people of Huntsville were invited, and a "transportation committee" had been created to arrange rides for ladies, who would be admitted free of charge.

On July 4 the "Camp Clay Crier" reported that Company 3486 was expecting 61 new recruits from north Alabama. Work at the rock quarry was progressing. A new air drill was facilitating the blasting and breaking up of rock. A rock crusher was expected, and the roads would soon be covered with rock. On June 24, construction had begun on a garage and workshop. The structures, when finished and furnished with all the modern tools needed for mechanical work, would serve as the repair shop for the trucks of Company 5402 and Company 3486.

On August 15, the "Camp Clay Crier" reported that the education program was being reorganized. Classes would be taught in the morning, afternoon, and evening. The men were working two shifts in the field, and several ladies had volunteered to teach courses while the foremen were at work. The classes would be less crowded with the new schedule. Mr. Greene, the CEA, had contacted the WPA to obtain cedar logs from trees being cut from the right-of-way of a road under WPA construction to join Huntsville to the park. The lumber was to be used by the woodworking class for chests, cabinets, and other items.

Two members of the newspaper staff, Johnie Brasfield and Leslie B.L. Dunn, were working on a special project collecting beetles. As of August 15, 1936, they had caught about 1,200 beetles. The September 18 "Camp Clay Crier" reported the beetle project had begun on August 3 under the supervision of Dr. Walter B. Jones, state geologist and director of the Alabama Museum of Natural History. The boys were searching for the rare and beautiful *Steniridea lodingii*, of which only four specimens had been caught, all from Monte Sano. Another rare beetle, *Dorcus brevis*, a stag beetle, had been found, and 18–20 specimens of *Geotropes ulkei* had been collected. In the 1930s, this scarab beetle was thought to be one of the rarest beetles known. The project was so successful Dr. Jones asked that it be extended through November 1.

The September 18 issue of the "Camp Clay Crier" summarized the project work of Camps TVA-P-12 and TVA-P-13. A horse barn made of frame construction with two stalls for seven horses, a covered shed, a hayloft, and a corral had been finished. A public recreation lodge of frame and stone construction was completed. The six-room superintendent's dwelling was completed with the exception of a terrace that was to be added. A service building for maintenance tools was completed, as well as a repair and blacksmith shop. Four cabins had been built and the foundations for three more begun. The picnic area was completed; table and bench combinations were already being used by park visitors. Plans for a parking area, a guardrail around the picnic area, and an overlook at Chalybeate Spring were awaiting approval. TVA architects had finished designs for a picnic shelter, a commissary, and a latrine building. These plans were to be submitted for the eighth period, which would begin October 1, 1936. Plans had been submitted to tear down the old pavilion at Inspiration Point and replace it with a tower and observatory platform.

Park Service and TVA officials inspected the work project on August 24, 1936. Project Conover was highly praised. Colonel Page Bunker, the state forester, announced that the park would be open to the public by June of 1937.

The September 18 issue of the "Camp Clay Crier" also reported several camp improvements. The "rock work" class had built a fishpond between the two camps; it was eight feet in diameter and three and a half feet deep. A rock pillar rising up from the middle of the pond provided a continuous spray of water. Water lilies and moss had been placed in the pond, and it would soon be stocked with fish. A native stone fireplace was planned for the recreation hall. A construction class had cut logs for a cabin to be built as a "clubhouse" for the leaders and assistant leaders in camp. The concrete class had finished construction of the entrance to the camp.

On October 16, 1936, the "Camp Clay Crier" reported that the entrance was finished with a curved rock wall on the side. The enrollees had built the entrance in their "odd hours." The natural well project had finally begun. The area around the well had been leveled and a platform built over the entrance. A windlass with 400-foot cable, capable of carrying five to seven men, was being built on the platform. The WPA had begun staking the mile-and-a-third road between the park and Pratt Avenue in Huntsville. WPA officials estimated the road construction would employ 200 men.

On January 26, 1937, the "Camp Clay Crier" reported that bad weather had slowed progress of the project during the first half of the eighth period. The rock crusher had been broken for two or three weeks but was back in "full swing." A great amount of work had been done at the nursery. Several miles of old roads had been obliterated in the park, covered with topsoil, and planted with young trees from the nursery. The existing trails in the park had been cleared of downed trees and debris. Surveying and mapping of Inspiration Point and the natural well had been completed, as had five trailside shelters. A swimming pool, 250 feet long by 50 feet wide, was being planned for Monte Sano Park.

According to the *CCC Camp Directory for Alabama*, Camp TVA-P-13 was turned over to the Park Service and designated Camp SP-16 after the eighth period.

Company 5432, Camp TVA-14, Stevenson, Alabama

The *CCC Camp Directory for Alabama* listed Camp TVA-14 as a newly established camp for the fifteenth period, which began April 1, 1940, as a Forest Service camp for the TVA, working on soil conservation.

Wade Gladden of Gadsden, who had joined Company 5432 on October 3, 1939, was detailed to Stevenson on August 16, 1940, to work on the construction of Camp TVA-14. He recalled that the CCC enrollees worked with civilian carpenters on the camp buildings and drilling the well. The enrollees lived in tents while the camp was being built. As soon as the camp construction was finished, Mr. Gladden went to work in the kitchen (Wade Gladden interview, February 8, 2002; see the CD).

On July 3, 1941, the *Progressive Age* reported that an advanced detachment of CCC enrollees from the Stevenson camp were building a new camp near Langston, Alabama, in the southern part of Jackson County, a side camp for 50 enrollees. The work was to be limited to private land suffering from severe sheet and gully erosion. The camp would also do reforestation and erosion control on TVA lands that had been previously terraced and that were a reasonable distance from the camp.

Private landowners in the vicinity of the Langston side camp were instructed to apply for CCC assistance at the county agent's office or at the CCC camp once it was established at South Sauta Creek. The landowners were to furnish materials such as brush, straw, logs, fencing, and teams of draft animals if needed. In return for the materials, the landowners would secure labor from the CCC enrollees to establish meadows at the ends of the terraces, planted with grass or *sericea lespedeza*. Landowners had to agree to maintain the work and to keep fire and stock out of the worked areas.

According to the *CCC Camp Directory for Alabama*, Camp TVA-14 was closed after the eighteenth period, which ended March 31, 1942.

Enrollees from Company 3474, Camp F-9, planting longleaf and slash pine seedlings on the Blue Pond Plantation, Conecuh National Forest, 1937. Photo courtesy of USDA Forest Service.

Enrollee from Company 3474, Camp F-9, Blue Pond Plantation, Conecuh National Forest, 1937. Photo courtesy of USDA Forest Service.

Enrollees from Company 3474, Camp F-9, building a bridge over Five Runs Creek, Conecuh National Forest, 1937. Photo courtesy of USDA Forest Service.

Project supervisor inspecting check dams in gully at Open Pond, Conecuh National Forest, 1937. Camp F-9 is seen in background. Photo courtesy of USDA Forest Service.

Enrollees from Company 3478 leaving Camp F-7, Chandler Springs, Alabama, Talladega National Forest, 1936. Photo courtesy of USDA Forest Service.

Enrollees from Company 3478 filling up backpack pumpers on way to forest fire, Talladega National Forest, 1936. Photo courtesy of USDA Forest Service.

Telephone line crew from Company 3477, Camp F-6, Heflin, Alabama, Talladega National Forest, March 20, 1937. Fred Phillip, construction foreman. Enrollees: Henry Taylor, Roy Bell, Freddie Jones, William Johnson, Brooks Kent, Odis Getaw, Virgil Weathers, Bradgy Perry, Sam Wilson, Norris Bush. Photo courtesy of National Association of CCC Alumni.

Watercolor painting of Camp F-1, Moulton, Alabama, Alabama National Forest, 1934, by Charles Foster. Photo courtesy of Charles Foster.

Enrollees of Company 3486, Camp TVA-P-13, Huntsville, Alabama. Note the "Education Dept." sign with E. W. Greene, camp educational advisor. Photo courtesy of National Association of CCC Alumni.

Gazebo at Geneva State Park, built by Company 2421-V at Camp SP-1. Photo courtesy of Patricia Whigham.

Enrollees of Company 2421 V, Camp SP 1, laying pipe at Geneva State Park. Photo courtesy of Patricia Whigham.

Enrollees of Company 2421-V, Camp SP-1, observing tractor constructing firebreak in Geneva State Park. Photo courtesy of Patricia Whigham.

Picnic shelter at Geneva State Park, constructed by enrollees of Company 2421-V. Photo courtesy of Patricia Whigham.

Enrollees of Company 2421-V surveying in Camp SP-1. Photo courtesy of Patricia Whigham.

Enrollees of Company 2421-V. Photograph appears to be of members of one of the barracks in camp. Photo courtesy of Patricia Whigham.

Caretaker's house with observation tower in background, Weogufka State Park. Structures built by Company 260, Camp SP-4. Photo courtesy of USDA Forest Service.

Camp Baltzell, side camp at Mound State Monument, 1935. Photo courtesy of the Dr. Walter B. Jones Photograph Collection, University of Alabama Museums.

Enrollees pouring the concrete foundation for the museum at Mound State Monument, 1937. Photo courtesy of the Dr. Walter B. Jones Photograph Collection, University of Alabama Museums.

Enrollees of Company 1485, Camp S-52 at Chunchila, Alabama, constructing a bridge. Photo courtesy of National Association of CCC Alumni.

Camp P-54, Company 2403 at Brewton, Alabama. Photo courtesy of National Association of CCC Alumni.

6
The CCC and the Alabama State Parks

A system of state parks in Alabama began in the 1920s. In 1925, Governor William W. Brandon appointed a State Park Committee (Burleson 1975:27). On September 27, 1927, the state legislature passed the State Land Act, giving the state authority to establish state parks. On December 22, 1930, the *Birmingham News* announced the establishment of the Talladega County State Park, 421 acres along the Coosa River. The park received little attention or development (Burleson 1975:33). By 1933, Alabama had 11 state parks, comprising approximately 6,000 acres: Talladega County, Cheaha, Geneva, Little River, Bromley, Sumter, St. Stephens, Fort Toulouse, The Lagoons, Weogufka, and Panther Creek (Burleson 1975:34).

In June 1935, the Alabama Commission of Forestry was seeking additional land gifts. The state could not afford the purchase of new land but recognized the importance of the work of the CCC. Alabama could lose several camps if suitable sites were not made available. On June 23, 1936, the Park, Parkway, and Recreational Area Study Act was passed, expanding the role of the National Park Service in park planning. On February 21, 1938, Governor Bibb Graves designated the Alabama Commission of Forestry to cooperate with the National Park Service in their nationwide study. CCC Director Robert Fechner wrote to Governor Graves that he hoped Alabama would "cooperate to the fullest extent possible in this study" as the results would "be the basis of future cooperation in all matters pertaining to Park and Recreational planning, development, operation, and maintenance, which, of course, will include any work which might be done by the Civilian Conservation Corps" (Burleson 1975:37–39).

Following the completion of the Park, Parkway and Recreational Area Study, long-term development plans were drawn for most of the state parks. Priorities were based on a park's importance: Gulf State Park, Cheaha State Park, DeSoto State Park, Monte Sano State Park, Chewacla State Park,

Valley Creek Regional Park, Oak Mountain State Park, Cedar Creek Regional Park, Little River Regional Park, Wheeler Regional Park (proposed by TVA), Chattahoochie Regional Park, Muscle Shoals and Wilson Parks (TVA), Weogufka Regional Park, Panther Creek Regional Park, and Chickasaw Regional Park (Burleson 1975:39–40).

On March 14, 1939, Governor Frank M. Dixon signed the Department of Conservation Act, and Dr. Walter B. Jones was appointed director of the newly created department. It was decided that rather than trying to develop and manage 14 parks in an uncoordinated manner, five of the most prominent parks would be selected for development in the first year: Cheaha, Monte Sano, and DeSoto State Parks were chosen for their outstanding mountain scenery, Gulf Shores State Park for its location and high rate of attendance, and Chewacla State Park to provide a balance in park distribution. All five parks had CCC camps operating satisfactory programs. It was expected that the parks would open to the public by June 1939. Panther Creek, Little River, and Weogufka were turned over to the Commission of Forestry to be operated as state forests (Burleson 1975:40–43).

On August 1, 1940, the *Cleburne News* carried an insert titled "Know Your Alabama," addressing the five state parks. More than 200,000 visitors had registered at Gulf Shores, Chewacla, Cheaha, Monte Sano, and DeSoto State Parks during the first year. These five parks, containing a total of 14,444 acres, had 57 cabins built of wood or stone, "fully equipped to meet the needs of vacationists, including stoves, iceboxes, furniture, dishes, kitchen utensils, and even towels." The cabins had a combined maximum capacity of 209 persons and rented for $9 a week. The Alabama Legislature had failed to provide operating funds, so a small gate fee of 10 cents for adults and 5 cents for children would be charged for the 1940 season. Everything else in the parks was free, except the rental costs of the cabins, bathing suits, and lockers.

Company 2421, Camp SP-1, Hacoda, Alabama

Company 2421 was organized on July 1, 1933, at Fort McClellan, made up of Spanish-American and World War I veterans, primarily from Alabama. After conditioning, they were sent to Geneva State Park at Hacoda. The work project, covering 3,200 acres, consisted of building roads, bridges, trails, cottages, and firebreaks and planting tropical trees and native shrubbery. The men lived in tents until barracks were built. The camp had its own water and electrical plant and was considered one of the best in the district for good health and morale (1934 CCC District G annual).

On July 8, 1934, the *Montgomery Advertiser* reported that 40 men were to receive honorable discharges and be sent home. The morale of the company suffered as the men preparing to leave were the heads of large families. The CCC had turned despair into hope, but the men would soon be turned out into the "cruel, cold world, with little chance for employment." President Roosevelt, however, had recently extended their enlistment period, and 30 of the 40 veterans remained in Company 2421. That September, the scene repeated itself, as 175 men were expecting to be honorably discharged. The *Montgomery Advertiser* reported on September 16 that the president had once again extended their enlistments through June 1, 1935.

On September 23, 1934, the *Montgomery Advertiser*'s staff correspondent Howard C. Smith visited Camp SP-1 on "Government Property Inspection Day." It was a very serious inspection, as the men would be charged for any missing property. Each man was issued two suits of clothing, a raincoat, an overcoat, underwear, toilet accessories, a bed, and bedding. Each item of clothing had to be accounted for and loaned items returned. Smith reported, "The 90-foot barracks looked like second-hand stores with fake auctioneers." Practical jokes were common. A flask filled with brown liquid found among the belongings of an enrollee, who stammered his innocence, turned out to be a soft drink upon closer inspection. The joking kept the mood at Geneva State Park light and happy as the 190-man company constructed a playground and recreational center under the direction of the Alabama Commission of Forestry and the U.S. Department of Interior. The park was receiving hundreds of visitors each week.

According to the *CCC Camp Directory for Alabama*, Camp SP-1 was not approved for the fifth period, which began April 1, 1935.

Company 468, Camp SP-2, Oxford, Alabama

Company 468 was organized on May 18, 1933, at Fort McClellan with junior enrollees from the northern counties of Alabama. After two weeks of conditioning, they were sent to their camp, nine miles southeast of Anniston, arriving on June 3. They lived in tents while they cleared the site and constructed the mess hall and barracks.

"Camp Cheaha" was originally designated as "Camp S-51" as a state forestry project. The forestry personnel arrived on June 13, and work began on the Oxford-Cheaha Road. By October 1, the mess hall and barracks were completed. On November 17, a storm hit the camp, demolishing the mess hall, water tank, and garage and knocking the barracks off their foundations. The wreckage was cleared immediately, and Company 468 ate their Thanksgiving dinner in a new mess hall (1934 CCC District D annual). The *Gadsden Times* reported on November 22 that nine members of Company 468 were hospitalized. Company Commander Captain William D. Britt was quoted as saying that the wind hit with sudden and amazing force.

On April 15, 1934, Captain Jack D. Haynie relieved Captain Britt, and the project was transferred to the State Parks with O. R. Head as the superintendent. By the time of the 1934 annual, Company 468 had completed 13 miles of road construction leading to the top of Cheaha Mountain. A stone tower on the highest peak in Alabama at 2,407 feet was nearing completion. A stone dam had been constructed, forming a reservoir with a capacity of 250,000 gallons. Sites were cleared for several stone overnight cottages (1934 CCC District D annual).

In August, the Oxford-Cheaha Road was completed to the point that trucks could get to the top of the mountain. William D. Sadler of Munford had enrolled in Company 468 on July 20, 1934, and was assigned to the dynamite crew widening the road to the park. He also ran the air hammer used for cutting through the bedrock. Enrollees working on the stone bridges, culverts, and retaining walls learned the art of stone masonry through on-the-job training. The leader of the work crew was the only man on the project experienced in masonry (William D. Sadler interview, April 27 and May 8, 2001; see the CD).

Camp SP-2's "Narrative Report to the National Park Service" dated December 1, 1934, recorded that the 13.7-mile road from the camp to the park had been widened to 18 feet. Arch culverts had been built from native stone at every drain except one (Hillibee Creek), which was to be spanned by a 20-foot semicircular arch bridge, also to be built of stone. The 40-foot stone tower was completed except for the roof and interior finishing. A new air compressor and road machine would make road construction easier.

A "Narrative Report" dated February 1, 1935, reported that winter weather had slowed progress. Company 468 was ready to begin construction of two miles of roadway down the west side of the mountain toward Camp SP-7 and Talladega. The caretaker's house was nearly completed, lacking the interior finishing and tile roof. Difficulties in hauling men and supplies up the mountain continued.

A Camp Inspection Report dated February 28, 1935, recorded 204 men in Company 468. The camp educational advisor, E. C. Merritt, reported that 175 men were participating in the education program, which had expanded and offered courses in practical arithmetic, instruction in reading, writing, and arithmetic for illiterates, tree culture, woodworking, bookkeeping, landscaping, business English, business law, English, and physical education.

A "Narrative Report" dated June 1, 1935, recorded that the stone tower and the caretaker's house were completed. The latter contained two bedrooms, living room, dining room, and kitchen and a bathroom with hot and cold water. Four stone overnight cabins were completed. Each had a bedroom, a bathroom, and a combination living and cooking room with fireplace, Dutch oven, and pantry with sink. Water was gravity-fed to the cabins and caretaker's house from the reservoir. Project superintendent O. R. Head expected to complete a 20-foot semicircular bridge over Hillabee Creek on the road between Camp SP-2 and the park. Work was also progressing on the road toward Camp SP-7 and Talladega. Designs were under way for a stone lodge and several more cabins.

A "Narrative Report" dated December 2, 1935, recorded that Company 468 had assisted Company 465-C at Camp SP-7 with their project work prior to Company 465's disbanding in late October. This work included road construction and construction of an earthen dam with a concrete core, creating Lake Cheaha. The beautiful mountain lake, completed with the exception of the spillway and apron, provided reflections of Pulpit Rock and Cheaha Mountain. Plans were submitted to build a bathhouse and other buildings around the lake.

According to a Camp Inspection Report dated December 18, 1935, there were 200 enrollees from Georgia, Florida, and Alabama under the command of Captain J. S. Pinkston. The work project contained 2,320 acres and consisted of improvements to Cheaha State Park under the supervision of O. R. Head. Camp SP-2 was equipped for recreation with a boxing ring, a basketball court, a volleyball court, a baseball diamond, and indoor equipment for the recreation hall. There were 327 books in the camp library, and 180 enrollees participated in the education program. Dances and a trip to Tuscaloosa to see a football game were listed as informal recreational activities. The company had access to a 16mm movie projector that showed "silent" movies. Company 468 was awarded the "Best Camp in District D" for the third quarter of 1935.

On March 31, 1936, Project Superintendent O. R. Head wrote a special report to the Park Service reporting accomplishments. A 14-mile mountainous road had been built from the camp to the park with two native stone bridges of masonry arch construction, over Hillabee and Dry Creeks. A stone bathhouse was 80 percent completed. Five stone overnight cabins had been built with tile roofs, individual septic tanks, and sewer disposal systems, and were fed water from a mountaintop reservoir of 200,000 gallons impounded by a stone dam. A second dam had created the six-acre Cheaha Lake. A four-room caretaker's house and a two-car garage had been constructed of stone. Fifteen miles of telephone line had been erected, connecting the park with Camp SP-2. Seventeen miles of roads had been built within the park and between the camp and the park. The roads were 22 feet wide with an average grade of only 8 percent. Three miles of trails had been constructed in the park.

According to Superintendent Head, the intention of the construction of buildings and structures in Cheaha State Park was to adhere to Park Service standards for architecture, engineering, and landscaping, to retain the natural appearance through preservation and protection, and to present the public with an educational benefit of science, history, and nature.

On April 3, Cheaha State Park was officially opened. The *Cleburne News* reported on April 16 that the principal speakers at the dedication ceremony were Robert Fechner, director of Emergency Conservation Work, and Colonel Richard Leiber, president of the National Conference of State Park Officials. On March 26, the paper had reported that a national convention of 250 foresters would be held in the park in connection with the dedication ceremony.

Company 468 served barbeque to 700 people at the dedication. During the three years that Company 468 had worked on Cheaha State Park, there had not been a single fatal accident. Given the road conditions in the early days of the project and the number of men transported, this was a remarkable record (1936 CCC District D annual).

In July, Company 468 transferred to Camp SP-7 at Munford. The camp buildings at Camp SP-2 were dismantled and relocated to the new location at Camp SP-7. Work continued at Cheaha State Park (William D. Sadler interview, April 27 and May 8, 2001; see the CD).

Company 230, Camp SP-3, Uriah, Alabama

Company 230 was organized on May 18, 1933, at Fort Jay, Governor's Island, New York, with junior enrollees from New York and New Jersey. After a month of conditioning, they were sent by train to Wyoming to work in the Ashley National Forest under the command of Captain Grose. On October 16, those men who did not return to New York were sent to Huxford, Alabama, arriving on October 20. They built their camp along a highway near Little River State Park. No sooner had Company 230 received 139 replacement from the Second Corps Area, they were called to fight forest fires, a frequent occurrence. Construction of the camp continued. With the barracks, mess hall, and recreation building completed, they moved from tents into wooden buildings.

During their first six months in Alabama, Company 230 worked on firebreak and road construction and stump removal. More replacements arrived in March 1934, and work began on an artificial lake and dam. Log cabins and a fire tower were constructed in the park. In the spring of 1934, the baseball team was hoping to win the district championship. There were only 17 members of the original company, and they were preparing to return to New York. They would "take their work elsewhere, and leave the company in the hands of those who joined later, to carry on where they left off" (1934 CCC District G annual).

According to the *CCC Camp Directory for Alabama*, Camp SP-3 was abandoned after the fourth period, which ended March 30, 1935. The camp would be reestablished at Little River State Park in January 1936 with Company 1432-C.

Company 1432, Camp SP-3, Uriah, Alabama

Company 1432 took pride in being one of the oldest companies in the CCC. The junior African-American company was organized at Fort Benning, Georgia, on May 29, 1933. In July, they were transferred to Clayton, Alabama, to work on a private forestry project. On January 15, 1936, Company 1432 was transferred to Uriah under the command of Captain John A. Laughlin. He was replaced by 1st Lt. Claude Barmer in February. Lt. Barmer was considered stern, straightforward, and capable. No one was more interested in the welfare and happiness of the men under his command, and Company 1432 improved by "leaps and bounds" under his leadership. The work project at Little River State Park was conducted under the supervision of the National Park Service with G. W. Rawls the project superintendent (1936 CCC District G annual).

According to the *CCC Camp Directory for Alabama*, Camp SP-3 was abandoned during the tenth period on January 1, 1938.

Company 260, Camp SP-4, Weogufka, Alabama

Company 260 was formed at the Plattsburg Barracks, New York, in April 1933. After several weeks of conditioning, enrollees were sent to Lewiston,

Idaho. On October 20, an advanced cadre of 15 men under the command of Lt. George H. Toepfer, USN, arrived in Weogufka and began clearing a site for a camp that was completed on January 10, 1934. On November 2, 1933, they received 175 new enrollees from Fort Dix, New Jersey. The project work began on November 13 on a state park under the supervision of Roy Duran, who was replaced by Stanton Ready. On March 15, 1934, Captain Guy D. Field, Infantry-Reserve, replaced Lt. Toepfer as company commander (1934 CCC District D annual).

The state park would be one of the most scenic places in Alabama, situated on Flagg Mountain at 1,149 feet above sea level. Just south of the camp was one of the largest yellow pine forests east of the Rocky Mountains. From a 52-foot observation tower under construction on the top of Flagg Mountain, the surrounding countryside could be seen for 60 miles. The men also constructed trails leading to scenic points, a road leading to the park, overnight cabins, and a museum. For recreation, Company 260 held dances in their recreation hall twice each month, enjoyed by the enrollees and local residents. The isolation of the camp taught every man in the company the necessity of using his own resources for work and pleasure. Company 260 took pride in their company slogan, "We can take it" (1934 CCC District D annual).

A Camp Inspection Report dated May 2, 1934, recorded 200 men, including 16 LEMs, under the command of Captain Field. The work project consisted of road and trail construction in the 400-acre state park under the supervision of Stanton Ready.

A "Narrative Report" dated November 30, 1934, recorded that the lookout tower being built of native stone, 40 percent completed, was already popular with visitors. A caretaker's house with halved logs and stone was under construction, as were four overnight cabins. Four miles of foot trails had been built, giving hikers and horseback riders access to all points of interest.

In December 1934, Company 260 began publishing a camp newspaper, "Reflector." Issues were archived at the University of Chicago from December 1934, February, April, May, Memorial Day, Fourth of July, and September 1935. It was published twice each month under the supervision of the camp educational advisor, L. O. Kyzar. The December 1934 issue reported that the education program offered courses in auto-mechanics, woodworking, photography, rock gardening, and garage building

A "Narrative Report" dated January 31, 1935, reported that the work on the lookout tower was progressing. The timbers were hand-hewn by the enrollees, and the framing was accomplished by them with the help of one skilled carpenter. The foreman was making every effort to have the enrollees do as many different jobs as possible. As a reward for mixing all of the mortar, an enrollee named Domalga from New York was allowed to go Montgomery with the E.C.W. truck for supplies. He visited the state capitol and stood where Jefferson Davis had been sworn in as president of the Confederacy. He boasted that very few Yankees had done that.

Work was also progressing on the four overnight cabins. The enrollees had never done any construction previously and were not even familiar with the tools, but they were interested in learning and were being taught masonry one at a time. The cabins were masonry rubble from foundation to window and rounded logs from window to rafter. The caretaker's house was also a combination of masonry and logs. The masonry for an open pavilion was completed, and the timbers for the roof were being framed.

The major road into the park was open to traffic but was not surfaced and had no guardrails. A truck trail as well as foot trails had been built to the cabins. Superintendent Ready concluded his report stating that the camp needed additional trucks. The work crews were trucked two and one-half miles to the project area, with their lunches brought at midday. The sand for the mortar was hauled to the site from 18 miles away and the stone from 10 miles away.

On February 15, 1935, Special Investigator Coney reported on his investigation regarding complaints sent to President Roosevelt in a letter dated January 12. The work schedule, inspections, food, excessive fines, and the fact that southern leaders were making the camp miserable for the northern enrollees were the subjects of the complaints. Coney found that work had been assigned to the enrollees beyond the 40-hours-a-week maximum. Fines had been imposed on the men without just cause. The food was found to be unsatisfactory, primarily due to a lack of variety and prevalence of beans and other starches. The meals and menus did not match; many items never appeared on the tables.

The excessive work hours were from Saturday and afternoon work on the construction of a small welfare building. Enrollees had been assigned to the project when not enough volunteered. Although the work was outside the eight-hour day and against CCC regulations, the District D Executive Officer at Fort McClellan upheld the company commander's employing the enrollees beyond the 40-hour week.

The complaint against the rated leaders focused on one senior leader who was thought to be a "rat or stool pigeon," as he had been formerly an informer for the local prohibition agents. The company commander, however, defended him, stating he was only disliked by "a small group of agitators." The discrimination against the Second Corps Area enrollees was based on the fact that Alabama enrollees made up 12.5 percent of the company and yet made up 50 percent of the rated men. The company commander also defended this situation, stating the best men had been promoted and it was difficult developing leadership qualities among the Second Corps Area men.

In spite of the investigation, the two February issues of the "Reflector" reported that Company 260 had won "Best Company" for District D. The arguments in the mess line had been resolved by having the enrollees run races; the winners got extra food. There had also been improvements made to the camp. The company bathhouse had been converted into a "Pompeian bath reminiscent of Ancient Rome with its glistening brass fixtures, mirrors and marbled floor." It was also reported that Project Superintendent Ready had been replaced by Roy Parke.

On April 29, 1935, Assistant Director McEntee forwarded Special Investigator Coney's March 5 report to the adjutant general at the War Department. McEntee concluded, "All the data in this case appears to bring out the fact that the Camp Commander was either incompetent or indifferent, and the Director respectfully requests the removal of the present Camp Commander and he not be assigned to any further duties in connection with the Civilian Conservation Corps."

A "Narrative Report" dated May 31, 1935, reported that 99 enrollees had returned to Fort Dix for discharge, reducing the company strength to 83. With overhead positions, there were only 45 boys in the field force. Work on the tower had been suspended, and the boys were taught masonry on the overnight cabins. The 45 enrollees in the field had made exceptional progress on other projects, laying 300 feet of four-inch sewer line and constructing two septic tanks. A dam had been built to create a "water hole" in an inaccessible area. The building materials had been hauled to the site by "bone carts" (a slang expression meaning carried on their backs). The dam was made of "Cyclopean Masonry" where "One Man Rock" and smaller rocks were embedded in the concrete grout. A 300-foot chute was constructed to deliver the concrete to the dam site. The dam was 35 feet long and averaged 4 feet high. It stored 50,000 gallons of water delivered by a hydraulic ram to a 1,500-gallon storage tank built on a wooden tower on a hill south of the cabins.

Cabin #1 was completed except for hanging the window shutters. It was built of longleaf pine logs, 11 inches in diameter, on masonry up to the windowsill. Cabin #2 was built of hand-hewn squared timbers, 7 by 10 inches, erected on masonry up to the windowsill. Cabin #3 was constructed of round logs, 8 inches in diameter, on masonry to the windowsill. The flagstone floor was not yet laid. Construction of Cabin #4 had not yet begun. The caretaker's house was nearly completed.

The tower had an outside dimension at the base of 18 feet by 18 feet, with an interior dimension of 10 feet by 10 feet. The walls were 4 feet thick for the first 16 feet of height. There was a one-foot "step back" at this point. The tower lacked two and one-half feet of masonry for completion, and construction of the lookout house was ready to begin. Sand and rock had been hauled to the site. The men were trucked 12 to 15 miles to the remote site of the park. They had also cut nearly two miles of firebreaks.

On June 15, 1935, "A letter from the field" was submitted to the National Park Service, presumably written by Project Superintendent Parke. The morale of 90 percent of the men improved as they adjusted to their new surroundings. The other 10 percent "is such as one would find in any stratum of society where large groups are economically destitute. Unrest, dissatisfaction, murmuring and fomentation find recruiting ground in this group." Cooperation between the army personnel, project supervisory personnel, and enrollees was less than ideal, but conditions were improving. The camp slogan summed up the situation: "We can take it."

Although summer had not yet arrived, the park had welcomed 1,500 visitors from as far away as Montgomery and Birmingham. The 50-foot tower on Flagg Mountain was the main attraction. The natural appearance of the park was preserved. "One who tries to improve on nature will merely show how presumptuous he can be." The park was a "Masterpiece of Nature."

The letter concluded with comments about the young men from New York and New Jersey adapting to the virgin forests of Alabama. "We work with city bred boys, unskilled and to whom the great outdoors, work tools, wild life, mountains and nature are a sealed book." The supervision of these boys took patience, with safety being stressed continually. "They need to be told that an axe can not cut granite." There were two tasks at hand, making a park and remaking manhood. Slowly, both were being accomplished.

The Fourth of July 1935 issue of the "Reflector" reported that Captain Field had been relieved of duty. In spite of Director Fechner's request to the War Department that Captain Field not be assigned to another CCC camp, he was transferred to Company 251, Camp TVA-P-4 at Wilson Dam. Lt. Louis Rosenburg, the mess officer, was also transferred to Company 251.

Lt. Ernest Howell, who had served previously under Captain Field, took command of Company 260.

In a "Narrative Report" dated July 31, 1935, Superintendent Parke stated that with Lt. Howell in command, cooperation between the army and Park Service personnel had been 100 percent. On July 17, the Second Corps Area enrollees were sent to western states, and work came to a standstill. The supervisory personnel and LEMs were doing surveying and carpentry. The tower was nearly completed, and two cabins were ready for occupation. The park had acquired another 170 acres, and fire hazard reduction and firebreak construction had been completed over this new area. The local people were happy to have a state park in their area and had donated stone, sand, and tools to the park.

With the Second Corps Area enrollees gone, Superintendent Parke reflected on their experience in Alabama: "There can be no greater transition in the United States than from a city like New York, especially among the poverty stricken classes and slums, to an almost virgin forest, purely agricultural region." While some of the enrollees had come from good homes, most had stopped their education at the grammar school level. Some were illiterate. Most were underfed, malnourished, or underweight. Almost all gained weight while in camp as a result of balanced rations, regulated eating and sleeping habits, outdoors work, and the change of environment. During the time that Company 260 was at Weogufka, six of the Second Corps Area enrollees married "local girls of good family." When married, the former enrollees thought the first thing to do was to get a good job and make a living.

Company 260 was transferred to Hawthorne, Nevada, arriving in late July 1935, and established Camp M-2. They continued the "Reflector," and the September 1935 issue reported that Company 260 went through many days of travel and constant change. Nevada was a very different environment than they had known in Alabama.

Company 4498, Camp SP-4, Weogufka, Alabama

A "Narrative Report" dated September 30, 1935, written by Superintendent Parke recorded that Company 4498 arrived at Camp SP-4 on August 13, 1935. The boys, coming mostly from Mississippi, were unconditioned. After conditioning, they were turned over to the Park Service for project work on September 3. They completed the stone foundation and placing of logs for Cabin #4 and laid the plumbing fixtures in Cabin #3. The lookout tower's floor was laid with a Coast and Geologic Bench Mark placed in the middle. The exterior masonry required that two men lower themselves on scaffolding. The exterior woodwork of the tower was scored with a blowtorch. The museum and open pavilion, attached to the tower, were finished. Materials to run a telephone line from the camp to the park, a distance of four miles, had been delivered. Full communications were expected to be in place by October 1.

On September 3, construction began on the park road down the south side of the mountain. Large stumps were pulled by caterpillar tractor; smaller ones were grubbed with pick and shovel. Blasting was necessary to remove rocks. The timber from the trees in the right-of-way, 18 to 20 inches in diameter, was used in building structures in the park, and smaller trees were used for posts in the guardrails and for fuel wood. A topographic survey of the park was also completed. During the "conditioning period," Lt. Howell had ordered a considerable amount of work at the camp. The bathhouse, mess hall, and kitchen received improvements. Footlockers were built in the barracks. A great amount of time was given to recreation, which was improving the men's conditioning and their morale.

Project Superintendent Parke reported that the farm boys from Mississippi were well suited to their work. A few were homesick, but they soon adjusted to camp life. A number of them were becoming skilled masons and carpenters. Work on the cabins was progressing. The first three were of a "dogtrot" design. Cabin #4 did not have the hallway between the rooms. Cabins #5 and #6 were being built out of 5-by-10-inch logs cut at a local sawmill. They contained a large living room, a bedroom, a kitchenette, a bath, and a toilet. Both cabins would be completed within ten work-days.

According to a Camp Inspection Report dated December 20, 1935, Company 4498 had 180 junior enrollees from Alabama and Mississippi under the command of 1st Lt. Ernest W. Howell. The work project, under the supervision of Roy E. Parke, consisted of improvements over a park area of 800 acres. In addition to indoor recreational equipment, a swimming pool and tennis court were under construction. Cleveland Harris, the CEA, reported that classes were offered at the elementary, high school, and college levels, as well as vocational courses. CEA Harris reported that 100 percent of Company 4498 was enrolled in the educational program, with 63 percent of the men in two or more classes. The company produced a camp newspaper called the "Flagg Mountain News." The December 20, 1935, issue was archived at the University of Chicago.

According to the *CCC Camp Directory for Alabama*, Camp SP-4 was closed during the sixth period, which ended March 31, 1936.

Company 472, Camp SP-5, Fort Payne, Alabama

Company 472 was established on May 20, 1933, at Fort McClellan with junior enrollees from Alabama. After their conditioning period, when they received their vaccinations, they were sent to Chula, Georgia, where they built firebreaks and fought forest fires. On November 14, the company was transferred to Fort Payne. They began construction of their camp within the city limits at an old ballpark. The company received 52 replacements at the beginning of the second period and was assigned 16 local experienced men. With the arrival of the foreman and trucks, they began constructing firebreaks across Lookout and Sand Mountains and fighting forest fires. By the end of the second period, Camp SP-5 was completed. Captain Howard H. Harris replaced Captain Brooks on March 15, 1934. Lt. S. S. Barksdale, who had been the commanding officer when the company was first organized, was assigned as the camp educational advisor. At the beginning of the third period, April 1, 1934, work began on a state park near Mentone under the supervision of the National Park Service (1934 CCC District D annual).

A Camp Inspection Report dated April 28, 1934, recorded 206 men under the command of Captain Harris. The work project, under the supervision of J. W. Lovelace, consisted of the development of the 520-acre DeSoto State Park, including construction of truck trails and campgrounds, timber stand improvement, and the development of a nursery. Recreational opportunities included playing baseball, running track, scouting and hiking, boxing, and horseshoes.

In July 1934, Bob Jones of Quinton, Alabama, enrolled in Company 472. The first project he worked on was the construction of a culvert across a small creek in the middle of the park. He was later sent out "scouting for rock" and found a source of beautiful sandstone in the northwestern portion of the park. It would be used in the construction of the park's buildings. As Mr. Jones was experienced with dynamite, he was put in charge of the rock quarry (Bob Jones interview, August 7, 2002; see the CD).

A Camp Inspection Report dated March 3, 1935, recorded 211 men under the command of Captain E. P. Scruggs. Desoto State Park was now 800 acres, and the new superintendent was B. F. Phillips. The work project consisted of construction of cabins and roads and a fence around the park and cleanup of the park area. Lt. Barksdale's education program had expanded, offering courses in elementary reading, writing, and arithmetic. Vocational and academic courses were offered in auto mechanics, typing, music, shorthand, business mathematics, radio operations, bookkeeping, first aid, personal hygiene, woodworking, elementary surveying, current events, and journalism. Approximately 82 percent of the enrollees were participating.

The journalism class published a semimonthly newspaper called the "Camp Beacon." Six issues between April and August 1935 were archived at the University of Chicago. The April 19 issue reported that the enrollees were planting 1,000 trees each day. The May 10 issue reported that Company 472 had received 20 new enrollees. They were going through conditioning, getting their inoculations against typhoid and smallpox, getting over homesickness, drawing their first canteen checks, and working in the camp area. The rookies were getting "razzed," and the newspaper reminded the older enrollees that they too had once been rookies. Twenty men were at Guntersville setting up tents for a new camp. The baseball team was undefeated.

The May 24 "Camp Beacon" reported that the camp infirmary had been expanded by 20 feet, giving the men more room for quarters. A 20-man crew was working in the "chert pit" getting material for surfacing the park's roads. On June 7, it was reported that another 20-man detail had left to begin construction of a new camp at Scottsboro. Company commander Captain Griffin had received a letter from the Exchange Division of the University of Illinois thanking Company 472 for the issues of the "Camp Beacon." Their library had requested newspapers from the CCC camps to be filed as historical records. The editors of the "Camp Beacon" asked, "We're wondering if some of the foolishness we are constantly putting in our papers will be held against us by future historians."

On June 24, 1935, Project Superintendent B. E. Phillips reported to the National Park Service that all of the work approved for the fourth period was completed. The fifth period work was delayed as the site plan for the park had been submitted late, but all the materials were in place. These projects included construction of a stone tower, power line, pump house, four additional cabins, and park roads. There were 181 enrollees and 14 LEMs in Company 472. They were lucky to have Alabama boys from farms, rural areas, or the mining districts. Mr. Phillips praised the army personnel for their discipline and executive experience. Fort Payne was "growing a more kindly feeling toward the C.C.C." The local people were becoming more interested in the park and were beginning to understand the purpose of the CCC.

The August 17 "Camp Beacon" reported that Mr. Phillips had been assigned superintendent of the project at Munford in addition to his responsibilities at Camp SP-5. Mr. Pace, a National Park Service foreman, was acting superintendent, but Mr. Phillips had overall supervision of both camps. Four more cabins and construction of an access road had been approved for work projects, and plans were being drawn for a dam across the river just below Cabin #10. Water and electric lines were approved to run to the six completed cabins. A double shift on the "chert haul" was averaging 45 loads per day. The park road would be finished in time for the approval of the new projects.

According to a Camp Inspection Report dated December 17, 1935, there were 203 enrollees from Alabama under the command of Captain Newell C. Griffin. The project work, under the supervision of B. E. Phillips, consisted of the development of the 2,460-acre DeSoto State Park. The new CEA, Carl Q. Baxter, had made arrangements for night classes at DeKalb High School, including English, typing, auto mechanics, shop mathematics, and radio. There had not been space in camp for an education building, and although the library had 413 books, Baxter felt the reading room was not adequate.

A "Narrative Report" dated January 20, 1936, recorded that snow and subfreezing weather had hampered work on the four cabins, foot trails, telephone lines, and park roads. The picnic shelter had been completed in November and was considered by Mr. Phillips "the best workmanship of any structures in DeSoto State Park." The lodge was of the same type of masonry. He considered the lodge "a much prettier job" and "the boys are becoming more proficient in masonry" and taking pride in the structure.

According to a "Narrative Report" dated February 29, 1936, six miles of foot trails had been built around the deep gorge formed by Little River called May's Gulf. Two small foot bridges, constructed of hewn white oak, had been built across small ravines. Six cabins were completed on the ridge overlooking Little River, and four more were planned to be finished by April 1. The lodge would accommodate 30 to 40 diners. Plans were proposed for a custodian or caretaker's house, a contact station, and a combination comfort station and bathhouse. A small dam was proposed across Little River to provide for fishing and bathing. At Camp SP-5, a camp office building and a grease shop and oil storage house had been built.

Woodrow Biddle of Fort Payne, Alabama, transferred to Company 472 on January 7, 1936. His first job was maintaining and driving the trucks. He later worked as a rock cutter for the caretaker's house. The blocks of stone were delivered from the quarry, and Mr. Biddle cut the rock to the final di mensions for placement (Woodrow Biddle interview, March 4, 2002; see the CD).

In a "Narrative Report" dated March 31, 1936, Mr. Phillips observed that the CCC program was growing in favor with the local people as they watched the development of the park. Cooperation was coming from different civic groups and from local and city government. The County Board of Revenue had offered chert, cement, and other materials. The enrollees of Company 472 were forming social ties with the community.

A Camp Inspection Report dated January 28, 1937, recorded 171 men from Alabama under the command of 1st Lt. Jesse B. DuBois. The work project, under the supervision of Mr. Phillips, had completed ten overnight cabins, five miles of foot trails, and six miles of cherted roads. A custodian's house and garage and a lodge constructed of native stone were completed. The park area had been fenced. It was expected that another two or three years were needed to complete the park.

On September 17, 1936, Colonel Milford W. Howard, a former congressman and adjacent landowner, had written to Senator Hugo Black, making "grave charges" against Project Superintendent Phillips, including personal use of government property and being "a man of bad morals." An investigation ensued over the next several months, and it was found that coal and fish bought for the camp had been delivered to Mr. Phillips's house. Meanwhile, Colonel Howard had a change of heart and wrote to Special Investigator J. S. Billups on January 30, 1937, stating that Mr. Phillips had "great possibilities" and asked that he be given a second chance, perhaps with just a demotion rather than being "turned out of a job—disgraced and barred from further government service."

On February 15, 1937, Colonel Howard wrote to Senator Hugo Black, informing him that Mr. Phillips had been discharged from the National Park Service. Colonel Howard asked Senator Black for mercy as well as justice on behalf of Mr. Phillips. On February 15, CCC Assistant Director James J. McEntee also wrote to Senator Black, stating that the matter had been sent to Conrad Wirth of the Park Service. Although the "amount involved does not appear to be of any considerable value, the principle is regarded of very vital importance." Mr. Phillips and two other men had been suspended from Emergency Conservation Work. McEntee wrote to Senator Black again on February 26, noting appreciation of Colonel Howard's sympathies but concluding that "to continue Mr. Phillips in the service of the CCC would be demoralizing to the enrollees." The CCC had to "guard the morals of the enrollees." There was no alternative left but to approve his discharge.

On May 12, 1937, B. E. Phillips wrote to CCC Director Fechner, explaining that he had began his career with the CCC as a junior foreman and had worked his way up through promotions. When he arrived at Camp SP-5, there was talk of ending the project and moving the camp. He had been advised to "do any reasonable thing that could be expected to expedite the program." He stated that every irregularity committed at Camp SP-5 had been done for the "specific purpose of bringing developments at this park up to, and beyond, that of any park in this vicinity." He asked Mr. Fechner for a second chance to show his ability to run a camp "without the slightest trace of irregularities."

On May 17, James J. McEntee wrote to Mr. Phillips, pointing out that the selection of superintendents and foremen was the jurisdiction of the Technical Services. Director Fechner would not interfere in their authority. He suggested that Mr. Phillips take up the matter with the National Park Service.

On July 21, 1937, the *Haleyville Spotlight* reported that a fire in downtown Fort Payne had destroyed a $40,000 building that had been occupied by six businesses. Three truckloads of CCC boys returning to Camp SP-5 stopped to assist the firemen in fighting the fire. Before it could be controlled, the entire CCC camp was summoned to help fight the blaze. "Pete" Leath of Fort Payne, Alabama, had joined Company 472 in 1936, and he recalled the fire in Fort Payne. Henry Harrelson, chief of the volunteer fire department, had only 10 or 12 men. The enrollees stayed with the fire the rest of the day (Milton "Pete" Leath interview, February 28, 2002; see the CD).

A Camp Inspection Report dated November 4, 1937, recorded 237 men under the command of Captain N. A. Athanson. The work project, under the supervision of Acting Project Supervisor Frank F. Berry, consisted of the development of DeSoto State Park, including fire presuppression and construction of the parkway drive, four more overnight cabins, and stone portals at the entrance of the park. Another ten months were needed to finish the approved projects. Memnon C. Scales, the new Camp Educational Advisor, reported 74 percent participation in his program.

According to a Camp Inspection Report dated September 19, 1938, there were 181 men under the command of 1st Lt. John F. Payne. The educational program had expanded, particularly the vocational courses, which now included poultry agriculture, auto mechanics, blasting and drilling, cabinet-making, carpentry, cooking, radio, landscaping, surveying, truck driving, and typing. The camp library had 520 books of text and reference subjects but none for recreational reading. Five daily newspapers and two weekly newspapers came to camp, along with ten copies of "Happy Days," the national CCC newspaper. Ninety percent of the enrollees were participating in the educational program. Thirty-nine enrollees had learned to read and write since October 14, 1937, and several men had returned home to attend high school and college. Thirty men had learned to build cabinets and perform carpentry work. The entire company was showing more interest in the educational program.

A Camp Inspection Report dated October 10, 1939, recorded 191 men under the command of Smith J. McCurry. The work project, under the supervision of George E. Cadman, consisted primarily of road construction. Other projects included construction of foot trails, guardrails along the roads, a contact station at the park entrance, and making signs and markers for the park road system. The education program under new CEA Luny J. Smith added weekly educational motion pictures and still films. Several trade and industries teachers had been assigned to the camp by the State Board of Education, and there were also six teachers from the local high school coming to camp during the afternoon to teach courses. The technical service personnel, the CEA, and enrollees taught classes at night. According to CEA Smith, a large majority of the men who participated in the program for several months showed improvements in academic learning, fitness for employment, and "general physical, mental, and social improvements."

Jim Griffin of Rainsville, Alabama, had arrived to Camp SP-5 in April 1939. He worked as a rock mason, cutting and laying stones for the cabins and picnic shelter. He recalled CEA Smith. He spent some time in the reading room and library in the camp and took a vocational course in sales and merchandising and regretted not taking more classes (Jim Griffin interview, March 11, 2002; see the CD).

A Camp Inspection Report dated September 3, 1940, recorded 186 men under the command of Smith J. McCurry. The work project, under the supervision of George E. Cadman, consisted of construction of a vehicle bridge, a dwelling, signs and markers, combination tables and benches, cabin furniture, truck trails, and minor roads. Recreational activities included softball, baseball, tennis, horseshoes, ping-pong, and basketball. Swimming facilities were available at Fort Payne.

Wayne A. Shaffer of Hartselle, Alabama, had enrolled in the CCC in Decatur in early 1939. He was sent to Camp SP-5, where he worked on crews constructing foot trails, roads, overnight cabins, and a picnic shelter. He ran the air compressor and drill at the rock quarry and worked on a survey crew with Thurmond Radford, the civil engineer. They surveyed both sides of the

Little River Canyon and built a road. Mr. Shaffer was the rod man on the survey crew. He also worked as an auto mechanic and as the first aid man in the infirmary. In the latter role, he would take temperatures, blood pressure, and pulses of enrollees coming into the infirmary and record this information for the doctor who visited the camp. Mr. Shaffer also administered some of the medicines. If an enrollee was really sick, he was sent to the hospital at Fort Oglethorpe, Georgia. When Mr. Shaffer came down with malarial fevers, he was given doses of "I-Q-S" (iodine, quinine, and strychnine), then cod liver oil, followed by large amounts of tomato juice.

Mr. Shaffer recalled that at the end of the day, the enrollees showered and changed clothes to go to supper. The food in camp was very good, as they had good cooks. After supper, they would gather between the barracks and listen to music. Company 472 had a "world champion" fiddler who played all types of music. He was joined by enrollees on guitar and banjo. Mr. Shaffer spent his free time in the reading room, practicing reading and writing on his own. He also recalled playing tennis against "Captain Smith," the company commander, and Mr. Smith, the CEA. Mr. Shaffer was at Camp SP-5 when it was disbanded in March 1941 (Wayne A. Shaffer interview, November 13, 2002; see the CD).

James Marona, Sr., of Trafford, Alabama, enrolled in the CCC in the winter of 1940 and was sent to Camp SP-5. He worked on the survey crew as a rod man. In his free time, he played baseball and walked into Fort Payne to see movies. When Camp SP-5 was abandoned in March 1941, Mr. Marona and most of the men transferred to Athens, Tennessee (James Morona Sr. interview, November 6, 2004; see the CD).

Company 259, Camp SP-6, Foley, Alabama

Company 259 was organized at the Plattsburg Barracks in New York. The junior enrollees from New York and New Jersey were sent to Camp F-9 in Hingham, Montana, on May 12, 1933, and transferred to Camp SP-2 at Munford, Alabama, on October 20 (NACCCA database).

A Camp Inspection Report dated May 2, 1934, recorded 188 enrollees under the command of Captain David E. Ackerman. The work project, under the supervision of Stanton H. Ready, consisted of the development of the 700-acre Cheaha State Park. The work was hard, as 128 new enrollees in the company were malnourished.

On May 3, *The Onlooker*, a weekly newspaper of Baldwin County, reported that a CCC camp was to be built 10 miles south of Foley. The camp would begin construction of a state park as soon as barracks and facilities were built. A 640-acre tract of state land had been acquired, including 300 acres of a 600-acre lake. The new park would be called "Gulf State Park." On June 7, *The Onlooker* reported that five Army officers and 25 CCC enrollees had arrived to begin construction of the camp. Plans were approved for seven camp buildings, two water systems, one picnic shelter, two piers, 20 acres of public camp grounds, 8.5 miles of foot trails, one-half mile of truck trails, and planting trees and shrubbery on 400 acres. It reported on June 14 that another 135 enrollees had arrived from Munford on June 11 by special train to augment the detachment already at the camp.

An undated "Narrative Report" recorded that camp construction was completed by August 31, 1934. The work project had begun on June 15. Ten miles of telephone line, three miles of roads, two miles of fence, a mile of foot trail, and 2.5 miles of firebreaks had been constructed. Fire hazard reduction, general cleanup of the park area, and beach improvement had been completed. The materials for the construction of the piers and cabins had been cut by the enrollees. Morale was very good, and the men were being "transformed into useful citizens and in addition to learning to use tools many good leaders were being developed."

According to a Camp Inspection Report dated January 5, 1935, there were 159 men from New York, New Jersey, and Alabama under the command of Captain David E. Ackerman. Sixty-three enrollees had been dishonorably discharged for refusing to work, one for theft, and another for eloping. Company morale was "a little below average." About 50 percent of the company had participated in a food riot on August 21, 1934, and another had been planned in December but failed to materialize. The work project, now under the supervision of William C. Connell, consisted of the development of Gulf State Park. With the camp so close to the Gulf Coast, fishing and swimming were major recreational activities. Basketball was the principal sport played. The recreation hall had ping-pong tables, a radio, a piano, several writing tables, and current magazines and newspapers.

The camp had been without an educational advisor for over a month. Assistant CEA Al Ruddy reported in December 1934. The camp surgeon taught first aid and sexual hygiene at the high school level, and Al Ruddy taught journalism. Vocational courses were taught on road construction and telephone line work. College level courses in forestry and surveying were taught by Mr. Schattenburg, landscaper, and Mr. Pace, engineer. *The Onlooker* printed the camp newspaper, called "Gulf Currents."

A "Narrative Report" dated January 1935 reported that the weather had been ideal for December and January, with the best progress made since the beginning of the project. Two miles of road construction, 2,000 feet of fence along the roads, and three-quarters of a mile of beach cleanup had been completed along the lake. Ten thousand bald cypress trees had been planted along with several hundred live oak and red cedars. Construction had begun on a caretaker's house and cabins along a road leading to the Gulf of Mexico.

On March 7, *The Onlooker* reported that a new dance floor laid at the CCC camp would be "initiated with one of the popular dances given for the enlisted personnel, officers and friends." The Dixie Melody Boys would provide the music. It was also reported that a shrine to the Virgin Mary was to be dedicated in the camp by Bishop Toolen of Mobile in a service open to the public.

A "Narrative Report" for February and March 1935 recorded that company strength had dropped over 50 percent during the last week of fourth period (March 1935); however, most of the project work had been completed. The caretaker's house was nearly finished. A 90-foot footbridge, crossing the lagoon and connecting the park area on the freshwater lake to the area fronting the Gulf Coast, was completed except for the handrail. The shrine to the Virgin Mary had been constructed by the enrollees in their free time. Governor Bibb Graves and the Alabama legislature had visited the park.

A Camp Inspection Report dated June 6, 1935, recorded 179 men under the command of Captain Ackerman. Company morale was good. It was noted that the mess had improved and was now satisfactory. Each enrollment brought a group of new enrollees, some of whom were undesirable because they had no intentions of following CCC regulations. They were "weeded out," and the remaining enrollees were "generally a contented lot." Relations between the enrollees and the local community were good.

L. G. Hill had replaced Mr. Connell as the project supervisor. The work on the 670-acre state park included road construction, cleanup of the beach and around the lake, construction of cottages and a caretaker's home, and general park improvements. CEA Ralph Carlisle reported that in addition to the vocational and academic courses offered, fieldtrips had been taken to Spanish Fort and other historical points of interest on Mobile Bay. The company baseball team had won games against teams from Chatom, Fort Barrancas, and Foley.

Project Supervisor Lawrence G. Hill submitted a "Narrative Report" on July 9, 1935. Many people were taking advantage of the recreational opportunities in the park. Freshwater and saltwater fishing were popular with local men and women. Visitors were coming from 200 to 300 hundred miles away. Bathing in the Gulf of Mexico was a popular pastime. The enrollees were becoming excellent swimmers. Mr. Hill predicted that Gulf State Park would become an extremely popular park once the bathhouse and cabins were completed. The piers in the freshwater lake would attract many people coming to fish through the fall and early winter. Some time was needed for the boys from New York to become adjusted to the heat. The glare of the white sand had been a problem, but there was little complaint after the boys had been issued sunglasses.

Company 259 abandoned Camp SP-6 in July 1935. Presumably, the enrollees from New York and New Jersey returned to the Plattsburg Barracks.

Company 1425, Camp SP-6, Foley, Alabama

Company 1425 was organized in May 1933 at Fort Benning, Georgia. They spent their first year at Dufuniak Springs, Florida, before transferring to Milton, Florida. Just as they were to begin project work, they were transferred to Foley. At Gulf State Park, under the supervision of Lawrence G. Hill, they worked on the construction of a huge recreational center and provided sanctuary to wildlife. Captain David W. Eddy was the company commander (1936 CCC District G annual).

A Camp Inspection Report dated January 11, 1936, recorded 216 enrollees from Alabama and Florida under the command of Captain Eddy. Project work in the 3,600-acre state park included construction of park roads, bridges, a custodian's house, a shelter house, a sewage and wastewater disposal system, foot and truck trails, beach improvement, fire hazard reduction, fire fighting, and old road obliteration. Camp SP-6 had an excellent recreation hall, equipped with a radio, a piano, two pool tables, a ping-pong table, and sets of checkers and dominoes. Outdoor equipment was furnished for baseball, basketball, boxing, horseshoes, and volleyball.

Charles E. Lockett's education report for December 1935 recorded that 82 percent of the enrollees were in the program. Courses were offered in reading, spelling, arithmetic, writing, piano, Spanish, penmanship, civil service, carpentry, forestry, typing, tractor upkeep, auto mechanics, blueprint reading, plumbing, bookkeeping, shorthand, current events, first aid, citizenship, traffic management, and the Bible. The Gordon Motor Company of Foley loaned auto mechanic films, and illustrative charts were obtained from Ford and Chevrolet. The carpentry class was building a cabin with logs donated by a private citizen. Mr. Lockett was working with local businessmen and luncheon clubs to assist in the educational program and to find employment for the enrollees. Future plans included more visual education, more field trips, and more detailed instruction for illiterates.

A "Narrative Report" dated January 31, 1936, reported that six cabins were completed, lacking only the plumbing fixtures. The roadwork in the park had been delayed by the worst rain and flooding in the past ten years. Alabama Governor Bibb Graves had taken occupancy of a vacation cottage within a half mile of the park and was showing great interest in the work. A barbeque in his honor, organized by his friends, was attended by 300 people in the park.

A "Narrative Report" for March 1936 recorded that Gulf State Park had expanded from 640 to approximately 1,500 acres. The park had half a mile of beach along the Gulf of Mexico, and eight miles of shoreline along lakes. Road construction was making the park accessible, except in areas designated for wildlife protection. Construction was proceeding on 12 cabins. A photograph in a "Narrative Report" for April 1936 showed a dugout canoe that had been found outside of the park. The canoe, made of heart cypress, was turned over to the State of Alabama.

The *Union Banner*, a weekly newspaper of Chilton County, reported on June 25, 1936, that the National Park Service had reported that a skeleton had been found near Foley. Archaeological excavations being conducted by Walter B. Jones of the Alabama Museum of Natural History had uncovered a flexed burial of a female "affirming the presences of aboriginal Indians on the Gulf Coast during the medieval period." Twenty enrollees for the CCC camp provided the labor. Dr. Jones thought this was the first burial excavated in the coastal area of Alabama by scientists.

The Onlooker reported on April 8, 1937, that Camp SP-6 had celebrated the fourth anniversary of the CCC with an open house on April 4. There had been 2,000 visitors to the park, and over 500 people ate a luncheon that featured a 225-pound birthday cake. The visitors were impressed with the work of the CCC enrollees, and "even the most skeptical had to admit that in training the nation's youth President Roosevelt had achieved an outstanding accomplishment." The enrollees had built cabins and bathhouses on the lake and nine miles of road and had planted 12,000 trees in the park.

On September 16, 1937, *The Onlooker* reported that the Foley Lions Club was helping enrollees find employment upon their honorable discharge. They had wired the international headquarters in Chicago asking that their local efforts be expanded nationwide. Company Commander Captain W. D. Morrison had taken personal responsibility for finding work for at least two enrollees. The editor of the camp newspaper, "Gulf Breeze," wired the national CCC newspaper, "Happy Days," asking for help. At the time, there were 90,000 enrollees nationwide who would reach their time limit for enlistment by September 30.

A Camp Inspection Report dated December 8, 1937, recorded 193 men under the command of navy Ensign Russell H. Dausman. The enrollees were from Alabama, Georgia, Florida, Mississippi, and Louisiana. The work project under Mr. Hill consisted of construction of roads, overnight cabins, signs and markers, boats, boathouses, and a fence around the park and was expected to be completed by September 1, 1938.

On December 30, 1937, *The Onlooker* reported that Company 1425's camp newspaper, the "Gulf Breeze," had won first prize as the best CCC newspaper in the nation, as judged by the education department in Washington, D.C. The monthly newspaper had developed a new headline system that had brought inquiries from several of the country's leading schools of journalism. The staff of the "Gulf Breeze" consisted of James D. Diamond, editor; R. J. Mitchell, business manager; "Red" Llody, reporter; and Eddie Kahalley, sports editor. The paper was printed at the plant of *The Onlooker.*

The Onlooker reported on January 20, 1938, that the Department of the Interior was experimenting with planting giant redwood trees at Gulf State Park. Over 100 seedlings had been shipped from Fruiton, California, and planted in the park about a half-mile from the Gulf of Mexico. It was uncertain if the trees would survive the local soil and climate.

According to a Camp Inspection Report dated October 11, 1938, there were 194 men under the command of 1st Lt. Herbert O. Jones Jr. The work project, under the supervision of Lawrence G. Hill, would take place within Gulf State Park, now comprising 4,500 acres and would include construction of a combination building facing the Gulf of Mexico, drilling a well and installing a water and sewage disposal system, building and surfacing roads, moving and planting trees, and lake and pond improvement. CEA J. A. Dale's education report recorded that there were 16 teachers, including senior enrollees and WPA teachers. Fifteen enrollees had learned to read and write, 5 had finished the sixth grade, and 12 were taking high school courses. Thirty-two had received civilian jobs because of their vocational training.

On May 11, 1939, *The Onlooker* announced that Gulf State Park would open for the season on May 20. Fifteen cabins were available along the shores of Big Lake, providing "modest" accommodations for 100 overnight guests. Boats were available for guests. The casino or combination building built between the Gulf of Mexico and freshwater lakes contained an assembly room, bathing houses, dining room, and other facilities and could accommodate 2,000 people. The interior was finished in a rustic style with a great fireplace at one end of the lounge room. Picnic grounds were also available.

In August, Company 1425 established a side camp at Fort Morgan. The *Tuscaloosa News* reported on August 22 that Dr. Walter B. Jones, state conservation commissioner, had announced that 25 enrollees from Gulf State Park had been transferred to the reclamation project at Fort Morgan. The National Park Service had conducted extensive restoration work on the fort with transient labor in 1938.

Nathan E. Davis enrolled in the CCC in December 1939 and was sent to Camp SP-6. He was one of the enrollees at the Fort Morgan side camp. He recalled that he worked on a crew landscaping the ditches around the fort, sloping the ditches, and placing sod. The men found numerous artifacts, many of which were later placed in the museum (Nathan E. Davis interview, October 7, 2003; see the CD).

A Camp Inspection Report dated October 5, 1939, recorded 196 men under the command of Joseph W. O'Connell, a reserve officer with civilian status who had 32 months of service in the CCC. The work project, under Mr. Hill, included improvements in the 4,522-acre Gulf State Park and the restoration of historical structures (likely at the Fort Morgan side camp). Outdoor recreational equipment was available for volleyball, softball, and baseball. "Sound motion pictures" were shown in camp every two weeks. There was a bowling alley in the camp in addition to the equipment in the recreation hall. Trucks were available for recreational trips.

According to a Camp Inspection Report dated August 22, 1940, there were 202 men under the command of Charles T. Holland, "CCC Subaltern," who had two years of service in the CCC. Company 1425 had a 32-man detail assigned to a side camp at Santa Rosa Island, Florida. Mr. Hill supervised the work project at Gulf State Park. CEA Julius A. Dale reported that 38 illiterate enrollees had learned to read and write and were raising their education levels. Enrollees continued to find employment after their training while in the CCC. It was noted that 176 enrollees from Camp SP-6 had gotten jobs as plumbers, carpenters, surveyors, and brick masons.

On January 9, 1941, *The Onlooker* reported that Gulf State Park was preparing for the 1941 season with five new cabins under construction. Even with 16 cabins that could accommodate 100 people, hundreds of families had been turned away during the spring and summer months. The casino was open throughout the winter. Meals were served in the dining room, and an orchestra played on Saturday and Sunday afternoons.

A Camp Inspection Report dated November 18, 1941, recorded 239 men under the command of J. A. Dale, formerly the camp educational advisor, who had 62 months of service in the CCC. The work project, under Mr. Hill, consisted of the construction of five cabins, a water supply and sewerage disposal system, three miles of road improvement, one mile of road construction, three miles of sand dune improvement, building tables, heavy chairs, and lounge chairs, landscaping the beach area, planting trees and shrubs, fire suppression on 6,000 acres, and pest control on 3,000 acres. The 22-man detail at Santa Rosa Island, Florida, was constructing a recreation area for the army under the supervision of foreman Elmer A. Harrell. An inspection of the side camp conducted on November 14 revealed sanitation problems and poor recreational and educational facilities. Before improvements could be made, the side camp was abandoned, as Company 1425 was to be replaced by a company of World War I veterans. Company 1425 abandoned Camp SP-6 on January 19, 1942.

Company 2436, Camp SP-6, Foley, Alabama

Company 2436 was organized on June 22, 1935, in Jasper, Tennessee, of World War I veterans (1937 CCC District "C" annual). They worked on several TVA projects before transferring to Camp SP-19 at Fort Payne, Alabama. They worked at DeSoto State Park for four months, leaving for Foley on January 16, 1942.

Company 2436 arrived at Gulf State Park on January 19, 1942. According to a memo written to Special Investigator J. S. Billups on January 23, it was expected that Company 2436 would have only between 30 and 40 men. According to the *CCC Camp Directory for Alabama*, Camp SP-6 was abandoned after the eighteenth period, which ended March 30, 1942.

Company 465, Camp SP-7, Munford, Alabama

Company 465 was organized on May 23, 1933, at Fort McClellan. After three weeks of conditioning, the junior African-American company was sent to Northport, Alabama, where they worked on a private forestry project under the supervision of George Drolet. They also established a side camp at Mound State Park. They transferred to Camp SP-7 on November 13, 1934 (1934 CCC District D annual).

A "Narrative Report" dated January 31, 1935, written by Project Superintendent W. P. Moon, described Camp SP-7 as located five miles south of Munford, "artistically arranged" on hilly terrain in a pine and hardwood forest. The camp had been built by a northern company in the fall of 1933. Company 465 was made up of enrollees mostly from Alabama, with a few from Mississippi. The supervisory personnel consisted of nine men from Alabama, engineers, ex-contractors, and construction and woods foremen, who were "of broad and varied experience and are thoroughly conversant with the habits and customs of colored boys." Cheaha State Park was located nine miles east of the camp over a "third rate road, which is all but impossible during wet weather." The work project consisted of construction of an earthen dam with a concrete core wall. The dam measured 30 feet high and 300 feet long, creating a five-acre lake to be used for fishing, boating, and swimming. Company 465 also constructed 2.5 miles of truck trails and secondary roads.

A Camp Inspection Report dated February 28, 1935, recorded 206 men under the command of Captain L. H. Hutchison. The work project, under the supervision of W. P. Moon, consisted of road and dam construction and general cleanup of the park. Equipment was available for baseball, basketball, horseshoes, boxing, tennis, volleyball, indoor baseball, and football. There were also magazines, newspapers, books, a piano, a radio, and indoor games for other recreation. T. H. Walker, camp educational advisor, reported that classes were offered in manual training, literacy instruction, arithmetic, reading, writing, first aid, auto mechanics, English, civics, history and government, cooking, music, and business arithmetic. Approximately 144 enrollees were participating in the educational program.

A "Narrative Report" dated May 31, 1935, recorded that the work for the last two months had focused on dam and road construction. Regardless of the unusually wet weather, they had been able to get in 40-hour work weeks. The work was still done primarily by hand. Company morale was high, except for a period when new replacements from Mississippi and Tennessee were homesick. As soon as they got out to the field, the homesickness disappeared. This problem would not recur, according to Mr. Moon, as all future replacements were to be from Alabama.

During the summer of 1935, the CCC expanded, and several cadres of enrollees were taken from Company 465 to form new "Junior-Colored" companies. With fewer men, the work focused on the dam with little accomplished elsewhere in the park. Camp SP 7 was to be abandoned by October 1, 1935.

According to a "Narrative Report" dated September 30, 1935, Mr. Moon resigned on July 31, 1935, and was replaced for a time by B. E. Phillips, from Camp SP-5. G. W. Rawls, a foreman, took over supervision when Mr. Phillips returned to Camp SP-5, and O. R. Head, the project supervisor at Camp SP-2, took over when Mr. Rawls transferred. Mr. Head reported that the dam was completed, creating a lake of about seven acres. He predicted the lake of "cold mountain water will no doubt be very popular with summer visitors." The park had already received many visitors in the past summer and fall. Mr. Head noted, "If and when an approach road from the west is built to the park, it will become one of the most popular places in this section of the state." A road to the top of the mountain provided views of 75 miles. "The vivid colors of autumn blend well with the heavy blue haze that is found in so many southern mountains."

On October 29, 1935, the *Talladega Daily Home* reported that the McElderry CCC Camp had been abandoned. The 157 enrollees were transferred to camps at Chandler Springs (F-7), Heflin (F-6), Greensboro (SCS-6), and Alexandria (SCS-8). Forty trucks of equipment and supplies were transferred to Fort McClellan.

Company 468, Camp SP-7, Munford, Alabama

Company 468 transferred from Camp SP-2 to Camp SP-7 on July 8, 1936. A Camp Inspection Report dated November 13, 1936, recorded 206 enrollees from Alabama, Florida, Georgia, Mississippi, and Texas under the command of Captain E. C. Babcock. The work project was under the dual control of the National Forests and State Parks. One-quarter of the enrollees were to work on Forest Service projects in the Talladega National Forest, primarily road construction. The other three-quarters were working in Cheaha State Park under the supervision of O. R. Head, primarily on road reconditioning and dam and lake area development.

"Pete" Leath was in Company 468 for two months during the summer of 1936 at Camp SP-7. He worked on the stone tower and on the construction of the road from Lineville to the park as well as a retaining wall around the lake and the bathhouse. Shortly after being put on a tractor crew, he was transferred to Camp SP-5 at Fort Payne (Milton Lawrence "Pete" Leath interview, February 28, 2002; see the CD).

A Camp Inspection Report dated March 18, 1937, recorded 180 men from Alabama under the command of Captain Roscoe W. Tanner. The work project, under Mr. Head, consisted of development of the 2,200-acre Cheaha State Park, including the construction of a lookout tower, five overnight cabins, a custodian's house, and a garage and bathhouse, all built out of native stone. Four miles of foot trails and 30 miles of park roads were 90 percent complete. Four thousand native shrubs and trees had been transplanted to the park area. The work project would be completed in June 1939.

Company 468 was still under agreement with the Forest Service. John S. Davis, junior civil engineer, wrote a letter on March 18, 1937, that the Forest Service was still using Camp SP-7 for their project work. The work included fire suppression and presuppression, construction of roads and trails, and investigation of areas for potential recreation for the public. Further, Camp SP-7 could be called on in emergencies to work in the Talladega National Forest.

On October 21, 1937, the *Cleburne News* reported that Company 468 was being transferred to Medford, Oregon. The company had left Anniston on a special train of four tourist cars and two baggage cars. They met a similar six-car unit at Birmingham carrying the camp to Bessemer. Lt. Charles E. Holmes transferred with Company 468 as company commander. The State Park and Forestry Service was to place a caretaker in Camp SP-7 to look after the property.

According to the *Official Annual Medford District, Civilian Conservation Corps, Ninth Corps Area, 1938*, Company 468 arrived at Medford, Oregon, on October 18, 1937, after five days of traveling and established Camp Prescott, SP-13.

Company 487, Camp SP-8, Bessemer, Alabama

Company 487 was organized at Fort McClellan in late May 1933 out of the first several thousand junior enrollees sent there for conditioning. On June 22, Company 487 was sent to Bessemer, where it established Camp P-62 and worked on a private forestry project (1934 CCC District D annual). In December 1933, the camp was changed to Camp S-62 and continued to operate as a state forestry project. In October 1934, the project was transferred to the Department of Interior and the work shifted to the development of Oak Mountain State Park (1936 CCC District D annual).

A "Narrative Report" dated January 31, 1935, recorded that the first work project was the building of a road into the park. The ruggedness of the terrain was problematic, but after many studies, a route was chosen connecting the park to the Montgomery-to-Birmingham highway. Construction began the second week of October 1934.

George Davis, who was born in Etowah County, had experience driving heavy machinery. He drove a caterpillar bulldozer on the road construction project and the truck with the midday meal for the crews and earned extra money running errands for the project surveyor (George Davis interview, August 21, 2002; see the CD).

According to a Camp Inspection Report dated March 2, 1935, there were 207 enrollees from Alabama under the command of Captain B. M. Parks. The work project, under the supervision of J. H. Glander, consisted of road construction, roadside clearing, and fire hazard reduction in the 950-acre Oak Mountain State Park. There was outdoor recreation equipment for basketball, baseball, tennis, volleyball, boxing, and horseshoes and indoor equipment consisting of a ping-pong table, a radio, magazines, newspapers, books, and indoor games. CEA Carl Q. Baxter's education program offered elementary instruction and auto mechanics.

In May 1935, Company 487 produced its first issue of a semimonthly newspaper, the "Camp Jester." The "First May Issue" reported that Captain Hubert T. Andrews had replaced Captain Parks and W. J. Connell was replacing Mr. Glander as the project supervisor. The "Second May Issue" reported that since October 1, 1934, Company 487 had constructed 7.5 miles of road and built a bridge. Additional projects proposed included construction of a one-acre lake and 10 cabins.

A "Narrative Report" dated May 31, 1935, reported that April and May had been ideal for work. Rain had "conveniently" fallen only on the weekends. Thirteen of the 20 miles between camp and park were over a gravel road that was described as "uncomfortably dusty" and required an hour's drive each way. Only six hours of work per day were being accomplished. In spite of the distance, the trucks were in excellent shape. Morale was "unusually good." A bus line had been made available to take enrollees the two miles into Bessemer. Coordination between army and supervisory personnel was "one hundred percent." The food in camp was "good and well prepared."

The "First June Issue" of the "Camp Jester" reported that a detail of 21 enrollees were establishing Camp SCS-7 at Clanton, Alabama. The baseball team would begin a 10-game schedule in June, playing against CCC teams from the camps at Weogufka, Camp Hill, and Dadeville.

On September 19, 1935, the *Shelby Reporter* related that 180 boys were rapidly developing Oak Mountain State Park. The project supervisor, W. J. Connell, was not only laying plans for the park but also training the young enrollees in every phase of the work. The enrollees were quick learners, interested in what they were doing and making excellent progress. The road leading into the park climbed up the mountain and leveled off into a parking lot, where trails led off in every direction. The work blended so well with the landscape, it looked as if no work had been done at all. The main attraction was a 30-foot waterfall. Stone staircases were constructed in the steeper areas with narrow trails. The view from the rim of Oak Mountain looking across the valley "belonged to a southern woodland scene, and these colors and shades are changing constantly almost under the clouds that cast their shadows down from above." Other projects under construction were a caretaker's house and an equipment house made of frame and fieldstone veneer. A stone bridge had been built over a small stream at the entrance of the park.

A "Narrative Report" dated September 30, 1935, recorded that three miles of road were completed between the park and the Birmingham-Montgomery highway and another 3.5 miles within the park. Plans were under way to connect the park road with the road being built by the National Park Service in the adjoining Recreational Development Area property. Work projects planned for the sixth period, beginning October 1, consisted of construction of a stone lookout tower and a group of six cabins, camping and picnic ground development, and completion of the park road system.

On October 10, 1935, the *Shelby County Reporter* related that 10,000 acres were being considered for a national park in Shelby County near Oak Mountain. It would enhance the state park and also serve as a game sanctuary.

A Camp Inspection Report dated December 6, 1935, recorded 192 enrollees from Alabama, Florida, and Mississippi under the command of Captain Hubert T. Andrews. The work project consisted of the development of the 940-acre Oak Mountain State Park. There were no approved projects at the time of the inspection. The majority of the company was being held in camp with some fire prevention work being conducted.

The December "Camp Jester," now being published monthly, reported that the Thanksgiving holiday had been celebrated with a dance in the recreation hall. Most of the enrollees were home, but those who had stayed in camp enjoyed a feast of roast turkey with all the trimmings. The caretaker's dwelling was nearly completed; it had two bedrooms, a living room, kitchen and dining room, and a bathroom. The exterior was painted green; the interior walls were stained with linseed oil. An equipment storage house was also nearly completed, with room for tools and an automobile.

A "Narrative Report" dated December 31, 1935, reported that very little project work had been approved for November and December. A great deal of fire prevention work had been done in the Recreational Development Area next to the park, and work had begun on a telephone line between the camp and park. During December, four buildings from the abandoned Camp SCS-3 were dismantled and relocated to a side camp at Moundville. Oak Mountain State Park was beginning to attract more visitors.

Project Supervisor Connell's "Narrative Report" of March 13, 1936, reported that work had been slowed because of bad weather, but the roads and trails were in good condition after two months of rain and snow. Three and one-half miles of telephone line had been completed, and a repair garage had been built in camp. Three cabins were expected to be completed by March 31. The structures and scenery of Oak Mountain State Park had been photographed by a Mr. Anderson from Washington, D.C., and a Mr. White had visited the park in February in preparation to filming it. Construction of the side camp at Moundville was nearly completed. Work would soon begin on the preparation for the soil for planting and erosion control. Three parking areas had been built along the park road for viewing the mountain scenery, and eight miles of foot trails were completed along the highest ridges from the parking area to Pea Vine Falls and the natural springs. Firebreak construction and fire hazard reduction work along the roadsides had been completed, and a topographic survey of the park had begun.

On April 6, 1936, the *Shelby County Reporter* announced that another 1,000 men were at work at Oak Mountain where the National Park Service was developing an 8,000-acre recreation camp. Artificial lakes and cottages were to be built for family use and other cottages for organized boys' and girls' camps. The National Park Service would employ men through the National Reemployment Service from the WPA rolls.

On May 28, 1936, the "Camp Jester" reported that 20 enrollees had been sent to Fort McClellan in preparation to being sent to a camp in Pennsylvania. Company 487 had received 21 replacements, mostly from Georgia. Oak Mountain State Park had been officially dedicated. The park had been completed in record time under Mr. Connell and was expected to be one of the finest in the area.

A Camp Inspection Report dated November 23, 1936, recorded 161 men from Alabama, Georgia, and Mississippi under the command of Captain Frank R. Crom. The development of the 940-acre park continued under Mr. Connell. The work at the side camp at Moundville was under the supervision of foreman R. E. Parks. CEA W. H. Malone reported that 90 percent of the company was participating in the education program, which offered academic and vocational courses.

A Camp Inspection Report dated March 19, 1937, recorded 155 men under the command of Captain Alexander H. Stephens. The project work under Mr. Connell included general park improvement as outlined in the park master plan. Completed work included the caretaker's dwelling, an equipment and storage house, one picnic shelter, two trailside shelters, a waste disposal system, a well and water lines to the cabins and dwelling, and eight miles of park roads with two vehicle bridges. Construction of a lodge of native stone was to begin in April. Up to this point, all structures had been frame construction with stone foundations and chimneys. The work in the park that had begun on October 5, 1934, was expected to be completed in June 1939. It was noted that Camp SP-8 had been named "Camp Hugo Black."

On April 2, 1937, Burton M. Graham, CCC liaison officer, wrote to Special Investigator J. S. Billups to report that Company 487 had only 150 men. An additional 30 enrollees would be sent during the procurement period of April 1–20 and would give considerable aid to the work at the camps at Bessemer and Moundville.

On April 6, 1937, Major William H. McCutcheon wrote to Special Investigator Billups reporting that some of the buildings at Camp SP-8 needed repair. It was one of the older camps and had been built out of green lumber with the poorest construction and workmanship. The floors and roofs were sagging and the sides were bulging. A survey of needed improvements was to be conducted at the Bessemer camp.

It is not known if the repairs were made before Company 487 was transferred to Yosemite National Park in October 1937. James A. Goodman of Montgomery had joined Company 487 in April 1935 and had earned the leader rating as a cook and mess steward. He had been detailed Camp Baltzell at Mound State Park in December 1935 and spent four months at the side camp with 50 enrollees. When Company 487 transferred to California, Mr. Goodman saw snow for the first time in his life. He also was able to go to the 1938 Rose Bowl in Pasadena to watch Alabama play California (John A. Goodman interview, December 13, 2001; see the CD).

On October 21, 1937, the *Shelby County Reporter* related that although the CCC camp at the state park had been discontinued, the work was continuing in the Oak Mountain Recreation Area. Relief workers from Birmingham were constructing cabins, lodges, a dining hall, an infirmary, and other quarters. The work by the CCC over the past three years included a group of vacation cabins, two picnic areas with fireplaces and shelters, a custodian's dwelling with storage and service structures, and water, sanitation, and telephone systems. Enrollees had built nine miles of park roads and nature trails leading to the picturesque sections of Oak Mountain, Pea Vine Falls, and the gorge. The article concluded that Oak Mountain and the recreation development area would eventually be combined to form an "outstanding playground."

Camp SP-9, Salt Springs State Park, Jackson, Alabama

Camp SP-9 was proposed for the fifth period, April 1, 1935, for Salt Springs State Park in Clarke County. The park contained 1,200 acres near Jackson, Alabama. The camp was never occupied (*The Civilian Conservation Corps and the National Park Service, 1933–1942: An Administrative History,* Appendix C).

Company 444, Camp SP-10, Selma, Alabama

Company 444 was established at Fort Moultrie, South Carolina, on June 2, 1933. The junior enrollees from Georgia were sent to Glencoe, Alabama, in June 1934, then to Camp Hill in October. In October 1935, Company 444 transferred to Valley Creek State Park, 17 miles northeast of Selma (1936 CCC District G annual).

A Camp Inspection Report dated January 7, 1936, recorded 213 men from Alabama, Georgia, Tennessee, Mississippi, Virginia, and South Carolina under the command of Captain William P. Brandon. The project work, under the supervision of Melford G. Cleveland, consisted of construction of park roads, foot trails, fences, overnight cabins, fire hazard reduction, and the clearing of land and construction of a large dam to build an artificial lake. The enrollees were also razing undesirable structures within the 700-acre park.

Camp SP-10 had several problems. Water had to be hauled from Selma. The men were carried to Selma three times each week for bathing. The grounds of the camp were badly eroded and the barracks in a "state of general disorder." Meals were served in mess kits because of the lack of water to wash plates. There was no camp educational advisor. Although there was equipment for baseball and basketball, including uniforms, and indoor equipment, the recreation hall was poorly lighted by only one light bulb.

A "Narrative Report" dated March 1, 1936, recorded that work during January and February had been severely slowed by continuous rain and subfreezing weather. Company 444 had only worked 28 out of the possible 50 work days. Progress had been made on the park roads, and work on two cabins was completed. Work on the lake bed could only be done during moderate weather. During February, the Alabama State Nurseries delivered 21,350 tree seedlings which had been planted. A Park Service blacksmith shop was nearly completed. The most outstanding development was the construction of three large springs with steps, benches, landings, and dams.

According to a Camp Inspection Report dated October 23, 1936, there were 163 men from Alabama, Georgia, Florida, Mississippi, and Louisiana under the command of 1st Lt. Gaines E. Maxwell. The work project, under Mr. Cleveland, consisted of park development and construction of roads, foot trails and bridges, guardrails on roadsides, and two log cabins on the edge of the proposed 60-acre lake. The water supply to the camp was not adequate; the camp buildings were scattered over rough terrain, and no efforts had been made to beautify the camp. The camp commander was seeking permission to purchase chinaware with the company ration savings.

The new CEA, C. E. Masters, reported that the educational program was offering courses for illiterates, courses at the elementary and high school levels, and vocational courses. Informal activities included guitar lessons, dancing, current events, journalism, and a course on everyday manners. (Issues of the "Valley Creek News" from 1936 and 1937 were archived at the University of Chicago.)

A Camp Inspection Report dated November 26, 1937, recorded 204 men under the command of 1st Lt. Jesse B. DuBois, the third commander since Captain Maxwell had left on April 27, 1937. Sim E. Pace was the new project supervisor. Valley Creek State Park was reported to be 1,500 acres in size, and the park project was not expected to be completed before March 1939. Since the end of September 1937, the Park Service had been trying to reestablish the side camp at Moundville. Eight trucks and other considerable equipment were still at the camp with foreman Henry O'Quinn looking after the equipment and drawing a salary of $166.66 per month. Special investigator J. C. Reddoch recommended that if the side camp was not reestablished, the trucks and foreman should be released.

By February 1938, Company 444 had completed the caretaker's house with hot and cold running water and hardwood floors. They had also built three rustic cabins with stone fireplaces. Thirty enrollees who had come to camp unable to read and write had been enrolled in the educational program, and they were now able to write letters home and read a newspaper. The side camp at Moundville was reestablished with 60 men under the supervision of Henry O'Quinn. The 1938 District D annual showed the enrollees at Moundville pouring concrete in the construction of the museum. It was the only concrete building built by CCC enrollees in Alabama (1938 CCC District D annual).

On June 1, 1938, Company 444 transferred to Moundville to establish a full camp, designated Camp SP-15.

Company 2420, Camp SP-10, Selma, Alabama

Company 2420, consisting of veterans of World War I from Alabama, Mississippi, Florida, and Georgia, established Camp P-60 at Chatom, Alabama, in July 1933 (1936 CCC District G annual). They transferred to Camp SP-10 on June 2, 1938 (NACCCA database).

A Camp Inspection Report dated August 30, 1938, recorded 184 men under the command of Captain J. C. Heidenreich. The work project, under the supervision of Sim E. Pace Jr. consisted of an area of 1,080 acres in Valley Creek State Park. The main project was the construction of a dam measuring 850 feet long, 100 feet wide at the base, 10 feet wide at the top, and 16 feet high. It was expected to create a 97-acre lake, and more than a year was needed to complete the dam. Volleyball was the only recreational activity in camp. Four trips were taken to Selma each week. There were checkers, dominoes, cards, and a pool table in the recreation hall. Company 2420 had been without an educational advisor for some time. The camp had no school building.

On September 21, 1938, Special Investigator Reddoch wrote to the director in Washington stating that an education advisor had been selected for Company 2420 and would be reporting to the camp around the first of October.

According to the *CCC Camp Directory for Alabama*, Camp SP-10 was abandoned after the twelfth period, which ended March 30, 1939. Company 2430 transferred to Cheaha State Park, where it established Camp SP-17 on June 20, 1939.

Company 230, Camp SP-11, Citronelle, Alabama

Company 230 transferred to Camp SP-11 in June 1935, working on the construction of the camp for one month. They had not begun any project work before being transferred to Nevada in July (1936 CCC District G annual).

Company 5412, Camp SP-11, Citronelle, Alabama

Company 5412 arrived at Camp SP-11 in the middle of August 1935. The camp was located "in the scrub pine and sand hills of South Alabama." The junior enrollees from West Florida spent two weeks in camp in conditioning. The company was supplemented by LEMs from Company 230 and a cadre of rated men from camps at Youngstown, Florida, and Chunchula, Alabama. By the fall of 1935, Company 5412 was beautifying the camp with evergreen shrubberies from local nurseries (1936 CCC District G annual).

On September 11, 1935, Special Investigator J. C. Reddoch wrote to CCC Assistant Director McEntee to report that some of the lumber used in the construction of Camp SP-11 was of inferior quality and likely green. There was no telephone connection and no recreational equipment in the camp. There was also no camp educational advisor. The work project consisted of the development of the 640-acre Cedar Creek State Park. Road construction was progressing slowly because of a lack of motor equipment. The project superintendent was trying to get a fourth truck for the project.

A Camp Inspection Report dated January 10, 1936, recorded 185 enrollees from Florida, Alabama, Mississippi, and Louisiana under the command of Captain Henry B. Hart. The work project, under the supervision of J. W. Lovelace, consisted of the construction of park roads, foot trails, vehicle bridges, one impounding and diversion dam, a fence around the park, telephone lines, picnic shelters, and the installation of a water system. Trees and shrubs were planted in the park area. A three-room education building, the recreational hall, and the officers' mess room and quarters were all being used for educational classes. All staff members were assisting in the program. Local teachers were volunteering to teach classes, and offerings included elementary school subjects and vocational classes. There was 86 percent participation in the educational program.

According to a Camp Inspection Report dated October 27, 1936, there were 168 men from Mississippi, Florida, Louisiana, Georgia, and Alabama under the command of 1st Lt. Rudesill. The work project was now under the supervision of Mr. Donovan. The construction of park roads, telephone lines, and a caretaker's dwelling was completed, and work was under way on the construction of a dam that would create a 23-acre lake. Company 5412 had uniforms for baseball and basketball teams and equipment for tennis and horseshoes plus two sets of boxing gloves. Indoor equipment consisted of a piano, two pool tables, a bowling alley, a Crosley radio, and two sets of dominoes, two sets of checkers, and a card table with two decks of cards.

Although Company 5412 had been without an educational advisor, 90 percent of the men were participating in the educational program. Courses were offered in literacy instruction and at the elementary and high school levels. Vocational courses were offered in bookkeeping and photography. The camp had no traveling library.

A Camp Inspection Report dated March 15, 1937, recorded 167 men under the command of 1st Lt. Marion B. Evans. The work project, under Mr. Donovan, consisted of the construction of a 25-acre lake, roads, a bathing beach, and a picnic area and the planting of native trees and shrubs. Ninety percent of the dam was completed. The bathing beach and picnic area were proposed. Roads and foot trails had been constructed, and 40,000 young trees and shrubs had been planted around the park, and fences and firebreaks had been built. The lake was located in a natural basin with a beautiful site for overnight cabins. The work project was estimated to be completed by April 1938.

Damon Fuqua, born in Brewton, Alabama, joined Company 5412 in May 1937. The project work consisted of developing Cedar Creek State Park. Mr. Fuqua operated a bulldozer in the construction of the dam, along with maintaining the park roads. He also worked on a crew that planted gallberry bushes in the ditches to control erosion. While in camp, Mr. Fuqua played on the company baseball team against teams from other CCC camps and area high schools. In December 1937, he transferred to Company 1425 at Camp SP-6 at Gulf State Park (Damon Fuqua interview, February 17, 2003; see the CD).

According to the *CCC Camp Directory for Alabama*, Camp SP-11 was abandoned during the tenth period, which ended March 30, 1938.

Company 4457, Camp SP-11, Citronelle, Alabama

The *CCC Camp Directory for Alabama* recorded that Camp SP-11 was reestablished during the thirteenth period, which began April 1, 1939. Company 4457 transferred to Camp SP-11 on August 1, 1939, from Georgia (NACCCA database).

A Camp Inspection Report dated October 6, 1939, recorded 165 men under the command of 1st Lt. David Mims Jr. Upon their arrival, they made camp improvements. The work project, under the supervision of Sim E. Pace, consisted of general park improvements and construction of park roads, a combination building and entrance portal, and a custodian's dwelling. They also did fire-suppression work. For recreation, sound motion pictures were shown in camp twice a month. Athletic equipment was available for baseball, volleyball, boxing, and horseshoes. The recreation hall was inadequately furnished, with only a few small tables and chairs.

CEA Grady Farley reported that courses were offered in literacy instruction and at elementary and high school levels. Vocational classes were available in auto mechanics, nursery cultivation, swine raising, truck driving, and woodworking. The camp library had approximately 2,000 volumes, and the camp received 7 daily newspapers and 25 magazines. Two nights a week were devoted to the classes. Enrollee participation was only 30 to 36 percent, but four enrollees had gained civilian employment.

According to a Camp Inspection Report dated August 14, 1940, there were 198 men under the command of Lt. Mims. The work project was progressing. CEA Farley's educational program had increased its enrollee participation to between 75 and 95 percent. Academic classes met daily and vocational classes twice a week. The camp had an unusual nursery project "which seemed to have considerable possibilities." During the third quarter of 1940, 17 men in Company 4457 had learned to read and write.

According to the *CCC Camp Directory for Alabama*, Camp SP-11 at Cedar Creek State Park was abandoned July 31, 1941, during the seventeenth period.

Company 4448, Camp SP-12, Auburn, Alabama

Company 4448 was established on August 18, 1935, from an initial cadre of 26 men from three camps in District H. Under the command of Captain William Massey, the cadre cleared a campsite area of cotton stalks, stumps, and rocks, then constructed the buildings. The work project was the construction of the 600-acre Chewacla State Park, located 4.5 miles south of Auburn, and was to begin on September 15, 1935 (1937 CCC District H annual).

A Camp Inspection Report dated January 2, 1936, recorded 167 enrollees from Florida, Georgia, and Alabama under the command of Captain Clifford S. Urwiller. The work project, under the supervision of W. J. Ryan, consisted of the construction of park roads, culverts, bridges, and a concrete dam that would create a 26-acre lake. The lake basin was being cleared. Recreational equipment was provided for baseball, basketball, volleyball, boxing, and horseshoes. "Moving pictures" were shown in camp frequently, and trips were arranged to see shows in Opelika twice a week. The company received 50 magazines and 5 daily newspapers.

CEA Royal Mattice's education report for December 1935 recorded that 18 courses were offered with 96 enrollees, or 58 percent of the company, attending. Another 100 enrollees received training while working on the project. J. W. Drake, junior foreman, taught a well-attended course in rock masonry and construction in the evenings. Four NYA teachers were furnished by the Alabama Polytechnic Institute. According to the Center for Research Libraries, Company 4448 began a camp newspaper in 1936 entitled "???" (three question marks were the name of the newspaper), to be changed to the "Chewacla News" in August 1936.

Claudis G. Beasley of Brewton, Alabama, enrolled in the CCC in the fall of 1935 and was sent to Camp SP-12. He worked on various projects in the development of Chewacla State Park and recalled working on the construction of the dam and buildings in the park. He also worked in the quarry, cutting rock for projects in the park. In his free time, he played baseball and "visited a little gal" in Opelika (Claudis Greene Beasley interview, October 20, 2003; see the CD).

Dan Williams enrolled in the CCC in Baton Rouge, Louisiana, in May 1936. The enrollees were sent by train to Auburn, then trucked to Chewacla State Park. He worked on the construction of the dam and clearing of the lake bed and planted grass along the banks of the park roads. In his spare time, he taught himself how to type. He was assigned to the camp surgeon but fainted during his first surgery. He eventually became the company clerk (Dan Williams interview, August 10, 2001; see the CD).

A Camp Inspection Record dated March 17, 1937, recorded 156 men from Alabama, Florida, Georgia, Louisiana, and Mississippi under the command of 1st Lt. Cena V. Fertitta. The all-masonry dam was completed, the bathing beach 90 percent completed, the custodian's dwelling 50 percent completed, and a 23-foot-long stone and masonry bridge 85 percent completed. Two and one-half miles of a scenic road and four miles of foot trails had been built. The work project was expected to be finished by January 1940.

According to the 1937 District H annual, the masonry dam contained 6 million pounds of rock. The lake was to be used for fishing and recreation. The custodian's dwelling, containing six rooms, was built of native stone quarried by the enrollees. The arch bridge over Moore's Mill Creek, at the head of the lake, was being constructed of reinforced concrete faced with stone. Plans were being made for overnight cabins, a large recreation building, and a bathhouse.

A Camp Inspection Report dated November 30, 1937, recorded 180 men from Alabama, Florida, Georgia, Louisiana, and Mississippi under the command of Captain Henry K. Toenes. The work project under W. J. Ryan was progressing. The masonry dam was completed, as were two miles of foot trails, a masonry bridge, 2.5 miles of roads, a custodian's dwelling, and two rock and concrete overnight cabins. Work had begun on five more cabins, a parking area, a picnic shelter, and 12 outdoor fireplaces. During July and August 1937, 22,887 people checked into Chewacla State Park.

In early 1938, J. L. Hall of Hope Hull enrolled in the CCC and was sent to Camp SP-12. He drove a truck taking crews and hauling materials to the work sites. He recalled a tennis court in camp and said that he enjoyed learning to play tennis while in the CCC. There were also pool tables and a ping-pong table in the recreation hall (J. L. Hall interview, November 21, 2002; see the CD).

According to a Camp Inspection Report dated September 29, 1938, there were 191 men under 1st Lt. Lazarus H. Todd. Flynn E. Hudson had replaced Mr. Ryan as the project superintendent. The main project was the bathhouse, which was expected to require 5,000 enrollee man-days and cost $3,500 in materials. A work detail was staying in camp to build an educational building, to extend the woodshop, and to hang a ceiling in the recreation hall. The new CEA, Thomas C. Harris, had expanded the educational program, adding high school level and vocational courses. He reported that courses ranged from reading and writing for semi-illiterates to academic work at the high school level. Every enrollee could find a vocational course that appealed to his interest. The army officers, the CEA, the assistant CEA, enrollees, and NYA teachers were offering the classes, and the technical personnel taught job training courses. Five nights a week were devoted to the educational program, which had grown steadily over eight months with 55 percent of the company participating.

A Camp Inspection Report dated September 11, 1939, recorded 192 men in Company 4448. They had been without a company commander since August 30. The subaltern, James N. Luton, had been in camp since August 29. He was experienced, interested, eager to receive suggestions, and willing to do whatever he could to improve the camp. The work project, under the supervision of Mr. Hudson, consisted of general park improvement and was progressing satisfactorily. Projects included the construction of fireplaces, a parking area, and combination tables and benches, extension of the park road, treatment of gullies in the park, tree inspection and pest control, educational and guide work at the contact station, and various improvements around the Bureau of Animal Industry experimental farm.

The educational program under CEA Harris continued its success. Ten courses were taught in camp and three at Alabama Polytechnic Institute (API) at Auburn. Twelve vocational classes were offered. Thirty-five enrollees had started college work at API since January 1, 1939, and now 12 men were attending college full time. Six men had been promoted from the literacy class to elementary school level.

According to a Camp Inspection Report dated November 7, 1940, there were 194 men under the command of Captain R. F. Holcomb. The work project, under Mr. Hudson, was just about completed. Additional work projects needed to be approved, or the enrollees were to be turned back to the army because of an insufficient work program. Forrest P. Mathews, the new camp educational advisor, reported that approximately 92 percent of the company was participating in the program. The camp library, with 800 volumes, was considered the most popular place in camp.

On December 2, 1940, Charles H. Kenlan, assistant to the director, wrote to the Department of Interior's representative to the CCC Advisory Council regarding the lack of work at Camp SP-12. H. E. Weatherwax, the acting representative for the department, responded to his letter on December 12, 1940. The National Park Service had been planning to terminate Camp SP-12 on September 30, 1940, and therefore only three months of work had been approved. Company 4448 was kept in Alabama as the National Park Service was trying to establish a camp at the Oak Mountain Recreation Demonstration Area. A revised work program at Chewacla State Park had been prepared, however, as the State of Alabama had acquired additional land in the park. This acquisition created work for the remainder of the fiscal year.

According to the *CCC Camp Directory for Alabama*, Camp SP-12 was abandoned after the sixteenth period, which ended March 31, 1941.

Company 4449, Camp SP-13, Gordon, Alabama

Company 4449 was established on August 11, 1935, when a cadre of 25 men from Vilas, Florida, arrived in Gordon, Alabama, under the command of Captain Homer L. Singletary. The camp was located a mile and a half west of the Chattahootchee River and a half-mile north of the Florida state line. On August 15, another 174 new enrollees arrived. After two weeks of conditioning, the company was turned over to Project Superintendent John A. Garrett to begin work on Alabama State Park No. 13. First Lt. Malcolm R. Wimbish relieved Captain Singletary at the end of November 1935 (1937 CCC District H annual).

A Camp Inspection Report dated January 3, 1936, recorded 170 men from Alabama, Florida, and Georgia under the command of Lt. Wimbish. The work project, under Mr. Garrett, consisted of the development of the 596-acre Chattahootchee State Park, including the construction of park roads, bridges, culverts, parking areas, cabins, a caretaker's dwelling, fireplaces, and foot trails. Fire hazard reduction work was being conducted throughout the park, and an earthen dam was to be built, creating a 23-acre lake. There was little indoor recreational equipment, only a piano and a radio, but there was equipment for baseball, volleyball, basketball, and horseshoes.

William Lawton Lamb, CEA, reported that the educational program offered courses at the elementary and high school levels. Vocational classes in first aid were offered. Mr. Lamb and the assistant CEA taught most of the classes, the company commander taught the safety class, and the camp doctor, Dr. W. H. Turner, taught one of the first aid courses. Systematic instruction on the job was given in cooking, interior decorating, concrete work, forestry, rock excavation, and music. Instruction was also given in the infirmary and company exchange. Seventy-three percent of the enrollees were participating in the education program. According to the Center for Research Libraries, Company 4449 produced a camp newspaper called "Chattahootchee Chatter" during 1936 and 1937.

On March 15, 1936, the company was notified that it would be disbanded by April 1. All but 75 enrollees were transferred to other companies. On March 24, the order was rescinded, and company strength had to be rebuilt. In early May, Lt. Marvin P. Hughes relieved Lt. Wimbish. The company mess officer and two leaders were transferred to the Third Corps Area to new companies being organized. On June 14, Chattahootchee State Park was opened to the public. Camp SP-13 had a visitors' day with field events and a baseball game (1937 CCC District H annual).

By the time of the writing of the 1937 annual, the 23-acre lake had just been completed with the construction of a 500-foot earthen dam. The lake was the centerpiece for recreational development. Islands in the lake and at both ends of the dam had been planted with native trees and shrubs, giving a natural look to the construction. One of several cabins proposed had been completed, as well as a custodian's dwelling and a storage and supply house. There were approximately five miles of roads and foot trails meandering through the park. The park entrance was a portal of fitted stones. A small sawmill had been located in the park, and the wood removed from the lake site was cut into timber for future construction projects (1937 CCC District H annual).

According to the *CCC Camp Directory for Alabama*, Camp SP-13 was abandoned during 1937. It was not approved for the tenth period, which began October 1, 1937.

Company 2445, Camp SP-14, Linden, Alabama

The *CCC Camp Directory for Alabama* recorded that Camp SP-14 was a new camp established during the fifth period, which began April 1, 1935, at Chickasaw State Park in Marengo County, Alabama. The *Democratic-Reporter*, a weekly newspaper for Linden, Alabama, reported on May 9 that Marengo

County was getting two CCC camps, one to work on gully restoration (SCS-11) and the other, four miles north of Linden in the sixteenth section, in reforestation.

On May 22, 1935, the paper announced that work on a new park had begun. The Alabama Commission of Forestry had sent advance personnel to Chewacla Park, Camp SP-12; Chattahootchee Park, Camp SP-13; and Chickasaw Park, Camp SP-14. Design for roads, trails, bridges, and other improvements was the first task at hand. Additional company members would arrive by July 1 or soon after.

According to a "Narrative Report" dated Januaury 1, 1936, Chickasaw State Park was located on U.S. Highway 43 between Linden and Demopolis. The 480-acre park contained one of the few remaining tracts of virgin pine timber in the state on property owned by the state since 1819 (sixteenth section of a township). Located between the famed Black Belt and the Coastal Plain, the park was "a gem of scenic beauty which every nature lover will enjoy."

Preliminary survey of the park began in May 1935. The camp was established, and project work began on August 22. A 2.6-mile road with bridges and culverts accessing desirable areas of the park was completed, but, because of the nature of the soils, it needed surfacing. A stock-proof fence around the park and along the highway on the east side of the park was completed. Open fields surrounded the park, so no firebreaks were needed. Adjacent landowners were cautioned regarding burning trash and clearing their fields. Only one fire had occurred during the fall season, and it was quickly extinguished. Other accomplishments included 1.3 miles of foot trails constructed, one foot bridge, two miles of roadside fire hazard reduction, cutting and transporting of fence posts to Cedar Creek State Park, and construction of an ECW equipment and supply house and garage. The report concluded with the recognition that the army officers had given park personnel close cooperation. The enrollees, African-American veterans, had displayed their willingness to finish the project. The county officials and citizens had extended every effort to assist in the work. The development of the park was a "pleasure to everyone connected with it."

A Camp Inspection Report dated January 8, 1936, recorded 184 men from Alabama, Mississippi, Tennessee, Florida, Georgia, Louisiana, and Maryland under the command of Captain John R. Porterfield. The work project, under the supervision of G. L. James, consisted of the construction of park roads, foot trails, foot and vehicle bridges, telephone lines, fencing, a bathhouse, a dwelling, and a trailside shelter, fire hazard reduction, landscaping, planting trees, sodding, and the obliteration of old roads and trails in the park. Company 2445 had outdoor equipment for boxing, baseball, basketball, and horseshoes, and indoor equipment included dominoes, checkers, and a radio. There was no education program in the camp as there had been no CEA since the beginning of the camp. There were, however, five ordained ministers in Company 2445, and a Bible class was taught each Sunday morning after services.

A "Narrative Report" dated March 1, 1936, recorded that rain during January and February had slowed work. With the warmer spring weather, people from the surrounding area were visiting the park. Every precaution was being taken to preserve the natural beauty of the virgin timber. To date, not a single fire had occurred in the park. The fieldwork for a topographic map was completed. The road through the park, 2.6 miles long, was completed, with the last half-mile needing gravel. Pine, oak, walnut, and cedar seedlings from the state nursery at Livingston had been planted over 40 acres. The picnic grounds were being developed in a naturally beautiful area. Water was supplied from an all-weather spring. Construction was under way on 2.7 miles of foot trails, which gave visitors "access to the most picturesque sections of the park area."

Two more undated "Narrative Reports" were written by Acting Project Superintendent W. J. Donovan, likely from mid-March 1936. The entire length of the park road had been graveled. A total of 3.2 miles of foot trails were completed, with three bridges constructed of hewn timber on one trail. The topographic map of the park was completed. The park area was enclosed in a stock-proof fence. A telephone line connected the camp to Linden and would be transferred to the caretaker's house when the house was completed. The house was designed to resemble classical architecture after an old residence in the local area and would be completed soon.

Acting Superintendent Thomas M. Reed submitted a "Narrative Report" to the National Park Service on March 31, 1936, with the notation "Discontinued." The park road was completed. The caretaker's house was ready to be occupied, and a garage of the same design had been built next to it. A water storage tank had been built, as had a water pump and pump house at the artesian well. Four fireplaces had been built within the park and a cattle guard at the entrance. All park roads had been sloped and sodded to prevent erosion. The grounds of the caretaker's house had been drained and landscaped. Poisonous weeds had been eradicated along the foot trails and in the picnic and parking areas.

According to the *CCC Camp Directory for Alabama*, Camp SP-14 was abandoned sometime after the sixth period, which ended March 31, 1936. On May 21, 1936, the *Democratic-Reporter* reported that a swimming pool was to be built at Chickasaw State Park by a detachment of 30 enrollees from Company 444 at Camp SP-10 at Selma. They would be stationed at Camp SP-14 while building the pool and picnic grounds.

Camp Baltzell Side Camp, Mound State Monument, Moundville, Alabama

Mound State Monument, or Moundville Archaeological Park as it is now called, is one of the major archaeological sites in the Southeast. The Alabama Museum of Natural History began work at the site in 1929. By 1932, efforts by Dr. Walter B. Jones and David DeJarnette led to the purchase of the site (Lyon 1996:185).

The initial work conducted at the monument by CCC enrollees was erosion control by Company 465 from Camp P-59 at Northport, Alabama. The junior African-American enrollees established Camp P-59 on June 22, 1933, for private forestry work in Tuscaloosa County. The work at Moundville was hampered by time lost in driving 36 miles over dangerous, unpaved roads (Baklanoff and Howington 1989:20). However, even with only a few short hours of work each day, they allowed Dr. Walter B. Jones to start on the most critical erosion-control projects (Garrison 2001:12).

On April 5, 1934, the *Tuscaloosa News* reported that Congressman William B. Oliver had given a speech at Moundville High School and announced that a "branch" CCC camp was being considered at Mound Park. It was to develop the Indian mounds into a national park that would attract tourists from all over the world. Congressman Oliver gave his full support to the development. There were presently 30 men at work at the camp.

On January 17, 1935, Dr. Jones photographed the erosion control dams that had been built east of Mound F, between Mounds A and R, and south of Mound E. He also photographed the side camp, consisting of seven small barracks and two wooden structures with pyramidal tent roofs in a row along a park road in front of one of the mounds (Walter B. Jones Photograph Collection, Alabama Museum of Natural History.)

On November 13, 1934, Company 465 transferred to Camp SP-7 but continued the side camp. A "Narrative Report" from Camp SP-7 dated March 1935 included the work at Camp Baltzell. Nine rock check dams had been erected in gullies, and another 12 were needed to stop erosion of the gully heads. The gullies had been planted with black locust trees and other seedlings, and the area had been sown with carpet grass to prevent erosion of the "plateau upon which the mounds are built." Approximately 30,000 seedlings had been planted, and a system of footpaths had been built, connecting the most attractive features of the park. Erosion control was still the primary work project.

Dr. Jones praised the work of the CCC enrollees but wrote in 1935, "It will not be humanly possible for a side camp to accomplish such a large task within any reasonable length of time." He asked Congressman Oliver to join with Senators Hugo Black and John Bankhead to lobby for a full camp. Dr. Jones also asked the National Park Service for help and changed the name of the site to "Mound State Monument" to use Park Service terminology. Dr. Jones and his wife, Hazel, began training CCC enrollees in the excavations (Garrison 2001:13–15).

The *Tuscaloosa News* reported on September 17, 1935, that Colonel Page Bunker, state forester, had announced that a full camp of 200 men was to be established at Mound Park by October 1. Dr. Jones, Congressman Oliver, and Colonel George F. Baltzell, district commander at Fort McClellan, had presented a strong argument. In the last year, a side camp of approximately 25 workers had constructed roads, saved the mounds from erosion, and began excavations under the supervision of Dr. Jones.

The full camp would have to wait. A new side camp was established on December 23, 1935. Dr. Jones visited the camp as it was being occupied (Dr. Walter B. Jones Papers, Houle Library, University of Alabama). It was occupied by a detachment from Company 487 at Camp SP-8 at Bessemer. A "Narrative Report" dated December 31, 1935, recorded that four buildings from the SCS camp at Camp Hill had been moved to Moundville during December. On January 2, 1936, Dr. Jones worked on correspondence with "Davis, artist for Happy Day, CCC Paper" (Jones Papers).

The January 11, 1936, edition of "Happy Days" contained an article titled "On the Trail With Davis–Alabama." Marshall Davis had visited the 50-man side camp. He described the mounds, suggesting that it may have taken thousands of years for the "dirt to get 57 feet high." The age of the mounds was unknown. Davis concluded by stating that Dr. Jones "will direct the excavation work and in general will shortly have the very hell dug out of the place." The CCC enrollees were under the supervision of two state park foremen. They also worked on controlling erosion, which was "eating away certain prize sections of this area." His article included a sketch of the side camp, showing eight barracks and no tents.

Another strong supporter of Dr. Jones's efforts for a full camp was James

Milton Mallory of Savannah, Georgia. Mallory, a dear friend of Dr. Jones, was described as an archaeologist, geologist, director of the Georgia Forestry Association, a member of the State Board of Forestry and Geological Development, vice president of the Society for Georgia Archaeology, and a regent of the Alabama Museum of Natural History. He was Dr. Jones's closest link to CCC Director Robert Fechner. When Arthur Kelley of the National Park Service was critical of the work at Moundville in November 1936, Mallory wrote to Dr. Jones to inform him that he had spent the day with Fechner and "took the occasion to acquaint Fechner of the whole situation." Mallory assured Dr. Jones that CCC Director Fechner was "very much interested in Moundville" (Jones Papers).

On May 24, 1937, Dr. Jones photographed the pouring of the first batch of concrete for the new museum building. On June 24, he photographed the progress of the construction, showing the concrete foundation walls coming along (Walter B. Jones Photograph Collection, Alabama Museum of Natural History). In October, Company 487 was transferred to Yosemite National Park in California. With the departure of Company 487's detachment at Camp Baltzell, Dr. Jones planned a trip to Washington, D.C., to make a personal call on CCC Director Fechner (Garrison 2001:15).

By January 1938, Company 444 had reestablished the side camp at Moundville. The 1938 District D annual reported that approximately 50 men were at Moundville under the supervision of foreman H. O'Quinn. Photographs show the progress of the museum and note that the museum was the only concrete building constructed by the CCC in Alabama. The burial mounds were reported to be over 2,000 years old. On January 19, the *Tuscaloosa News* reported that Company 444 had established a side camp at Moundville to excavate the mounds and build a concrete museum. Fifty enrollees were assigned to the side camp with Henry O'Quinn as their foreman.

In March 1938, the National Park Service finally placed a full camp at Moundville. On March 14, Dr. Jones wrote to Dr. Charles I. Silin at Tulane University, stating that he would not be attending a geology meeting as he could not afford to leave Alabama as the full CCC camp was being established at Moundville. They were beginning a cooperative WPA project on archaeological research, involving nearly $200,000. Dr. Jones thought this would be the largest project granted for scientific research in the entire New Deal program. On April 22, Dr. Jones wrote to Mr. and Mrs. Gandrud of Fort Myers, Florida, reporting that the new buildings for the full camp were completed. They had requested that the men be transferred to the full camp. The full camp would "greatly step-up our program here" (Jones Papers).

On June 1, Company 444 transferred from Camp SP-10 to Moundville and established Camp SP-15. The work began in earnest with the 200 men. Under the supervision of James DeJarnette, the enrollees graded the land with mules and scoops, terraced the slopes, and reduced the flow of water by spreading it across a wider area. The water was diverted into a series of concrete drains and storm sewers. To further prevent erosion, grass was seeded and trees and shrubs planted (Garrison 2001:15).

Company 444, Camp SP-15, Moundville, Alabama

A Camp Inspection Report dated August 3, 1938, recorded 183 men under the command of 1st Lt. F.P. Langbehn. Camp SP-15 retained the name "Camp Baltzell." The work project, under James T. DeJarnette, consisted of preserving, restoring, and exhibiting a primitive Indian village of 26 mounds and several manmade lakes. The enrollees were restoring the mounds to their original size and cleaning out the lakes that had filled with sediments during the last century of cultivation. The work on the museum was 30 percent completed.

Camp recreational activities consisted of interbarracks competitions in softball and horseshoes. The recreation hall was inadequately furnished. Two recreational trips were made each week to Tuscaloosa.

CEA Mel H. Hassell's educational report for August 31, 1938, recorded that courses were offered at the elementary and high school levels. Special emphasis was placed on vocational training, especially in woodworking and agricultural subjects. Fifty enrollees had been promoted in the elementary grades, 12 had been taught heavy equipment operation, and 3 were competent woodworkers. Additional job training courses were offered in construction, archaeological reconnaissance and investigation, and restoration of historical monuments.

B. H. "Tubby" Hall enrolled in the CCC at Tuscaloosa in June 1938 and arrived at Moundville as the barracks for the full camp were being completed. He had finished high school and assisted Mr. Hassell in teaching enrollees in reading and writing. He worked as a laborer with a shovel on the excavations. Whenever the enrollees found an artifact, the supervisors worked with trowels to recover it carefully (B. H. Hall interview, December 4, 2003; see the CD).

On September 8, 1938, Dr. Jones wrote to museum regent Erskine Ramsey that a third wall section of the concrete museum had been poured. The enrollees performed all of the tasks involved in the construction: "The CCC boys built the forms, tied the steel, washed the sand and gravel, ran the mixer, and poured concrete for the facility that was to house one of the premier archaeological collections in the United States." Dr. Jones wrote in a press release on the museum, it was "to their everlasting credit that there is probably no better concrete job anywhere" (Garrison 2001:17).

When Olin Hurst of Lineville arrived at Camp SP-15 in 1938, work on the museum was well under way. He worked on the construction of the cement frames, poured concrete, and did carpentry work. When he noticed that a saw had become dull and was not cutting properly, he informed his leader that he knew how to sharpen saws. He was moved into the blacksmith shop and told to keep the saws sharpened and properly set and was promoted to assistant leader (Olin Hurst interview, July 21, 2005; see the CD).

On January 18, 1939, James Mallory wrote to Dr. Jones suggesting that it was time to invite CCC Director Fechner to the dedication of the museum. Fechner was planning a trip through the South, and the dedication could be worked into that trip. Dr. Jones wrote to Mallory on February 1, 1939, that there was "an enormous amount of work before us. . . . Mound State Monument is booming and we are using a lot of the boys on excavations in the new road location which is to lead to the Museum. We immediately ran into numerous burials, house structures, etc." He concluded, "James [DeJarnette] is pouring the roof section over the clear story this week. Most of the interior tile work is finished, and they will be ready for the plaster job very shortly now." He expected the museum to be ready by the middle of May and wrote to Mallory on February 2, "We must not let anything interfere with Mr. Fechner's visit to the dedication of the museum. I am holding the meeting at such a time that he can be there" (Jones Papers).

On March 12, Mallory wrote to Dr. Jones, who was now commissioner of the Department of Conservation, that CCC Director Fechner was "sore as a pup over the neglect of the Georgia parks." Georgia had proposed two state parks in each of their 159 counties and would charge no admission. Dr. Jones responded to Mallory on March 14 with his thoughts on Alabama's state parks: "I am going to try to put our State Park system on a self-sustaining basis, after two years of public support. Parks like Little River will probably never support themselves, but we do have a half dozen that might support themselves." He also updated Mallory on the museum: "The museum will be ready for its dedication the latter part of May . . . the boys have done a whale of a job on the Museum" (Jones Papers).

The *Tuscaloosa News* reported on April 3, 1939, that the "Mound Pageant" was to be staged at Moundville on April 14, depicting the lives and customs of the mound builders. The article included an overview of the work at the park. The CCC had established a camp and "wonderful work has been done by the camp members, such as sodding the mounds to prevent erosion and restoring them in their former build, planting flowering shrubs in the ravines, building little rustic bridges which connect the spots of beauty, erecting tables and chairs for the many people which have picnics there, building a museum to house the relics and artifacts found in the mounds, and many other things worthy of praise."

On April 14, the *Tuscaloosa News* reported that the pageant was "based on the lives of the ancient mound-builders who lived in this town on the banks of the Warrior River hundreds of thousands of years ago—long before the advent of American Indians." It would be held on the Central Mound with 750 schoolchildren of Hale County appearing in the program.

Mrs. Pearl George of Akron, Alabama, participated in the pageant as a schoolgirl. The children "reenacted" the building of the mound, carrying small tin pails. She recalled that the pageant was performed for the CCC boys as well as the general public. She had met Dewey George at Camp SP-15 in late 1938 or early 1939. Dewey worked on construction of the park roads, restoration of two of the lakes, and maintenance of the mounds. He also worked on the excavations. Pearl and Dewey married four days after his discharge in 1940 (Pearl George interview, November 29, 2001; see the CD).

On May 9, the *Tuscaloosa News* announced that the dedication ceremony for the Museum at Mound Park would be on May 16. The museum had taken two years to build and cost $50,000. According to Dr. Jones, it was to house the materials from one of the five most important archaeological sites in the United States. The museum was to be "completely lighted by an indirect system and a ventilation system changes air every three minutes." The Moundville Museum was "a monument to the industry and the fine spirits of the CCC boys themselves."

According to "Tubby" Hall, work on the museum had fallen behind schedule, and as the opening was approaching all of the CCC boys worked on the museum, working nonstop for the last 36 hours or so. Mr. Hall also worked on the friezes, which were made in the basement of Smith Hall at the University of Alabama's Museum of Natural History. The friezes, with the trophy head and long bone motif, were made under the supervision of Dr. Jones (B. H. Hall interview, December 4, 2003; see the CD).

On May 16, the museum at Mound State Monument was dedicated and opened to the public. According to the ceremony program, Erskine Ramsey, chairman of the University of Alabama Board of Regents, presided, Moundville's Mayor Rochelle Phares gave the welcome, Robert Fechner presented the museum to Dr. Jones, and the University of Alabama band provided the music. The *Tuscaloosa News* reported the next day that 600 people attended. In presenting the keys of the museum to Dr. Jones, CCC Director Fechner said the object of the CCC was to "accomplish work of a constructive nature without competing with private industry." The work at Moundville was a perfect example.

Herbert Evison of the National Park Service described the museum in the May 1939 issue of *The Regional Review*: "Of monolithic reinforced concrete construction, the new museum, designed in the aid of interpretation of one of the most remarkable archaeological sites in America, backs upon and looks out from a group of ancient mounds." James DeJarnette described the skull and long bones decorating the museum. The ornamentation of the doors and frieze was accomplished with plaster waste molds constructed on the job. Twenty-nine molds and reverse molds were used to create the 58 sets of design in the frieze. Private construction experts had predicted that this could not be done. Evison concluded his article, "The archaeologists exploring the site 2,000 years from now are likely to find most of it [the museum] still here. It was built to last."

A Camp Inspection Report dated October 2, 1939, recorded 161 men under the command of Lt. William C. Hornsey, a civilian commander. The work project, under James DeJarnette, consisted of archaeological reconnaissance and investigations, with excavations being made around the mounds. Minor work was still being done on the museum. Cases were needed for artifact exhibits. Archaeological investigations were needed for park roads. Routine surveys, both linear and topographic, were needed in the park. Pine trees in the park with saw-fly larvae had to be eradicated. The mounds needed more erosion-control work, and the aboriginal lakes still needed to be restored and filled. New enrollees were receiving fire fighting and fire presuppression training. Other projects included construction of a water system, a drainage system, a caretaker's house, a comfort station, an administration building, barns, fences, fireplaces, and table and bench combinations, and moving and planting trees and shrubs.

CEA Mel H. Hassell reported that there were three traveling libraries with a total of 277 books, a reference library with 53 books, and a permanent library with 233 books. There were 200 "additional books" in camp. Six daily newspapers and 31 different monthly magazines were delivered to camp. Twenty enrollees had learned to read and write during the last year.

On October 12, 1939, Paul Wilkerson wrote to Dr. Jones from Washington, D.C., informing him that the Motion Picture Laboratory of the Interior Department had closed. In 1934, Director Fechner had agreed to pay for motion pictures out of CCC funds. The laboratory had closed in June 1939 when Fechner learned that non-CCC activities had been filmed. Wilkerson estimated that a million feet of film, including footage of Moundville, had been shot, but it was all in a jumble, and none of Fechner's aides dared mention the subject. Wilkerson wanted Dr. Jones to have at least the Moundville footage, if not all of the Alabama footage. On October 26, Dr. Jones forwarded the letter to James Mallory, and asked him if he could call the matter to Director Fechner's attention. The Moundville footage was titled "Temples of Peace." Mallory responded to Dr. Jones on November 5 that he did not want to write Fechner about the film at the present time (Jones Papers).

On January 1, 1940, the *Tuscaloosa News* had two articles on the death of Robert Fechner at age sixty-three of complications of heart and lung ailments. Fechner had been the honored guest at Mound Park the previous spring, and he had been "greatly interested in the work done by the Alabama Museum and the CCC camp in the development of the historic Mound Park."

On February 12, Charles H. Kenlan, now the assistant to Director James J. McEntee, wrote to Lt. Hornsey at Camp SP-15 after a tour through the South: "The project at Moundville is indeed interesting and I am sure will furnish present and future historians with additional facts. . . . I felt delighted to witness among the enrolled—and officered—personnel the high state of morale, good mess, and corresponding advantages, which reflect on proper administration."

Odis Tucker enrolled in the CCC at Demopolis in January 1940 but had to wait until his eighteenth birthday before joining Company 444 that March. When he arrived at Moundville, his first job was cutting the grass on the mounds with a sling blade. He later got a job working with the gravel operation in the park. Sand and gravel was taken from the river and sorted for construction projects; it was also trucked to other state park projects (Odis Tucker interview, November 20, 2001; see the CD).

Sydney Barringer of Coker, Alabama, also joined Company 444 in March 1940. His primary job at Moundville was running the boiler for the tar used on the roof of the museum. Every morning he would coat his face with Vaseline to keep it from blistering. Mr. Barringer recalled that enrollees rotated on kitchen duty. Towels were tied to the bunks of the enrollees picked for KP. They had to wake up at 5:30 in the morning, while the rest of the company woke at 6:00. Occasionally, the towels were moved to another bunk (Sydney Barringer interview, November 27, 2001; see the CD).

A Camp Inspection Report dated August 26, 1940, recorded 203 men under the command of Lt. William C. Hornsey. The work project under James DeJarnette was described as interesting and progressing more satisfactorily. Recreational activities consisted of baseball, softball, shooting pool, horseshoes, swimming, and trips to Tuscaloosa. CEA Hassell reported approximately 1,000 volumes in the traveling, permanent, and reference libraries. Another 20 enrollees had learned to read a newspaper and write during the last 12 months. Ninety percent of the enrollees were taking vocational and elementary school level courses.

William Bell of Ashland enrolled in the CCC in the summer of 1940 and was sent to Camp SP-15. He worked on the excavation of two lakes in the park. Once the lakes were dug to a certain depth, the ponds were fed with artesian wells. He also worked on the park roads, sloping the banks with a square shovel. Whenever an enrollee found a piece of pottery, bone, or other artifact, he would mark it with a survey pin. A team of four or five enrollees who had been specially trained in archaeology would excavate the artifact (William T. Bell interview, June 4, 2001; see the CD).

A Camp Inspection Report dated October 21, 1940, recorded 184 men under the command of Lt. Hornsey. The work project was described as very satisfactory. Special investigator Billups noted that the bathhouse, barracks, mess hall, kitchen, and quarters were all spotless "and cleaned to the last detail of sanitation." Company 444 had "a morale superior to other companies" with a remarkable record of discharges. The company mess was "superior in its preparation of food and its choice of foods." The education system was reported as "fine working."

On January 14, 1941, the *Tuscaloosa News* reported that a fire had destroyed the educational building in the Moundville camp. The fire, of undetermined origin, had started in the ceiling while class was in progress at 7:15 in the morning. The camp fire department had prevented it from spreading to other structures, and most of the equipment in the building was saved. There were another 20 buildings and approximately 150 enrollees in the camp at the time of the fire.

According to a Camp Inspection Report dated October 3, 1941, there were 170 men under the command of 1st Lt. Simon A. Stricklen. Forty-nine enrollees were in Mobile, constructing a recreation center for the army, and this detail was expected to complete their work by November 1. The work project at Moundville was under the supervision of Charles L. Beard, acting superintendent. Work was still needed in the restoration of the historic structures, construction of roads and fences, moving and planting trees and shrubs, seeding and sodding, construction of the administration building, and the archaeological investigations.

CEA Hassell reported that the educational and vocational classes continued. Five classes were offered in National Defense Training, including metal working, auto mechanics, simple electricity, carpentry, and typing. The State Board of Education financed four of the National Defense courses. Seventy-five enrollees were devoting 15 hours each week to these courses. Ten hours were given from their "free time," and five hours came from project work hours. Between February 3 and June 13, 1941, Company 444 had discharged 100 enrollees from the classes of simple electricity, auto mechanics, carpentry, and metal working to accept civilian employment or to work in the repair shops in the area.

An article from a local newspaper was attached to the inspection report, stating that the boys from the camp were attending local churches in a body and creating a closer cooperation between the camp and the town. There had been a "slight stand offish attitude towards the camp." "It was a touching sight—one whole side of the church filled with boys, clean and neat in their khaki. . . . Lt. Stricklen is to be congratulated in entering into the community life of this town by bringing his boys to our churches."

W. C. Stone, raised in Perry County, had joined Company 444 in the spring of 1939. When he first arrived at Moundville, he worked on a crew planting shrubs and trees in the park and maintaining the mounds. He also worked in the supply room and on KP. He made baker and then second cook, which also had the rank of an assistant leader, and then first cook, which earned him leader rank and $45 per month. He recalled that Moundville was a wonderful camp. The local people made the boys feel welcomed, and they visited the camp regularly. He also recalled that he was cutting meat, preparing breakfast on the morning of December 7, 1941, when he heard on the radio that Pearl Harbor had been attacked. The camp was closed soon after (W. C. Stone interview, December 14, 2001; see the CD).

According to the *CCC Camp Directory for Alabama*, Camp SP-15 was abandoned after the eighteenth period, which ended March 30, 1942.

Company 3486, Camp SP-16, Huntsville, Alabama

In April 1937, at the beginning of the ninth period, Camp TVA-P-13 was turned over to the Alabama State Parks. Lt. James A. Hamlin took over the command of Company 3486, and H. S. Hanover remained as the project superintendent (1936 CCC District D annual).

The camp newspaper, "Camp Clay Crier," changed to the "Camp Clay Broadcast." The August 7, 1937, issue recorded a number of improvements that had been made to the camp buildings, and a new oil house had been built and painted. The camp educational program under E. W. Greene had improved, seeing an increase in participation and a broadening of subjects. Company 3486 had received 36 new enrollees in July. They had "discontinued their education early in life," and the program wanted to "stimulate their interests" in education. The drama club continued to perform for the local radio station, WBHP, in Huntsville. The class presented a drama each Monday evening. Musical groups from camp performed, and Mr. Conover and staff members gave talks over the radio. The plays were sponsored by the WPA Recreation Project of Madison County under the supervision of Miss Nancy Pierce.

The October 15, 1937, issue of the "Camp Clay Broadcast" was dedicated to the new enrollees. The rookies were assured that their homesickness would soon fade. They were told that in addition to the $30 each month, there was a great sense of good will and accomplishment in working hard all day and coming home to a good shower and a decent bed. The rookies were also warned that they could expect to be asked to go to the supply room looking for sky hooks, striped paint, cement stretchers, bunk ladders, and meal tickets. They would be asked to watch the flagpole, go after company cows, and carry garbage a mile to the company hogs (all common pranks). They might not sleep very comfortably when their beds had been short-sheeted.

During September 1937, the educational program had reached 100 percent participation with every enrollee in at least one class. The National Park Service had cancelled the dramatics, as transportation could no longer be provided for Miss Pierce. Nearly every enrollee had expressed interest in woodworking and auto mechanics. A new course entitled "CCC Administration" was being offered, taught by the company commander. Teachers from local schools were giving lectures in the camp. Company 3486 was hoping to be the top basketball team in the district for 1937.

A Camp Inspection Report dated November 9, 1937, recorded 199 men from Alabama, Georgia, Florida, and Mississippi under the command of 1st Lt. James A. Hamlin. The work project under Mr. Conover consisted of the development of the 2,000-acre Monte Sano State Park, and road construction was the main project. Other work included the construction of two stone cabins, a stone and wood shelter, and a parking area, installation of a sewer system for the cabins and public lodge, and operation and maintenance of the park nursery. Another six months were estimated to be needed to complete the approved work projects.

Worley Jackson of Gadsden transferred to Company 3486 around April 1937 from Company 472 at DeSoto State Park. He worked in the rock quarry running a jackhammer while they were building the park roads. He recalled that the jackhammer had to be taken apart and cleaned each night. Mr. Jackson also drove the water truck that watered the road (Worley R. Jackson interview, February 27, 2002; see the CD).

The November 25, 1937, issue of the "Camp Clay Broadcast" was dedicated to Donald Taylor, an enrollee who had died in mid-October. The camp was preparing for Thanksgiving and printed the menu of roast turkey with all the trimmings. Ensign James U. Horn, U.S. Navy, had arrived in camp, assigned as the junior officer. His wife was going to teach English grammar and give instruction on the proper conduct of a gentleman. Great progress was being made on the Monte Sano Parkway, including surfacing and grading and sloping and planting the banks to prevent erosion. The rock crusher had been in almost constant operation, employing more enrollees than any other project. Two stone cabins were nearly completed as was the overlook and shelter at the picnic area. The transition from a TVA project to a state park project was over. Instructions were now coming from Montgomery rather than Knoxville. Company 3486 had been weakened by the desertions of the "new boys" from October, but the company was slowly building strength, receiving enrollees from other camps.

The December 16, 1937, issue of the "Camp Clay Broadcast" reported that bad weather had slowed the work project. Mr. Ford's work crew had finished the second building at the picnic area. Mr. Hathcote, junior foreman, had finished constructing a sled with a 150-foot runway for hauling rocks up steep inclines. A six-foot sled operated by a tractor ran up a four-foot-wide runway. The woodworking shop was busy with Christmas orders for furniture and improvements in the recreation hall. Items ordered by the camp and district personnel included cedar chests, candlesticks, a radio table, a dressing table, a swagger stick, and a walnut chest. The enrollees were certain to have spending money for Christmas.

The camp educational program had received national recognition. Ray Hoyt, the editor of "Happy Days," offered Company 3486 the opportunity to write a story of 1,500–2,000 words on the success of their education program. The manuscript would appear with photographs in an upcoming issue of the national CCC newspaper.

B. H. Nunnelley of Helena, Alabama, enrolled in the CCC on October 15, 1937. When he arrived at Camp SP-16, he worked on a crew that was sent throughout the park looking for large rocks to be used in construction projects. After two or three months of this work, he was promoted to assistant leader and made the assistant camp educational advisor. His responsibilities included keeping records for the CEA and starting the fires in the educational building for the morning classes. Classes were also held after supper. Mr. Nunnelley organized recreation trips on the weekends and helped organize the sports teams. After a year, he was promoted to leader and made the company clerk (B. H. Nunnelley interview, March 7, 2002; see the CD).

The January 25, 1938, issue of the "Camp Clay Broadcast" reported the educational program was receiving another building to be used for classes, making a total of one workshop, five 20-by-20-foot classrooms, a remodeled reading room, and two new libraries. Miss Nancy Pierce, the WPA instructor for dramatics, music, and public speaking, was returning to camp. For the last two months, classes had been held at her house, and the local radio station had continued to broadcast dramatic presentations.

Lt. John H. Metterich replaced Lt. Hamlin on January 10, 1938, as company commander. He addressed the company as "an old friend giving worthy council" and expected the men to be "gentlemen worthy of membership in this great organization." No man should "stoop so low as to drink intoxicating liquor, especially in camp." Lt. Metterich also stated that participation in the educational program was the duty of every man in the company.

On February 25, 1938, the "Camp Clay Broadcast" appeared for the first time in set type rather than typed and mimeographed. Ten local merchants advertised in the newspaper to offset the cost of printing. In spite of bad weather with snow and ice, the company trucks had never had a "wreck of any importance." The crews took pride in their work, and there was a healthy rivalry between them. Mr. Hathcote's crew was working on the parking area at the top of the Dummy Line, an abandoned railroad line. Two different types of stone cabins were being built under the supervision of Mr. Gunn and Leader Alexander. The largest crew was at the rock quarry under the supervision of Leader Grady Robinson. The rock crusher was working at maximum efficiency under the supervision of Mr. Faulkner. Mr. Ford's crew had done some beautiful work in the park, and Mr. Davis's crew was getting the roads in the park in excellent shape. Mr. Chamberlain's crew with Assistant Leader Franklin was sloping the banks of the roads and maintaining the nursery. Mr. Hampton and Mr. Sheckles were keeping the machine shop and blacksmith shop busy. The aging fleet of trucks were kept running. It was estimated that there was still two years' worth of work to be done in the park.

The 1938 District D annual recorded that Monte Sano State Park had registered 13,000 visitors from 25 states in two months during the summer of 1937. The Natural Well, 350 feet deep, was entered by stairs or an elevator. Work on the well, however, would have to wait until the completion of the park. Park plans called for 15 more cabins. A 75,000-gallon water tank, the superintendent's house, and a public lodge had been completed. Five miles of roads had been built in the park. A total of 9,000 feet of three-inch water line and 33,000 feet of sewer line had been laid.

The educational program had received "major consideration." Thirty-three classes were taught in camp by the foremen, technical staff, and WPA teachers. Evening classes were attended at the vocational school in Huntsville. The woodworking shop specialized in training the men to make cedar chests and other furniture. Records were kept on each enrollee, and an office in Huntsville was established to track job vacancies. This project was shared with the enrollees of Camp TVA-7 and had the cooperation of the businessmen and civic groups of Huntsville.

The April 20, 1938, issue of the camp newspaper, now called the "Monte Sano Broadcast," announced that Monte Sano State Park was to be dedicated in early summer, with Colonel Page S. Bunker, state director of parks, officiating. The new park entrance was to open soon. Road construction on the Dummy Line would be the official route to the park, connecting Pratt Avenue and eliminating the need to drive around the mountain past the camp. The road was one of the more difficult projects, requiring the dynamiting of the mountainside to create a roadbed. It would open to the public as soon as the dogwoods and redbuds were in full bloom. It would be "one of the most beautiful parts of the park and one of the most attractive drives in north Alabama."

A Camp Inspection Report dated September 14, 1938, recorded 192 men under the command of 1st Lt. Carl A. Clayatt. The work project under Mr. Conover included the construction and surfacing of roads in the 2,000-acre park, constructing a 75,000-gallon concrete water tank, installing water and sewer lines, building incinerators, and making furniture for the cabins.

For recreation, the enrollees played softball, touch football, and baseball in camp. Transportation was not available for recreation outside of camp. The recreation hall had two pool tables. Two motion pictures were shown each month, and the company held a dance each month.

A "Special Report on Agriculture" prepared by CEA Edgar W. Greene gave details on the agricultural projects in camp. Two mornings each week, an hour was dedicated to these projects. The four company leaders and Mr. Greene were instructing the courses, which were financed out of the company exchange. A poultry project was raising Rhode Island Reds and Plymouth Rocks. The company mess had purchased 1,236 chicks, planning to raise them to eating size. The project was $50 in the red and had suffered a 25 percent mortality rate, but there were 250 broilers at nearly two pounds each and ready to sell and another 495 chicks.

The garden project was two years old but in a poor area, with only a spring and summer garden producing. It had netted a profit of $105 in its two years. It was currently planted in winter vegetables and cover crops in the poorer sections. The swine project, the newest, was located some distance from the camp in a well-shaded and well-drained area. There were six hogs, two of them "thoroughbreds." The project planned to study the thoroughbreds and nonblooded pigs under the same conditions. A bee culture project was one of the most fascinating parts of the program, with more enrollees signed up than all of the others.

Company 3486 had a 60-by-20-foot woodworking shop. Photography and blueprint making were also taught in the building. Two groups of 20 enrollees were being trained, and the shop was opened at all times with an instructor present. In the last year, enrollees had made more than 500 articles, including cedar chests, upholstered divans, chests of drawers, radio tables, and lights of all kinds. The enrollees paid for the wood and then owned the finished item. The estimated cost of the items built during the last year was placed at $1,000.

According to a Camp Inspection Report dated October 12, 1939, there were 180 men under the command of 1st Lt. Leonard H. Lyons. Robert W. Challen had replaced Mr. Conover as the project superintendent. A list of approved projects recorded that the community center building, measuring 130 by 50 feet, was 15 percent completed. The new entrance road was 3,600 feet long and nearly 50 percent completed. The bridle path was three miles long, circling from the horse barn through the Big Sinks Valley and back to the barn. One mile of the trail was 12 feet wide and two miles were 6 feet wide. A parking area at the community center was completed except for a small amount of fine grading on the paths. The contact station was completed with the exception of some lettering on the portals. The banks along the William B. Bankhead Parkway were to be mulched with straw to prevent erosion. A topographic survey of the park had been approved. Construction of a 2,000-person amphitheatre was to begin immediately. The last approved project was the training of all enrollees over the age of eighteen years to fight forest fires.

For recreation, the enrollees could shoot pool and play ping-pong, checkers, dominoes, and cards in the recreation hall. There was also a radio. For outdoor recreation, there was equipment for boxing, softball, volleyball, and basketball. "Sound motion pictures" were played in camp twice each month. Trucks were available for recreational trips to town twice a week. There were approximately 400 books in the camp library; four daily newspapers were received and the "standard list" of magazines, and the camp had a subscription to "Happy Days," the national weekly CCC newspaper.

A Camp Inspection Report dated November 27, 1940, recorded 203 men under the command of 1st Lt. Joseph M. Davis. The work project, under the supervision of Mr. Challen, was progressing satisfactorily. The enrollees were taking trips to Huntsville weekly for "picture shows" and to see basketball games. The recreational opportunities in camp consisted of horseshoes, volleyball, tag football, checkers, and shooting pool. A motion picture was shown in camp weekly.

CEA Albert S. Johnson's educational report recorded that three courses had been added for beginners in arithmetic, reading, and writing. The camp library had 727 books in the traveling, reference, and two permanent libraries. Academic classes were offered in literacy instruction and at the elementary and high school levels. Vocational classes were offered at all levels. The classes were planned to meet the greatest need of the enrollees. The daily attendance for the educational program was 191 enrollees. The aim of the program was to remove illiteracy, to develop knowledge and skills necessary for national defense and in various trades and agricultural projects, and to develop a desire in each enrollee to be a "self-supporting substantial citizen."

According to the *CCC Camp Directory for Alabama*, Camp SP-16 was abandoned during the sixteenth period, which ended March 31, 1941.

Company 2420, Camp SP-17, Munford, Alabama

Company 2420, a company of World War I veterans, transferred from Camp SP-10 at Selma during the twelfth period to Camp SP 7 at Munford. On

April 6, 1939, the *Cleburne News* reported that a new camp was to be built near Cheaha Lake and would be occupied by the company of veterans presently occupying the camp near Munford. According to the *Historical Record of CCC Camp Buildings*, during May and June 1939, the structures from Camp F-7 at Chandler Springs were dismantled and transported to Camp SP-17 at Munford. Camp SP-17 was established on June 20, 1939.

A Camp Inspection Report dated September 15, 1939, recorded 186 men under the command of Edwin Phillips (civilian status). The work project, under the supervision of Oliver R. Head, was confined to the 2,500-acre Cheaha State Park. Included were general surveys of the park, construction of the main road and Using Road in the camp, a survey of the parkway connecting Cheaha State Park to the paved highway, one-half mile of telephone line connecting the camp to existing lines, fire presuppression in cooperation with the U.S. Forest Service, training of enrollees in fire tower observation and fire fighting, extension of the park road from Cheaha Tower to Bald Rock, work on the parkway between Cheaha Lake and Cheaha Tower, construction of truck trails and an entrance to Cabins #6 and #7, construction of the walkways around Cheaha Tower, development of the picnic grounds at Cheaha Lake bathhouse, development of a parking area at Cheaha Tower, construction of a combination building at Cheaha Tower, and several more projects connected to the water system in the park.

For recreation, the men were shown motion pictures in camp twice each month. Equipment was available for volleyball, basketball, and baseball, but there was no area in the camp cleared to play these games. The recreation hall was furnished with a pool table, a ping-pong table, dominoes, checkers, and playing cards. Trucks were provided for recreational trips four times each week. Camp SP-17 had no educational program. Courses were offered in citizenship, woodworking, and first aid, but there had been no educational advisor since July 17, 1939. A new CEA had reported on September 11 but had immediately gone on leave and was reassigned to another camp while away.

Special Investigator J. C. Reddoch noted in his inspection that 2,085 man-days had been lost from project work in the construction of the camp. Work was still needed to complete the clearing of the camp area and cleaning inside several of the buildings. In the library, books were still in crates. The company commander was experienced, but very poor progress had been made in the camp establishment. On October 9, 1939, Charles H. Kenlan, assistant director of the CCC, wrote to the adjutant general in Washington inquiring if the 2,085 man-days of enrollee labor in building Camp SP-17 were in accordance with regulations. The acting assistant adjutant general at the Fourth Corps Area Headquarters in Atlanta responded. After a study of the topography, quality of soil, and other factors of the camp site, the amount of enrollee labor was deemed reasonable. Further, the ratio of enrollee labor to skilled civilians employed in camp construction was in accordance with CCC regulations.

A Camp Inspection Report dated November 18, 1940, recorded 191 men under the command of Captain Marseille Boullemet. The work project, under O. R. Head, was progressing satisfactorily. For recreation, there were horseshoes, tossing a medicine ball, fishing, and indoor games available in the camp and the park. Recreation trips were taken to Munford and Talladega each week.

There was still no camp educational advisor. Under the leadership of Assistant CEA Harry H. Miller, courses were offered in reading, writing, and arithmetic at the elementary school level and arithmetic and English at the high school level. Vocational courses were offered in raising poultry and swine, auto mechanics, bee culture, CCC administration, mess management, woodworking, and carpentry. The daily attendance was 161 men. The camp officers and technical personal taught the courses four nights each week. There were 380 books in the library, and the camp received 9 newspapers.

On September 17, 1941, Project Superintendent O. R. Head submitted a work proposal for the construction of rangers' quarters. Up to this point, the park rangers had been living in the overnight cabins, but their own quarters would allow the overnight cabins to be used by the public. The project would require 3,000 man-days, cost an estimated $1,534, and be completed by April 1942. The project was approved on September 27.

Frank Boullemet of Oxford recalled his father's military career. Captain Marseille Boullemet had served as a flyer in the signal corps during World War I and had remained in the army. His service with the CCC began in 1933 as a motor transportation officer at Fort McClellan. He arrived at Camp SP-17 while the camp was still under construction. Among the many projects, the veterans also worked on restocking the deer population in the park and the Talladega National Forest. The deer were captured in North Carolina and then released. Company 2420 also planted Virginia pine trees in the park. This species was selected because it was able to survive wind. Many of the veterans were skilled in construction and were allowed to work in the areas in which they had expertise.

Most of the men in Company 2420 were in their late forties, from the northern counties of Alabama but also from Selma and Montgomery. They were all "down on their luck," primarily tenant farmers. Many of the men had been wounded during the war, and several veterans died in camp from conditions related to their war experiences. Most of the men had wives and families. Captain Boullemet had a very liberal policy of allowing the men to go to Munford on the weekends to visit their families. He realized that the veterans had to be handled differently from the junior enrollees. Extra housing was built in Munford for the families of the CCC enrollees. Most of the officers lived in Talladega (Frank A. Boullemet interview, May 10 and June 2, 2001; see the CD).

Mrs. Emma Jean McCain of Ashland recalled that her father, Grover Cleveland Johnson, came home each weekend. He said that the work in the CCC was the easiest he had ever done, although it did involve a lot of heavy lifting. He had respiratory problems upon returning from the war, and the family always thought he had been gassed during the war. He would wheeze loudly whenever he exerted himself. Mr. Johnson's enrollment in the CCC was due to expire on February 28, 1942, after serving a year. On his last day, he suffered a heart attack while working on Bald Rock Lodge. He was sent to the hospital at Fort McClellan, where he died on March 14, 1942 (Emma Jean McCain interview, June 6, 2001; see the CD).

A Camp Inspection Report dated October 15, 1941, recorded 147 men under Captain Boullemet. The work project, under the supervision of O. R. Head, was being performed efficiently and according to approved plans. Twelve miles of park roads had been graded and surfaced. The 18-room lodge, with baths, was 95 percent complete. Parking areas at the lodge and cabins were under construction. A septic tank with dosing chamber, distribution boxes, and disposal field was under way for the lodge. Power lines were being built over the park area. A 1,000-foot waterline was under construction between the pump house and the lodge. The new parkway from Cheaha State Park to Munford, 8.5 miles long, had been initiated. The grading and surfacing of the roadway to the cabins with crushed stone was 30 percent completed. Two recreational trips each week to Talladega were available for the men. A movie was shown twice monthly. Croquet and table tennis were available in camp.

The educational program was largely vocational, with some courses offered at lower school levels. The classes tended to be informal, with the instructor leading the group in discussions and demonstrations. Vocational courses were offered in woodworking, poultry and game management, bee culture, photography, and auto mechanics. Academic courses were offered in literacy training, remedial English, and history and current events. The daily attendance was 78 enrollees. The benefits of the program could be seen in the interest in the educational facilities in camp and in the general morale of the company.

On November 12, 1941, *Our Mountain Home* reported that the hotel at Cheaha State Park was expected to be completed in the spring, and it would add to the drawing power of the park throughout the Deep South. It was being built on a knoll on the Bald Rock Trail, just a little lower in elevation than Cheaha Tower, which was built on the highest point in the state. Mrs. P. J. Fitzgerald, wife of the park supervisor, stated that the veterans were busy on the interior of the structure. The exterior was completed except for extending the terrace in front of the building. It was being built out of native stone with a tile roof and paneled pine walls. The roof of the dining room was distinctive with tremendous beams and a huge rock chimney coming up from a large, rustic fireplace. The hotel was to have 14 rooms, a number of them with connecting baths. In general design, the hotel followed the design of the cabins. The residential portion of the hotel was of two-story construction, the rest one-story. Construction of the hotel began in the autumn of 1940.

The November 12 article also reported that ground had been broken for rangers' quarters, a large structure that would provide quarters for forest rangers assigned to the park. The paving of the parkway was also nearing completion.

According to the *CCC Camp Directory for Alabama*, Camp SP-17 was abandoned sometime during the eighteenth period, which ended March 31, 1942.

Company 2436, Camp SP-19, Fort Payne, Alabama

Company 2436 was a company of World War I veterans organized on June 22, 1935, in Jasper, Tennessee. After working on several TVA projects, they transferred to Camp SP-19 on September 10, 1941. According to a Camp Inspection Report dated October 27, 1941, there were 169 men under the command of 1st Lt. Claude G. Richey. The work project, under the supervision of George E. Cadman, was the continued development of DeSoto State Park. Their first project was the dismantling of Camp SP-5 while constructing their new camp. Using worn-out trucks and having delays in the arrival of building materials slowed the work. They had, however, completed the right-of-way for the parkway between DeSoto State Park and May's

Gulf and constructed a telephone line between their camp and the state park. Other projects included construction of a playground, an aviation field, cabin furniture, a road between the park and May's Gulf, the Straight Creek rock bridge, a road from Camp SP-19 to the main road, and foot bridges, and realigning and cherting the main park road and sodding the road banks,

Recreational activities consisted of weekly dances and "moving pictures." Outdoor recreational equipment was available for archery, badminton, softball, and horseshoes, and indoors there were checkers, cards, and a pool table. Trucks were available for recreational trips into Fort Payne. There was no educational advisor in camp. The officers conducted classes in reading and writing, arithmetic, poultry, first aid, and safety. The average daily attendance was 140 men. There were 362 volumes in the permanent library, and the camp received 3 newspapers.

Company 2436 was transferred to Camp SP-6 at Foley on January 19, 1942.

7
The CCC and State Forests, Private Forests, and Others

Although the State Commission of Forestry was established in 1907, little was accomplished owing to a lack of funding. The commission was revitalized in 1923 by the provision of legislative funding and the appointment of Colonel Page S. Bunker as state forester (Burleson 1975:29). On March 14, 1939, the Department of Conservation Act of 1939 created the Alabama Department of Conservation, eliminating several older boards and commissions. Dr. Walter B. Jones was appointed the first director (Burleson 1975: 40–41). The Alabama Commission of Forestry, and later the Division of Forestry under the Department of Conservation, used the CCC to assist in the statewide plan to protect Alabama's forested lands, both for state-owned and privately owned forests.

By 1943, Alabama had over 18 million acres of forested land. Over 9 million acres were under organized protection of the state Division of Forestry. The ultimate goal of this division was to place all state and privately owned acres under protection (Alabama Department of Conservation 1944:7–8). The State of Alabama was producing a tree crop estimated at $150 million annually. The people of Alabama were just beginning to understand the value of the tree crop to the state's industry and to realize the importance of the forests to the state's economic and social welfare. The major focus of the Division of Forestry was the protection of the forested lands from uncontrolled forest fires (Alabama Department of Conservation 1944:11).

State Forestry Projects

Company 468, Camp S-51, Oxford, Alabama

(See Camp SP-2)

Company 1485, Camp S-52, Chunchula, Alabama

Camp S-52 was located 20 miles north of Mobile, in the "center of a natural game and forestry region" (1936 CCC District G annual). Company 1485 was established at Fort Barrancas, Florida, and, after two weeks of conditioning, entrained for Rendell, Alabama, on June 14, 1933. The junior company was under the command of Captain E. G. Welch. For the first six months the enrollees were housed in a group of brick kilns. Four barracks were eventually built in camp with two large and four small houses. In January 1934, a washroom and bathhouse was built. Prior to this, the enrollees had bathed in a nearby creek. In February 1934, a combination mess hall and recreation hall was constructed. The educational program offered electrical engineering, surveying, and high school level courses. The company baseball team was successful in 1934. There was also a tennis court in camp and an excellent swimming hole near the camp (1934 CCC District G annual).

Company 1485 published the "Chunchula Siren" in 1935, then called their camp newspaper the "Siren" in late 1935 and 1936 (Center for Research Libraries, University of Chicago). The work project, under the supervision of C. F. Attaway, consisted of the construction of truck trails, firebreaks, and telephone lines and included fire hazard reduction and fire suppression and prevention. In April 1934, Captain Nicholas A. Athanason replaced Captain John Soule, who had replaced Captain Welch. Under Captain Athanason many improvements were made to the educational program, which had consisted of night school courses. On June 16, 1934, O.R. Cottle became the first camp educational advisor.

Company 1485 provided great service to the local community. Several automobile wrecks near the camp required attention from the camp's men trained in first aid. Enrollees also recovered a body from the river after rescue attempts by civilians failed. The first aid men gave artificial respiration for three hours until a physician arrived.

In January 1936, a side camp was established in Baldwin County near Bay Minette with 50 men working on a private forestry project at the recently abandoned Camp P-61. By the time of the writing of the 1936 annual, the detachment had completed its work and was preparing to return to Camp S-52 (1936 CCC District G annual).

According to the *CCC Camp Directory for Alabama*, Camp S-52 was abandoned after the twelfth period, which ended March 31, 1939. Company 1485 was transferred to Camp P-77 at Uriah, Alabama, on May 1, 1939 (NACCCA database).

Company 1483, Camp S-53, Florala, Alabama

On June 15, 1933, the *Florala News* announced that "Camp Covington" was to be established on the Opp Highway just past the Overhead Bridge. It would take several days to get the camp in "good habitable condition" for the 180 young men and officers who had arrived on the Crestview-Georgiana train with five passenger coaches and a luggage car. The fieldwork was to be conducted in a radius of several miles from camp.

On July 20, 1933, the *Florala News* explained the type of forestry work that could be conducted by the CCC on privately owned land. According to State Forester Page S. Bunker, the government was "prepared to do certain work on private lands to put them into condition for increased and continuous production of timber." Colonel Bunker had received many requests from landowners. The activities authorized included the construction of firebreaks, wood observation towers, truck trails, telephone lines, emergency fire control landing fields, and protective structures such as cabins and tool sheds. The CCC could also reduce fire hazards, control insect epidemics, fight forest fires, and control erosion and floods. Planting trees on private land was not authorized. Landowners were to maintain and continue the work started by the CCC crews.

A Camp Inspection Report dated September 21, 1933, recorded 188 junior enrollees from Alabama under the command of Lt. S. H. Morrow. Camp S-53 was located eight miles north of Florala. The work project, under M. G. Cleveland, consisted of cutting fire trails and building roads and bridges over 90,000 acres of private land. The camp was in good condition, with clean mess hall, kitchen, and tents.

The "Camp Covington News" appearing in the October 12, 1933, edition of the *Florala News* reported that Mrs. Parker had arranged a play entitled "Cicero Steps Out," which included the participation of many local ladies. A new company commander, Captain Ciani, had arrived in camp and was liked by everyone. The article concluded with the boys extending their appreciation to the people of Florala for their kindness.

On January 18, 1934, the *Florala News* reported that Camp Covington had become a beautiful little city and the public was invited to visit. The tent city had been transformed to a camp with wooden structures. Four barracks, each accommodating 50 men, officers' quarters, and foresters' quarters had been built. A water system had been installed with hot and cold water running into a shower house. Many other improvements had been made, adding to the comfort and welfare of the company. The work was done by civilian labor from Florala. Company strength was brought up to 200 men through the enrollment of local men from Andalusia and Florala. An educational program was being started with elementary and high school classes.

According to a Camp Inspection Report dated March 30, 1934, there were 191 men under the command of 2nd Lt. J. B. Moore. The work project under Mr. Cleveland consisted of the construction of truck trails, firebreaks, and telephone lines on 110,000 acres of private land and 10,000 acres of state land. "Winter construction" in camp had been completed on January 10, 1934. For recreation, there was equipment for baseball, volleyball, boxing, tennis, and horseshoes. The general condition of the enrollees was good, with only two serious accidents having occurred. The prevalent ailment was the common cold. The average weight gain for the enrollees was 16 pounds.

On April 12, 1934, the *Florala News* had an article titled "Company 1483 Ala. S-53 CCC Notes." Captain D. W. Phillips was the new company commander. He was married to the former Miss Beulah Dauphin from Florala. The baseball team was drawing interest, with games scheduled against teams from DeFuniak Springs and Florala. The ladies from Florala had performed another one-act play in camp.

On June 7, 1934, the *Florala News* carried an article entitled "CCC Camp News," written by enrollee Lewis B. Watson. Lt. Moore and his wife had chaperoned a fishing party at Camp Walton with 30 enrollees attending. The biweekly dance held the previous weekend had been attended by over 500 people with the Florala Orchestra providing the music. It was also reported that several enrollees had attended a dance at the Veterans' CCC camp at Hacoda (Camp SP-1). The veterans were welcomed at the next dance held at Camp S-53.

Enrollee Watson had also written the company history appearing in the 1934 annual. He recounted the arrival of the first 206 men on June 15, 1933: "For many weeks, during the rainy season, the boys slept in tents, and ate out in the open, their meals were cooked on an outdoor army field range." One of the first projects was to build a road to connect Camp S-53 with the veterans' camp at Hacoda. Water for the camp had been a problem. After three dry wells were drilled, water was hauled from the nearest town. Professor R. F. Scarborough's educational program offered classes from first grade through the first year of college.

The "CCC Camp News" appearing in the August 2, 1934, edition of the *Florala News* was written by Robert Rodgers. On July 29, Company 1483 had received 97 new enrollees from Birmingham. The new men showed promise in a baseball game against the "old members" and good speed through "the belt line," which was a good sign for the track team. (Hazing was against

CCC regulations.) Captain Phillips and CEA Scarborough explained the educational program to the new men.

Enrollee Lewis B. Watson wrote the "CCC Camp News" appearing in the August 30, 1934, edition of the *Florala News*. Lt. Baxley was being transferred to Fort Barrancas. Lt. Vinson was to take over the duties of medical officer at both Camp S-53 and SP-1 at Hacoda. Several of the boys were suffering from homesickness. A bus was chartered to Birmingham. The "sniffing of smoke and exhaust" was the remedy, and all but one enrollee returned to camp. This enrollee returned the following week when he got hungry. The American Legion Post at Opp loaned the camp materials to make a boxing ring. The boys were boxing each night to see who would go to Pensacola to represent the camp as for the best boxer in District G. Boxing matches, wrestling matches, and minstrel shows were held in camp to raise money for equipment for the company football team.

The "CCC Camp News" appearing in the September 13, 1934, edition of the *Florala News* reported that funds were still needed for the football team that had begun practicing. Rumors were flying "fast and furious" about the company being transferred to the "deep swamps of Mississippi." It was expected that the move would be after October 1. "Since the boys have cut down, knocked down, sawed down, sat down and worn off all the lightwood stumps in Covington County, they are wondering if they will have a similar detail in the mud bogs of Mississippi."

A Camp Inspection Report dated November 10, 1934, recorded 165 men from Alabama and Florida under the command of Captain Phillips. Twenty-five men were on an advanced detail to Meridian, Mississippi. The project work, under Mr. Cleveland, consisted of constructing truck trails, firebreaks, and telephone lines. Company 1483 would soon be moving to Camp SES-1 at Meridian.

On November 29, 1934, the *Florala News* reported that Camp S-53 had moved to Meridian, Mississippi, "lock, stock, and barrel." Whether the camp was to be reoccupied was not known. The move was presumed to have been ordered because the conservation work had been completed in the area. However, there were many other federal projects that could be done, making further use of the camp. The people of Florala regretted the camp leaving. The camp had added "considerable to the life and activity of this section."

Company 467, Camp S-56, Townley, Alabama

Company 467, consisting of junior enrollees from Alabama, was established at Fort McClellan in May 1933, with Captain Burns in command. "After a final physical examination, the boys took the oath of enrollment and were initiated into the Forest Army." After two weeks of conditioning, they were entrained for Townley, Alabama. The company, now under the command of Captain S. C. Harrison, cleared the campsite of weeds and brush and erected tents. The work project began in the middle of June. Under the supervision of George Drolet, it consisted of "building truck trails and fire lanes over the mountains and fighting fires." In October, C. D. Hardins took over as the project superintendent, and in November, Captain John H. Ratliff took command of the company. On May 17, 1934, Company 467 was transferred to Sumter County, Alabama, and established Camp P-73 (1934 CCC District D annual).

Company 487, Camps S-62 and P-62, Bessemer, Alabama

(See Camp SP-8)

Private Forestry Projects

Company 2403, Camp P-54, Brewton, Alabama

On June 9, 1933, the *Montgomery Advertiser* reported that a CCC camp was coming to Brewton. The work was to be confined to the construction of firebreaks, fire towers, telephone lines, and truck roads. It was reported on June 22 that the camp was to open soon, as work on the camp would be completed within the week. City water was to be connected to the camp, which was located on the west side of Burnt Corn Creek. The camp was to house 200 enrollees and officers, and the people of Brewton were making every effort to make the camp's sanitation and recreation facilities comfortable.

A Camp Inspection Report dated March 31, 1934, recorded 181 enrollees from Alabama under the command of Captain F. W. Konemann. The camp was established on June 28, 1934. The work project, under the supervision of Acting Superintendent E. J. Ford, was spread over 200,000 acres of privately owned land. For recreation, there was equipment for baseball, basketball, boxing, horseshoes, and volleyball. CEA E. R. Smith had not yet organized the educational program. The camp "winter construction" had been completed as of March 15. Local laborers had been paid 40 cents per hour.

Camp P-54 was located "among the pines on a small promontory of ground just off U.S. Highway 31, within a stone's throw of the City of Brewton." The work project of conservation and reforestation was supervised by 10 foresters, furnished and paid by the state Division of Forestry. All experienced woodsmen, each was in charge of a crew of 26 enrollees. CCC Leader Howard O. Yelverton, author of the company history for the 1934 annual, considered the camp educational program as "by far the most important and far-reaching feature of the CCC camps." The conduct and morale of the enrollees was above average. The men appeared to be "a happy, healthy and contented lot." There had been only one desertion since the opening of the camp. The success of the camp was due to the army and forestry personnel. The camp was fortunate in being located near Brewton, as the people of the community had shown friendliness (1934 CCC District G annual).

Camp P-54 was abandoned in July 1934. Eighty-nine enrollees were discharged and sent home on June 30. "Special Order No. 82" provided transportation home for the enrollees through the Quartermaster Corps. Jesse C. Wright, who had enrolled in the CCC at Fort Barrancas on May 25, 1933, was sent home to Evergreen. He was also given a letter of introduction from Captain Konemann, recommending his services and stating that Mr. Wright had been "prompt and willing to execute orders." He had worked on a reforestation crew (Gordon Wright interview, May 22, 2001; see the CD).

Owen H. Carroll of Brewton was also sent home by "Special Order No. 82." He had enrolled in the CCC on May 2, 1933, and transferred to Company 2403 from Company 1403. While at the camp at Brewton, he worked as the camp medic. When he returned home from Camp P-54, he immediately reenlisted for another six months in Company 468 at Cheaha State Park (Owen H. Carroll interview, June 2, 2001, and January 24, 2002; see the CD).

Company 479, Camp P-55, Vredenburgh

Company 479, one of the original companies formed at Fort McClellan in May 1933, was established on May 25. After being fed and clothed, about 100 men were led down the company street past tents with a plank marked with the company number. Another 100 men joined them the following day, and the company was placed under the command of Captain John A. Andrews. On June 24, they left for Vredenburgh, 200 miles away. They arrived at six o'clock the next morning and began erecting their tents in a heavy rain. On June 27, Forest Superintendent E. J. Finnell reported for duty. On June 30, work began on construction of a mess hall. After several weeks, baseball games, boxing, and track meets were organized for recreation. Trips were taken to Camden, the nearest town of any size, to see picture shows. On August 29, 1933, one of the first educational programs established began under U. H. Hassell (1934 CCC District G annual).

The 1934 annual recorded that O. B. Harkins had replaced Mr. Finnell as project superintendent. Company 479 was proud of its work "in the woods."

They were also proud of their camp: "It had its own laws, its own characteristics. We boast of all modern conveniences of a modest home. Hot water, electricity, radios, telephones, automobiles, stoves, heaters, a company canteen, hospital, welfare building, and many other things which go to make up a splendid community."

On December 4, 1934, Company 479 was transferred to Camp F-18 at Newton, Mississippi (1936 CCC District G annual).

Company 2423, Camp P-57, Glencoe, Alabama

On June 11, 1933, the *Gadsden Times* reported that representatives from the army and Alabama Polytechnic Institute at Auburn were looking for a suitable site for a CCC camp near Glencoe. The camp was to do erosion control and reforestation in Cherokee, Calhoun, St. Clair, DeKalb and Etowah counties. On July 6, it was reported that the camp would likely be manned by World War I veterans. Enrollment of approximately 600 former servicemen had begun to fill three camps in Alabama.

On July 23, 1933, the *Gadsden Times* reported, "Negro Veterans Train Near Glencoe for Soil Fight." During the past week, 150 veterans had established the camp and project work would begin soon. The veterans were from Alabama, Georgia, and Mississippi, with the largest portion from Birmingham. The company was under the command of Major (Sereno E.) Brett. The project work was supervised by J. H. Wilson of Auburn. Personnel from Alabama Polytechnic Institute, in cooperation with the U.S. Department of Agriculture and the Etowah County farm agent, provided technical supervision. The men were housed in tents, seven men to each tent. Each man was issued a mess kit and other necessary articles. The mess hall and kitchen were housed in a frame building. A separate building had been put up for officers. A supply house had been built. Water for the camp was provided by a 150-foot well. The entire grounds were clean and in excellent shape. The atmosphere in camp was one of a "big wholesome family." A baseball team had been organized to play against "several colored teams of the district."

Camp P-57, also designated as Camp PE-57, for "private erosion," was located at the Glencoe Rifle Range of the Alabama National Guard. The project work was soil conservation and building terraces and check dams out of native stone on the surrounding hills. The veterans were highly commended for their fine workmanship. They also fought forest fires (1937 CCC District C annual).

On September 11, 1933, the *Gadsden Times* reported that barracks had been built for 200 men along with a larger mess hall. A ten-truck garage was under construction, and a bathhouse was nearing completion. A 5,000-gallon water tank had been installed, providing water through pipes to the camp buildings. These improvements were indications that the camp would remain in operation for several years.

On November 12, the *Gadsden Times* reported that the work of the camp at Glencoe was furnishing a model for restoring soil fertility. Federal engineers in New Orleans had attempted to have the camp work changed, but Congressman Miles C. Allgood, who was in close touch with President Roosevelt's soil erosion plan, had blocked the move. Congressman Allgood was quoted as saying, "Alabama had 10,000 acres of land that has been damaged by erosion. That means one-third of the area of this state has been washed clean of its topsoil. The only way to restore the fertility of these semi-waste lands is being demonstrated by this government camp at Glencoe and it will remain as it is."

In March 1934, the people of Gadsden made an appeal to the CCC to keep the camp at Glencoe when they heard rumors of it being moved. The *Gadsden Times* reported on March 13 that the Chamber of Commerce wired Senators Hugo Black and John H. Bankhead and Congressman Allgood to stop the move. On the fourteenth, the paper reported that Congressman Allgood assured the chamber that the move was just a rumor. He had spoken to the Forest Service and the matter was settled. Wires had been received from Rotary, Kiwanas, Business and Professional Women's Club, Lions, Civitan, and the Women's Club of Gadsden supporting the CCC camp.

A Camp Inspection Report dated April 27, 1934, recorded 170 men from Alabama, Georgia, Mississippi, and Florida under the command of Lt. G. H. Toepfer, U.S. Navy. The work project, under Alex Taylor, consisted of soil erosion control on 5,000 acres of privately owned land by the construction of masonry check dams, control ditches, and tree plantings. Recreational equipment was available for baseball, horseshoes, volleyball, and boxing, but, although there were some classes offered in camp, there was no educational program. 1st Lt. J. E. Griffith, Medical Reserve, visited the camp three times each week. The physical condition of the World War I veterans was good. The most common illness was "chronic complaints." Special Investigator Neill McL. Coney Jr. noted that the relationship with the local citizens surrounding the camp was very satisfactory.

An incident with the caretaker of the rifle range, however, had compelled the men to write a letter to Director Fechner on May 14, 1934. They stated that after the caretaker's daughter perceived an insult from members of the company, her father came into camp, armed, and threatened the lives of the entire company. Lt. Toepfer, the company commander, had made no effort to protect the men. Special Investigator Coney reported on June 6, 1934, that the nineteen-year-old daughter had been driving cows from the pasture past the men, who were sitting in front of their barracks. The men testified that they were not aware of her, and, further, they did not know that she was a female, as she was dressed in overalls. Her father came into camp and threatened to "blow them to pieces if they insulted his daughter again." The caretaker had a chronic abdominal affliction and frequently held his hand to his abdomen. This gesture may have been interpreted as showing that he had a weapon concealed under his shirt. The investigation could not determine if the daughter had been insulted. It could not be proven that the caretaker had a weapon. Lt. Toepfer had been replaced by Captain Roger W. Autry, but eyewitnesses from the camp and technical staff stated that Lt. Toepfer had not refused to protect the men, nor had he permitted civilians to enter camp without authorization.

Coney concluded that the whole incident may have been a misunderstanding. In view of the conflicting stories, he was of the opinion that the original letter may have been part of "a systematic programme of Communistic propaganda" as "communistic agitation has been prominent among Alabama negros since the Scottsboro trial, and that Communistic broadsides have been found in circulation in Gadsden, Ala., which is some four miles from this camp."

Captain Autry, the new company commander, wrote to Coney on June 5, 1934, asking for a copy of the original letter. He wanted to determine the seriousness of the charges, to determine if a member of his company had insulted a white woman, and to "combat communistic activity."

On June 12, 1934, Assistant Director McEntee wrote to Special Investigator Coney acknowledging his June 6 report. McEntee was glad the complaint was unfounded, and the matter was closed as far as his office was concerned. However, he reminded Coney that it was the policy of the department that the interests of the government be protected at all times in the operations of the CCC camps and that individual enrollees also be protected and not subjected to injustice of any kind. While communistic activities needed to be checked in the camps, from the hundreds of reports McEntee had read, he was inclined to believe that there was "a disposition to accuse men, who have a complaint, of being communistic." McEntee had "no sympathy with that idea." The men in the camps had a right to have a grievance, either real or fancied, and a right to make a complaint without fear of reprisal. McEntee was aware that some communistic propaganda had been circulating in camps from a group from New York. He told Coney, "Drop me a report when you find actual evidence of this."

On June 17, 1934, the *Gadsden Times* reported that Company 2423 had been transferred to Corinth, Mississippi, and was to be replaced by Company 444.

Company 444, Camp P-57, Glencoe, Alabama

On June 14, 1934, Company 444 was transferred from Commerce, Georgia, to Glencoe. The work project, under the supervision of Alex Taylor, consisted of soil erosion prevention in the mountainous area (1934 CCC District D annual). On June 17, the *Gadsden Times* reported that the new Glencoe company was under the command of Captain William P. Brandon. The crew of engineers that had been in charge of the project work with Company 2423 had remained in camp. Company 444 would continue the work, which would take two months to complete.

On July 1, sixteen local boys joined the Georgia boys, bringing the company strength closer to the authorized 200 enrollees. A better educational program was being organized. Those who wanted to take advantage of the program would be more successful and find out what kind of work they were most suited for. The enrollees under the supervision of the civil and agricultural engineers were steadily improving the local farms, and even more improvements were expected, as there was an indefinite number of farms that could use terraces and check dams. As efficiency increased, more farmers were willing to trust the terracing of their land to the enrollees. Interest was increasing in the soil improvement measures (1934 CCC District D annual).

On September 16, 1934, the *Gadsden Times* reported that the Glencoe Camp was being transferred to Dadeville. It was not known if it would be replaced. The work on soil erosion was completed for the present, and the camp was moving to Tallapoosa County, where erosion prevention was badly needed. "While located here the camp has accomplished a great deal of valuable work in changing creek channels, doing private terracing and work to prevent the waste of soils, agricultural leaders declared." The camp had also provided a boost to the local economy by providing a market for several of the large warehouses that supplied food to the camp.

Company 1432, Camp P-58, Clayton, Alabama

Company 1432 was organized on May 29, 1933, with junior African-American enrollees at Fort Benning and Captain L. D. Tharp the commanding officer.

Initially, the company consisted of an administrative group and 72 enrollees. When the company strength reached 211 enrollees, they were moved to Clayton (1936 CCC District G annual). Camp P-58 was established on June 23, 1933 (NACCCA database).

The work project, conducted on land owned by A. B. Robertson, was originally supervised by George N. Mitcham and later by Thomas D. Alldredge. In July 1933, Captain Tharp was replaced by Captain A. D. Tisdale. Between 1934 and 1935, Company 1432 had four commanding officers: Lt. J. E. Rohrer, Captain William P. Brandon, Captain Fred M. Condo, and Captain Anthony F. Stecher. These officers were loved and respected by the men and gave their best to make the company better. In August 1935, Company 1432 was rated one of the two best in District H. On January 15, 1936, Company 1432 transferred to Camp SP-3 (1936 CCC District G annual).

Company 465, Camp P-59, Northport, Alabama

Company 465 was organized on May 23, 1933, at Fort McClellan with junior African-American enrollees under the command of Captain Hoyt. After three weeks of conditioning, they were moved to Northport. They slept the first night in a sage field wrapped in blankets under a large oak tree, which later would stand in the middle of the camp. The next morning, trees and bushes were cleared and tents erected. Log cabins were built for the officers and foresters, barracks for the enrollees; then work began on the main office, mess hall, doctor's office, recreation hall, and other camp buildings. The work project, under the supervision of George Drolet, consisted of building roads and truck trails. By the fall of 1933, the work focused on fighting forest fires (1934 CCC District D annual). Company 465 also maintained a side camp at Moundville.

CEA Professor C. B. Gamble organized an educational program that offered a wide variety of courses. Company 465 produced a biweekly newspaper called "Our Little World," written and typed by the enrollees and mimeographed by Professor Gamble at the University of Alabama. Recreational activities included swimming, boxing, wrestling, tennis, croquet, basketball, football, volleyball, and baseball. The camp also hosted dances and barbeques once a month (1934 CCC District D annual).

On February 14, 1934, the *Tuscaloosa News* reported a serious disturbance in camp. Two enrollees refused to work and attacked a foreman. When the fight was broken up by a forestry supervisor, the foreman and supervisor were threatened. "Unrest became general," and the enrollees decided to strike. Two foremen who refused to join the strike were threatened with lynching by the enrollees. The army officers contacted the sheriff's office to restore order. The *Gadsden Times* reported "order was restored by chasing the belligerent group into the woods."

The next day, the *Tuscaloosa News* reported that 150 enrollees were discharged from the camp, cutting company strength down to one-fourth of its authorized size. Of the 50 or so enrollees who fled into the woods, a number had straggled back to camp, and more were expected to return to face their discharge. The remaining members of the company resumed their project work.

On March 16, the paper reported that only 95 enrollees had been discharged for their part "in an insurrection." The article also announced that the camp was appealing to the residents of Tuscaloosa County for assistance in battling forest fires. They urged the people spotting forest fires to call the Chamber of Commerce, who would then forward the information to camp officials.

On March 26, the paper announced that the CCC camp at Northport had been "placed in telephonic contact with the outside world." People could now call the camp directly with news of forest fires by calling "County Line 3203" and reduce the response time. The enrollees of Camp P-59 had extinguished a large number of fires, saving thousands of dollars worth of timber.

On June 26, the paper reported that Captain Robert A. Lewis had arrived in camp to take command. Captain Lewis, from Birmingham, had served a year at a Forest Service CCC camp in northern Alabama. He replaced Captain R. A. Rooks, who had transferred to Savannah, Georgia.

The *Tuscaloosa News* reported on September 5 that word had been received that Camp P-59 was to be moved by October 1. Protests had been filed by the civic organizations in Tuscaloosa County to stall the move. The Chamber of Commerce filed a protest with officials in Washington, and the Rotary Club and City Commission adopted resolutions calling for the retention of the camp. The Tuscaloosa Board of Revenue was expected to join the appeal. Several individuals sent protests via airmail. Colonel Bunker, state forester, telegraphed Washington urging that the camp remain in Tuscaloosa County and even recommended a permanent camp.

In spite of the protests, Company 465 was transferred on November 13, 1934, to Camp SP-7 to work at Cheaha State Park On November 16, the *Tuscaloosa News* reported that in the nineteen and a half months that Company 465 had been at Camp P-59, they had constructed more than 40 miles of roads in Tuscaloosa County and had carried out a great deal of fire prevention work. It was recommended that the camp be reoccupied the following April as a park camp. A caretaker was placed in the camp to protect the permanent barracks that had been built there.

Company 2420, Camp P-60, Chatom, Alabama

Company 2420 was a veteran company organized at Fort McClellan. After a conditioning period, 143 men and three officers were sent by train to Chatom on July 18, 1933. Under the command of Captain R. B. Cole, they began building Camp P-60 one mile from Chatom on Highway 29 on approximately 40 acres. The work was divided into details, one group clearing the thick undergrowth as the other began construction on the mess and recreation halls. A well was drilled to 225 feet, and a reservoir constructed to hold 1,500 gallons. The well produced 15 gallons per minute.

By August 1933, the camp was completed and the work project began under E. M. Harkins, superintendent of the Forestry Department. Less than a year after the establishment of the camp, 60 miles of telephone lines had been erected, 50 miles of truck trails and 192 miles of firebreaks built, 387 miles of fire hazard reduction completed, and five bridges and two fire towers and dwellings for the watchmen constructed. It was hoped to have roads constructed to be able to get within a mile of any fire in the county. The men had equipment for baseball and other sports. Magazines and newspapers arrived daily for the recreation hall. An educational program was organized on May 1, 1934, and many classes were held each week in advanced studies. As a veteran company, Company 2420 had men from many walks of life, and there was no difficulty finding first-class cooks and other company personnel (1934 CCC District G annual).

By 1936, Company 2420 attempted to have all 600,000 acres of Washington County under its protection. Through April 5, 1936, only 11,250 acres had burned, representing less than 2 percent of the total area in their work project. Mr. Harkins was still the project superintendent, but the company had gone through 16 commanders since the establishment of the camp. By the time of the 1936 annual, Company 2420 had built three fire tower dwellings, two fire towers, 89 miles of telephone lines, 308 miles of firebreaks, and 229 miles of truck trails and had completed 339 miles of fire hazard reduction, spent 10,385 man-days at fire suppression and 2,960 man-days of tower duty, and gathered 1,365 bushels of pine cones for seed collection. When Washington County was hit with a worm screw plague, the enrollees built 500 fly traps and burned over 2,000 carcasses of cattle (1936 CCC District G annual).

According to the *CCC Camp Directory for Alabama*, Camp P-60 was abandoned sometime after the tenth period, which ended March 31, 1938.

Company 484, Camp P-61, Bay Minette, Alabama

The Onlooker, the weekly newspaper of Baldwin County, announced the news of a CCC camp at Bay Minette on June 8, 1933. It was one of the first eight approved for Alabama. On June 29, the paper reported that an entire company of 225 officers and men had established a CCC camp two miles south of Bay Minette. The men would be living in tents. The work project included all parts of Baldwin County.

Company 484 was organized at Fort McClellan during the first week of June 1933. After three weeks of conditioning and shots, enrollees boarded a train for Baldwin County. Arriving in a pouring rain, they were taken to a vacant field two and one-miles from town on Highway 31. The situation improved when the people of Bay Minette offered hot coffee. Through a rainy first month, the men built their camp. The walk to town was considered long, in spite of the picture show and pretty girls. "Notwithstanding this disadvantage, many of the boys may be seen on the highway every night" (1934 CCC District G annual).

On July 6, *The Onlooker* announced that the Bay Minette's Lion's Club was cooperating with Captain W. S. Paul, camp commander, in selecting a camp name. A committee had been selected to pick a name from those submitted by the citizens of the county. On August 17, 1933, the paper announced that the camp had been appropriately named "Camp Baldwin."

On August 18, Company 484 was awarded the title of the best camp in District G and the second best camp in the Fourth Corps Area. Lt. Dean Blanchard, U.S. Navy, took command after Captain Paul transferred. In May 1934, Captain Lytton C. Campbell of the Aviation Reserves relieved Lt. Blanchard. As soon as the camp was completed, the work project began under Project Superintendent F. P. Propst. Working in the woods was new to most of the enrollees, most of whom were from middle and northern Alabama counties. "But learning to handle axes, shovels, and saws; building towers, bridges, and truck trails, was strenuous and exciting work. In just a little while blistered hands and sore backs were a thing of the past." The company baseball team, playing local teams and other CCC teams, went undefeated. The basketball team, also undefeated, won the district championship (1934 CCC District G annual).

John H. Guinn was selected as an "extra" for the Marengo County quota in the summer of 1933. He was sent to the Federal Building in Mobile just in case one of the other boys did not pass. When he arrived at Camp P-61, he spent two weeks in conditioning, then worked on a crew cutting access roads for fire trucks. After a year, he began working with the civil engineer, operating the transit and laying out roads, and was promoted to assistant leader. During the fire season, Mr. Guinn patrolled all of Baldwin County. He also manned the towers, most of them 70-foot wooden towers, but there were also the taller steel towers. Mr. Guinn played on the company baseball team, which used a camp diamond built in a 40-acre pecan grove. Mr. Guinn recalled that there was some friction between the CCC enrollees and the young local men. The locals didn't like the idea of the young ladies being invited to social events at the camp. The local merchants seemed to like the business the camp brought, and the enrollees went into town for church services on Sundays (John H. Guinn interview, November 18, 2002; see the CD).

On October 24, 1934, *The Onlooker* reported that 45 observation towers had been built in Alabama on state and privately owned land. The state owned 13 steel towers, three towers of pole construction, and one stone tower. Private landowners, in cooperation with the State Commission of Forestry and federal agencies, had built five steel towers, 12 towers of sawed timber, and 11 towers of pole construction. Baldwin County had 15 towers. Several more towers were being considered.

According to the *CCC Camp Directory for Alabama*, Camp P-61 was abandoned during the sixth period, which ended March 31, 1936.

Company 1415, Camp P-63, Jackson, Alabama

Company 1415 was organized at Fort Benning, Georgia, on May 20, 1933, with junior African-American enrollees, mostly from Alabama. Captain Joseph T. Zak was the company commander. For most of June, they were held at the Logging Camp at Fort Benning. The company left Fort Benning on June 28 and arrived at Jackson, Alabama, the following day. They began erecting tents "in temporary places and manner" while the officers planned the layout of the camp. The next day, the enrollees began clearing ground for tents, company streets, and camp buildings. On June 5, another 28 men joined from Fort Benning, bringing the company strength to 206 men. W. P. Moon was the project superintendent. By September, "work in the forest was under rapid progress" (1934 CCC District D annual).

According to the 1936 annual, Company 1415 was originally scheduled to be stationed at Chatom, Alabama, but owing to numerous complaints by the citizens of Chatom, the company was temporarily stationed at the logging camp at Fort Benning. When the company arrived at Jackson, they were "given a cordial welcome by the citizens." Company 1415 was transferred to Camp F-13 at Morton, Mississippi, in late November 1934 (1936 CCC District G annual).

Company 467, Camp P-73, York, Alabama

Company 467 was another of the original companies formed at Fort McClellan in May 1933. After a year at Camp S-56 at Townley, they were transferred to Camp P-73 in Sumter County. Because there was an inadequate water supply, the camp was moved to the "beautiful little city of York" on June 8, 1934. Captain W. G. Campbell assumed command as the camp was nearing completion (1934 CCC District D annual).

On May 30, the *Tuscaloosa News* reported that Congressman William B. Oliver had cut through the red tape to have the CCC enrollees from Camp P-73 assist in cleanup efforts after a tornado. At the time, CCC regulations did not permit this kind of work. The 1936 District D annual stated that the assistance with the cleanup "earned the highest commendation of the city officials, and the lasting friendship of the citizens." The people of York accepted the CCC camp.

On December 12, 1935, the *Tuscaloosa News* reported that Colonel E. F. Allison, the South's foremost conservationist, had hosted a deer hunt on his 120,000-acre holdings of the Allison Lumber Company for the 200 CCC enrollees of Camp P-73. The enrollees had been working on his land. After the deer hunt, there was a barbeque dinner, and Colonel Allison spoke on the subjects of conservation and hunter safety.

The work project, under the supervision of E. J. Finnell, consisted of fire prevention on 400,000 acres of privately owned land in Choctaw and Sumter counties. The project included the land owned by the Allison Lumber Company, which was "noted as one of the most efficiently handled private land projects in the country." Company 467 had constructed 40 miles of truck trails, 40 creosote-piling bridges, and a steel fire tower to add to the existing towers. They also connected the towers with 25 miles of telephone line. Nearly 7,000 man-days had been spent working at the Alabama State Forestry Nursery. Only 1,337 man-days had been spent fighting forest fires, which was indicative of the effectiveness of their fire control work (1936 CCC District D annual).

During 1937, Company 467 had constructed a 120-foot steel fire tower, built a 120-foot steel fire tower, created a six-acre lake to irrigate the state nursery, and produced and packed 2,500,000 seedlings at the nursery. Com pany 467 constructed two water supply systems with reservoirs to assist in fire fighting and started four five-acre stand improvement demonstration plots. They mapped 288,404 acres of land, showing timber quality, as well as houses, fences, roads, churches, and streams. They collected 18 bushels of conifer and one ton of hardwood seeds. Their fire control work increased the awareness of the people in that part of Alabama of the importance of protecting their natural resources. In the education program, under CEA Rush B. Johnson, 40 men who had come into camp unable to read or write had been taught to do both, 28 had learned to cook, and 12 had become qualified lifesavers. Another 12 men had been trained as heavy machine operators (1938 CCC District D annual).

According to the *CCC Camp Directory for Alabama*, Camp P-73 was abandoned after the eleventh period, which ended September 30, 1938.

Company 4434, Camp P-75, Chapman, Alabama

Company 4434 was a junior African-American company formed at Chapman on June 19, 1935, with army personnel and 25 enrollees from Florida. Captain Harry Austin was company commander. D. E. Hampe was the project supervisor with seven forestry foremen on his staff. On July 15, another 175 enrollees from Montgomery joined the company. On July 18, work began on construction of the camp, which was located in "the middle of a dense pine forest" and hardly considered inviting. By mid-August the camp was completed, and the company turned over to the Using Service for project work. Company 4434 built truck trails, bridges, lookout towers, and other forest protection projects. The educational program, under CEA Earl Smith, had 100 percent participation. Enrollees who came to camp unable to read their names were enrolled in reading and writing classes. The carpentry class built chairs, desks, cabinets, and other furniture (1936 CCC District G annual).

A Camp Inspection Report dated January 5, 1936, recorded 212 men from Alabama, Florida, Georgia, and North Carolina under the command of Captain Harry Austin. The work project, under Mr. Hampe, was scattered over an area of 1,157 square miles and consisted of the construction of roads, bridges, lookout towers, cabins, latrines, fences, and telephone lines. Other projects included seed collection, road maintenance, and fire hazard reduction. Recreational equipment was available for baseball, basketball, boxing, and horseshoes. There were also four sets of checkers and four "decks" of dominoes. The recreation hall was poorly equipped, with only a few tables, two stoves, and several steel chairs. The company radio was kept at the Post Exchange.

CEA Earl Smith was receiving excellent cooperation from the army officers and forestry personnel. Classes were offered in writing, arithmetic, geography, carpentry, blacksmithing, auto mechanics, engineering, first aid, glee club, hygiene, forestry, and (sports) coaching. Additional "on-the-job" training was giving in cooking, engineering, machine operation, bridge and road construction, and tractor driving. The outstanding achievement for December 1935 was by the men in the writing class, who were given Christmas cards to write home to their parents. For 25 of 26 enrollees, it was the first time they had written home.

According to a Camp Inspection Report dated November 30, 1936, there were 160 men from Alabama under the command of Captain T. W. Rogers. The work project, supervised by J. J. Patton, consisted of the construction of truck trails, fire towers, and telephone lines. The camp education program was now under CEA A. T. Wilson. Nearly all of the enrollees were participating in the program, and 95 percent were taking job training. During 1936 and 1937 the journalism class produced a camp newspaper called "Two Spots" (Center for Research Libraries, University of Chicago).

A Camp Inspection Report dated December 6, 1937, recorded 192 men from Alabama, Florida, and North Carolina under the command of Captain Rogers. The work project, under Acting Superintendent J. Fred Pomeroy Jr. covered an area of 1,090 square miles in Butler, Lowndes and Conecuh counties. Company 4434 had sent a detachment to a side camp at Brewton (former Camp P-54), where they were building truck trails, a fire tower, telephone lines, a combination garage/tool storage building, and an office building and doing general cleanup of Camp P-54 (that had been abandoned in the fall of 1934).

According to a Camp Inspection Report dated October 3, 1938, there were 202 men under the command of 1st Lt. George C. Ray. The work project, under Acting Project Superintendent Robert M. Wedgeworth, was over 690,000 acres (1,078 square miles), with approximately half of the area the property of the W. T. Smith Lumber Company. The work consisted of construction of truck trails, telephone lines, and lookout towers. CEA Alpheus T. Wilson had added vocational classes in landscaping, mechanics, heavy equipment, mess management, office methods, painting, timber construction, and typing. The illiterates in the company were learning to read and write. All of the carpenters had acquired their knowledge through vocational classes. Tractor operators, tower and bridge construction crews, and the company blacksmith had all been taught their trade through the program. One enrollee was "absent without permission" to attend the University of Chicago on a scholarship.

A Camp Inspection Report dated September 22, 1939, recorded 195 men under the command of John D. Ficklen, a civilian. Fifty-one men were erecting a new camp at Brewton, which consisted of building a bathhouse, oil house, grease rack, combination building, and blacksmith shop and was expected to be completed in ten days. The work project, under E. J. Finnell, was nearing completion, and the company was expected to be transferred by October 1. The project had covered 690,000 acres in Butler, Conecuh, Monroe, Escambia, Lowndes, and Crenshaw counties. CEA Wilson's educational program had expanded again, offering academic courses for the illiterate and at the elementary and high school levels. Vocational courses were offered in agriculture, auto mechanics, beekeeping, carpentry, electricity, forestry, furniture making, office management, poultry and swine care, and truck driving. There were 1,001 books in the camp library, and the camp received four newspapers. Courses were taught four nights and five days each week, and attendance was 100 percent.

Special Investigator J. C. Reddoch noted that the camp was below average. The barracks, recreation hall, and supply hall were in poor condition. Bedbugs, a common nuisance in the camps, were noted in the barracks. The company commander was indifferent to the regulations. Laundry records were falsified, and no records were being kept for the supply room. The deficiencies were forwarded to the War Department on October 25, 1939. On December 13, the acting assistant adjutant general wrote the Fourth Corps Area commanding officer assuring him that the deficiencies had been corrected. However, by this time, Company 4434 had been moved.

According to the *CCC Camp Directory for Alabama*, Camp P-75 was abandoned on December 1, 1939, and Company 4434 was transferred to Camp P-78 at Brewton on December 3 (NACCCA database).

Company 4435, Camp P-76, Vredenburgh, Alabama

Company 4435, a junior African-American company organized on July 20, 1935, established Camp SCS-4 at Troy and Brundidge (1936 CCC District G annual). It transferred to Camp P-76 on September 20, 1938 (NACCCA database). The camp was located eight miles west of town, in northern Monroe County. The work project was private forestry projects, likely in Monroe and Wilcox counties. According to the *CCC Camp Directory for Alabama*,

Camp P-76 was approved for the nineteenth period, the final period for the CCC, which ended June 30, 1942.

Company 1485, Camp P-77, Uriah, Alabama

Company 1485 transferred to Uriah on May 1, 1939, establishing Camp P-77 at the old Camp SP-3. The project work was private forestry. Bruce Mantel of Brewton, Alabama, enrolled in the CCC on May 26, 1941, between his junior and senior years of high school and spent six weeks or so at Camp P-77. He worked on soil erosion projects on private land (Bruce Mantel interview, November 18, 2003; see the CD). James Mills of Brewton enrolled in the CCC in June with his younger brother, "looking for adventure," and spent a month or so in Camp P-77. He began working on a road surveying crew. He was promoted to leader and ran the company canteen in camp for a short time, but he found running the canteen too confining and returned to the surveying crew (James Mills interview, October 28, 2003; see the CD).

Company 1485 was disbanded in July 1941. On July 11, Company 3477 transferred to Camp P-77 from Camp F-12 at Piedmont.

Company 3477, Camp P-77, Uriah, Alabama

Company 3477, a junior African-American company, transferred to Camp P-77 on July 11, 1941. They worked on private forestry projects for four months. On November 16, 1941, they transferred to Camp SCS-14 at Dothan (NACCCA database).

Company 4434, Camp P-78, Brewton, Alabama

Company 4434, a junior African-American company, transferred to Camp P-78 from Camp P-75 at Chapman on December 3, 1939. The *CCC Camp Directory for Alabama* noted that Camp P-78 was a new camp rather than the reestablishment of Camp P-54 at Brewton. The work project was private forestry in Escambia County.

According to a Camp Inspection Report dated August 16, 1940, there were 202 men under the command of John D. Ficklen. The project work, under Edward J. Finnell, was progressing satisfactorily and was beneficial to the enrollees. Recreational activities consisted of volleyball and baseball, and a horseshoe court was under construction. Boxing gloves had been purchased, and there were ping-pong and pool tables in the recreation hall along with checkers and card tables. The camp was only a mile from Brewton, and the enrollees could walk to town where they had the use of a recreation center.

The educational program, under CEA Alpheus T. Wilson, offered courses Monday through Thursday in the mornings and evenings. The program had taught about 45 enrollees to read and write during the last fiscal year, and many enrollees had become interested in a vocation. Two enrollees had been trained as radio operators, ten as carpenters. Several had returned home to help their families raise their standard of living.

A Camp Inspection Report dated September 20, 1940, recorded 200 men under the command of John D. Ficklen. The work project continued satisfactorily under Mr. Finnell. Recreational activities consisted of baseball, softball, bowling, boxing, shooting pool, and horseshoes. Mr. Wilson's educational program offered courses at the literacy level and at elementary and high school levels. Vocational courses were offered in agriculture, poultry raising, auto mechanics, bees, carpentry, cooking, furniture making, radio operation, swine care, tractor operation, truck driving, photography, and office management. There were 1,011 books in the 20-by-30-foot camp library. Two newspapers and the "authorized list of magazines" were received. CEA Wilson wrote, "Illiterates are being improved academically, and a large number of enrollees are becoming interested in various vocations as a means of making a living. We are trying to develop good citizens, who are more efficient academically and vocationally."

According to the *CCC Camp Directory for Alabama*, Camp P-78 was an approved camp for the eighteenth period, which ended March 31, 1942.

Company 1490, Camp P-79, Robertsdale, Alabama

On March 7, 1940, *The Onlooker* announced that another CCC camp was being considered for reforestation and fire protection in Baldwin County. To protect the forested lands, the county had been divided into four districts, and "Forest Riders" patrolled the forests, protecting several thousand acres. Additional fire towers were being considered. Landowners were charged six cents per acre for this protection.

The Onlooker reported on March 14 that Congressman George Grant had sent word from Washington that the CCC camp was approved. Construction of barracks for 200 men would begin at once. Robertsdale Mayor Amos Garrett said the CCC camp "would be received with elation by the business men and other persons in the city." On May 2, *The Onlooker* reported that the mess hall and barracks were completed. The camp was located in the "Elsanor section" of Robertsdale (about five miles east of town on Highway 90). *The Onlooker* reported on July 11 that the newly constructed camp would receive its enrollees on July 15. The roads in camp would have to be repaired by either the CCC boys or the county before project work could begin.

The Onlooker reported on April 3, 1941, that Camp P-79 was planning a celebration for the eighth anniversary of the CCC on April 6 with an open house. Camp Commander Captain Moxley L. Beck and Project Superintendent William Lee invited the public to visit the camp, see the project work, and the work accomplished by the national defense classes. The day would include speeches by prominent citizens, a horseshoe pitching tournament, and a softball game against the local Robertsdale team.

On May 15, *The Onlooker* reported that another open house had been held on May 13. With 80 percent of the company from Mobile County, a large crowd of "Mobile Folks" attended. Captain Beck had stated that many educators had been present to look at the work of the national defense classes.

According to the *CCC Camp Directory for Alabama*, Camp P-79 was shown as an approved camp for the eighteenth period, which ended March 31, 1942.

Company 5488, Camp P-80, Dadeville, Alabama

Company 5488 established Camp P-80 at Dadeville on July 6, 1940 (NACCCA database). The *CCC Camp Directory for Alabama* noted that Camp P-80 was established at the old Camp SCS-2. The junior enrollees worked on a reforestation and fire protection project on private land in Tallapoosa County. Camp P-80 was abandoned after the seventeenth period, which ended September 30, 1941.

Company 3490, Camp P-81, Bessemer, Alabama

Company 3490 established Camp P-81 on August 8, 1940. A Camp Inspection Report dated August 27, 1940, recorded 200 men under the command of John C. McCrary. The junior company had moved from Houston, Mississippi, and 90 percent of the enrollees were from Mississippi. At the time of the inspection, 50 men were working on the construction of the camp. The project work, under James D. Huckaby, was progressing satisfactorily for a new camp. Equipment was available for baseball, softball, volleyball, table tennis, horseshoes, and swimming. Recreational trips were taken to Bessemer and Birmingham.

The educational program, under CEA Albert E. Hughes, offered classes at the literacy level and elementary and high school levels. Vocational courses were offered in bee culture, poultry raising, swine production, gardening, carpentry, radio, bookkeeping, auto mechanics, cooking and baking, professional training, teacher training, foreman training, and leader training. The camp had traveling, permanent, and reference libraries. Ninety-five percent of the enrollees were taking academic courses, and all of the men were enrolled in vocational courses, except for those in the literacy level courses.

A Camp Inspection Report dated September 22, 1941, recorded 190 men under the command of John C. McCrary. The work project under Mr. Huckaby was being performed efficiently. Recreational activities consisted of motion pictures shown in camp each week and trips taken to Bessemer. Educational classes were offered four nights each week. With no educational advisor in camp, the classes were taught by four WPA teachers, administrative personnel, technical personnel, and the enrollees.

A follow-up report dated November 24 reported the company strength down to 121 men, with eight enrollees leaving the company each week to receive outside employment and desertions averaging three a week. In spite of this, the camp and project work were considered to be "making the progress we would desire." The educational advisor reported more work was being accomplished by the national defense classes than ever before.

A Camp Inspection Report dated April 10, 1942, recorded that Company 3490 had only 86 men. The project work, under the supervision of James E. Davis, was contained in an area within a 25-mile radius. Construction of a dwelling, garage, office, oil house, and explosives magazine were all completed. Five lookout towers were completed, another was under construction, and four more towers were to be built. Forty-seven miles of telephone line were completed and another 37 miles under construction. Eight miles of truck trails were completed, three miles under construction, and another 30 miles proposed. During the last quarter year, 426 man-days had been spent in fire protection work. The educational program was stressing national defense, first aid, the elimination of illiteracy, and food production. Enrollees were getting jobs through their national defense training, and the illiterates were learning to read and write. Health and safety was being taught, as well as citizenship and patriotism.

According to the *CCC Camp Directory for Alabama*, Camp P-81 was abandoned sometime after the eighteenth period, which ended March 31, 1942.

Fort McClellan, District D Headquarters, Overhead and Supply

Fort McClellan in Anniston, Alabama, was the headquarters for District D of the Fourth Corps Area. Both military and civilian personnel worked there in the administration of the CCC. The departments included administration, quartermaster receiving and shipping, and the District D surgeon's staff

(1934 CCC District D annual). There was also a motor transportation and finance section (1938 CCC District D annual). Other personnel included district chaplains, district inspectors, and the district educational advisor.

In addition to the overhead personnel, there was also a supply company stationed at Fort McClellan. Thirty men were selected for their "fitness for the duties of headquarters" from the first group of enrollees assembled for conditioning in May 1933. On July 12, the supply company moved to tents erected near the station hospital. The enrollees were from Alabama, Mississippi, Louisiana, and Texas. Their company strength was increased to 85 men as more duties were shifted from army to CCC personnel (1934 CCC District D annual). By 1936, company strength had increased to 185 men, which allowed for more rated men. The supply company contained both junior and veteran enrollees from Alabama, Georgia, Florida, Mississippi, Tennessee, and Louisiana. Their baseball team won the 1935 District D Championship. In September 1935, a recreation hall, a reading room, and canteen were added to their camp area (1936 CCC District D annual).

Fort McClellan contained nearly 20,000 acres of land on the military reservation. In addition to the district overhead and supply personnel, there were also CCC companies stationed at the fort conducting reforestation and fire protection projects.

Company 475, Camp Army-1 and Army-2, Fort McClellan

Company 475 was a junior African-American company organized on May 21, 1933, at Fort McClellan under the command of Captain G. H. Cushman. Captain Cushman was relieved by Captain E. G. Cowan on June 20, who was in turn relieved by Lt. Horace Speed Jr. The camp "was surrounded by mountains and nothing prevails but an atmosphere of health and contentment." All 220 men were enrolled in the educational program, receiving vocational training. The main concern of the educational program was to eradicate illiteracy but also to promote citizenship, vocational training, and health and hygiene. Recreational activities included swimming, boxing, and indoor baseball. The company basketball team won 75 out of 77 games (1934 CCC District D annual).

A Camp Inspection Report dated April 30, 1934, recorded 220 men under Lt. Speed. The work project, under his supervision, consisted of road construction and maintenance, the reduction of fire hazards, and timber thinning on the 19,500-acre military reservation. Recreational equipment was available for baseball, basketball, volleyball, football, boxing, horseshoes, croquet, cards, dominoes, and checkers. CEA R.C.M. Flynnt's educational program offered courses in literacy instruction, citizenship, and hygiene. The physical condition of the men was very good, with measles and mumps the most common illnesses. The average weight gain among enrollees was 20 pounds.

A Camp Inspection Report dated February 27, 1935, recorded 218 men from Alabama and Mississippi under the command of 1st Lt. V. D. Whatley. Reforestation, landscaping, and the construction of a landing field had been added to the work project, which was supervised by Lt. Whatley. The educational program, under CEA R. L. Hood, had expanded to include classes in reading, writing, spelling, geography, masonry, carpentry, leather working, current events, citizenship, safety, first aid, and agriculture. Only 58 percent of the men were enrolled in the educational program.

According to a Camp Inspection Report dated December 7, 1935, there were 207 men from Alabama, Florida, Mississippi, and Kentucky under the command of Captain F. A. Ingram. The work project, under the supervision of A. J. Freeborg, consisted of road construction and maintenance, timber stand improvement, soil erosion work, construction of check dams, and the salvaging of timber cut from the roads under construction. Outdoor recreational equipment was available for baseball, basketball, football, tennis, volleyball, croquet, and horseshoes. Indoor equipment consisted of indoor baseball, dominoes, three sets of boxing gloves, four sets of checkers and boards, and two "Monday Morning" football games.

The *CCC Camp Directory for Alabama* recorded that Company 475 shifted to the Camp Army-2 project on February 3, 1936. Camp Army-2 was established on August 24, 1935. The initial company at Camp Army-2 was not recorded. Captain F. H. Ingram, Project Supervisor Arthur J. Freeborg, and CEA Robert L. Hood remained with Company 475 when it took over the Camp Army-2 project work. According to the 1936 District D annual, Company 475 was called out to fight numerous forest fires on the reservation, often all night long, and after a few hours of sleep, the men returned to either project work or to the fire. Between May 1935 and the writing of the 1936 annual, Company 475 had constructed 10 miles of forest roads and trails, and built a firebreak around the perimeter of the reservation (1936 CCC District D annual).

According to the *CCC Camp Directory for Alabama*, Camp Army-2 was disbanded after the tenth period, which ended March 31, 1938.

Company 4407, Camp Army-1, Fort McClellan, Alabama

Camp Army-1 was briefly reopened on October 25, 1937, after having been unoccupied for nearly two years, by Company 4470, a junior African-American company. A Camp Inspection Report dated November 3, 1937, recorded 216 men under the command of Captain Eldon A. Pruett. The work project, supervised by the technical personnel from Company 475 at Camp Army-2, consisted of clearing a range for target practice and infantry maneuvers on the military reservation, and some landscaping. There were four to six months of work to be done.

Company 4407 had been moved twice during October 1937. On October 11, it was moved from Haughton to Calhoun, Louisiana, then again on the twenty-fifth because of opposition by the local citizens who did not want an African-American company in their town. According to the district commander, Company 4407 was to be moved from Fort McClellan in the near future, as many of the enrollees wanted to return to Louisiana.

The Biological Survey and the Fish and Wildlife Service

The Bureau of Biological Survey was established in 1905 in the Department of Agriculture to manage the nation's wildlife refuges, enforce wildlife laws, and conserve the dwindling populations of migratory birds. It was moved into the Department of Interior along with the Bureau of Fisheries in 1939, and the two agencies were combined in 1940 to create the Fish and Wildlife Service (http://www.fws.gov.who 12/7/02).

The CCC worked on two main types of projects for the Fish and Wildlife Service: improvement of wildlife habitat and construction of administrative facilities. The CCC constructed 44 of the more than 200 wildlife refuges in the country. "The enrollees constructed dams, dikes, and other water impoundments, planted cover vegetation and millions of trees for windbreaks, stabilized stream banks, erected many fire lookout towers, and fences, installed telephone lines, and built fire breaks" (Cohen 1980:93).

The Wheeler Wildlife Refuge, located on the outskirts of Decatur, Alabama, was created in 1938 as an experimental home for waterfowl along the Tennessee River where wild geese and ducks winter (http://www.decaturcvb.org/Pages/Press/refuge.html 12/7/02). The refuge was created along the edge of the Wheeler Reservoir that had been created by the Wheeler Dam built by the TVA in 1936.

A quarterly "Narrative Report" for February–April 1939 submitted to the Department of Interior stated that the work at the refuge consisted of marking the boundary, which WPA crews were working on. The rest of the project work was pending a final agreement between the Bureau of Biological Survey and the TVA. The WPA crews would continue to work on the boundaries. A CCC camp was to be established in October. It was advised to have the WPA work continue so the CCC crew could concentrate on constructing their camp headquarters.

On March 31, 1939, the Bureau of Biological Survey was granted a CCC camp at Hartselle, formerly Camp TVA-9, which had been abandoned in 1935. The project would take a company of 200 men two and one-half years to complete. It included the construction of the headquarters site, refuge boundary posting and fencing, improving truck trails, clearing and marking stream channels for patrol and navigation, and development of recreational areas including camping and picnic grounds, fishing and boating camps, landing docks, planting water and upland species of cover plants, fire protection, construction of wood duck boxes, various mapping projects, fire suppression, and soil erosion control.

According to a "Narrative Report" for May–July 1939, during June the army began making improvements to the buildings of old Camp TVA-9 in preparation to the arrival of the CCC company in October. The buildings were rewired, reroofed, and painted. A new barracks was built and several buildings enlarged. Three garages and a service building were planned for the Biological Survey's equipment.

On September 19, 1939, the Bureau of Biological Survey and the TVA agreed to allow the bureau to manage 18,000 acres of upland to be reserved for wildlife management and another 4,200 acres for agriculture. A "Narrative Report" for August–October 1939 stated that this agreement gave the Biological Survey the refuge area on the Wheeler Reservoir for the work planned for the CCC and the WPA.

Company 3403, Camp BS-1 and Camp FWS-1, Hartselle, Alabama

A "Narrative Report" for August–October 1939 recorded that Company 3403 arrived at Camp BS-1 on October 3, 1939, from Washington, North Carolina, with 99 enrollees. Another 115 new enrollees arrived in camp on October 18. The *Decatur Daily* reported on October 19, 1939, that the Hartselle CCC camp had reopened with 99 men from North Carolina and another 100 from Wilson Dam. Fifteen more men were expected by the end of the week. The narrative report recorded that the supervisory personnel included T. E. Kimbrough as project superintendent and Captain Henry B. Watson as commanding officer. During October 1939, the army personnel were busy preparing the camp buildings for winter. The enrollees worked on projects in the camp, including constructing a 600-foot entrance road and landscaping the camp. The work project was waiting for the arrival of nine new trucks, as there were only four stake trucks available, and more were needed to carry the men to the work areas.

According to a "Narrative Report" for November 1939–January 1940, the CCC enrollees and WPA workers had begun to "place this new and underdeveloped area in position to benefit migratory waterfowl and other wildlife." The CCC project had been handicapped by a lack of approved projects and plans, and the work had been mostly confined to construction of a truck trail. The weather during November and December had been too "unsettled for field work." Several new buildings had been erected in camp, along with new roads, and landscaping had been added. To fence in the CCC camp area, 500 posts had been acquired from the TVA. Cooperative forest and wildlife plans were completed, proposing to plant 500,000 trees and shrubs in the refuge. Other work included the construction of 1,000 check dams, 10 miles of truck trail clearing, and another 10 of grading and ditching, and the construction of a heeling seedling bed with a capacity of 500,000 seedlings.

Approximately 500,000 trees were planted on the refuge during the next three months by the CCC enrollees from the camps at Hartselle, Athens, and Huntsville. The "Narrative Report" for February–April 1940 recorded that rain had made the roads almost impassable, and the planting was further slowed by the lack of proper equipment and experience. The enrollees from Camp BS-1 also began planting seeds of aquatic plants. The foundations for the headquarters buildings were staked out. Several temporary bridges were built to give cooperative farmers access to waterfowl planting areas. The fencing project was still a concern: "Tenant farmers of the poorest class" lived around the refuge, and they had neither the financial means nor the inclination to fence their pastures. The livestock, especially hogs, were damaging the refuge. Fencing in the sensitive areas appeared to be the answer. It had been hoped the CCC enrollees and WPA employees could fence the more important sections, but the bureau was looking for the TVA to fence in the Indian Creek area in exchange for CCC man-days.

A narrative report for May–April 1940 recorded that the CCC projects were taking shape. The CCC crews and the cooperating farmers had utilized the sunny days to complete their planting. The enrollees also continued to work on the south side truck trail, with another 4 miles cleared and 12 miles graded. Two quarry sites had been located for a portable rock crusher to provide surfacing material. The excavation for the basement of the headquarters building was finished. The foundation was completed and framing had begun on the service building. Edwin Green, a CCC biologist assigned to the project, was conducting studies with Dr. Pinfound and Mr. Hall of the TVA on methods of controlling obnoxious weeds. Photographs in the report showed the CCC enrollees building wood duck boxes and receiving fire fighting training.

During August and through October 1940, clear, warm weather allowed the CCC crews, cooperative farmers, and refuge personnel to accomplish a great deal of work. A CCC fire patrol, using a refuge truck, regularly patrolled the refuge on weekends. Fire protection on the Wheeler Reservoir was conducted in cooperation with the TVA, and a new fire plan was being drafted between the TVA and the newly formed Fish and Wildlife Service. The wood duck boxes, built by the CCC enrollees, were erected throughout the refuge.

The enrollees from Camp FWS-1 (now the Fish and Wildlife Service) continued to work on the south side truck trail, improving it with crushed rock. Work on the administrative buildings, water supply, and sewerage system was progressing. The enrollees had collected 50 pounds of square-stem rush seed from a private pond near Somerville, Alabama. The seeds were to be planted on the refuge during the fall. Work project plans had been submitted on September 25 for soil conservation work on the Wheeler Refuge. The Fish and Wildlife Service and the TVA had made plans for building water control structures on the refuge for the reduction of malaria hazards and the improvement of waterfowl habitats. The work, to be done by either CCC or WPA labor, had to be approved by the TVA to ensure that the structures did not interfere with the production of hydroelectric power.

According to the Wheeler Wildlife Refuge's 1940 annual report, CCC enrollees had completed the preliminary work at the headquarters site, including the partial completion of the power line, pump house, and foundation excavations of the manager's residence and service building. They had built 10 miles of graded truck trail, cleared another 16 miles of road, and constructed two bridges. They had constructed 1,000 check dams for erosion control, planted 500,000 trees and shrubs at the refuge, and planted 140 experimental food plots for aquatic waterfowl. Six temporary patrol bridges had been built and 32 acres of habitat improvement had been completed in quail demonstration areas. Biologists Atkeson and Steenis had provided the technical supervision for the wildlife projects, including forestry, food and cover, aquatic plantings, soil erosion control, and habitat improvement. Biologist John H. Steenis had arrived at the refuge on April 15, 1940. He had conducted a cooperative study with the TVA and other agencies on the relationship between certain aquatic plants and mosquito larvae. Edwin Green, camp biologist at the Hartselle CCC camp, was experimenting with various techniques in controlling the overgrowth of lotus.

According to the "Narrative Report" for November 1940–January 1941, work was progressing slowly on the headquarters site. The well house and water system and 70 percent of the sewer system were completed. It was expected that the refuge headquarters would be finished and ready for occupancy by May 1941. Thirty to 50 enrollees, two foremen, and three to five skilled employees were working on the project. Progress continued on the south side truck trail. The enrollees were making good progress in the construction of the concrete culverts that were to replace wooden culverts. Six corrals had been built and were showing the local farmers that trespassing livestock would not be tolerated on the refuge. The corrals were having "a decided influence in reducing the amount of stock trespassing." The majority of the local farmers appreciated the efforts to reduce trespassing livestock.

A "Narrative Report" for February–April 1942 recorded that the refuge biologists had been transferred or assigned to other projects. Refuge biologist Atkeson was mostly working at Noxubee, Mississippi. There was no supervision for the CCC and WPA biological projects. However, the weather had been mild so no time had been lost. The enrollees of Camp FWS-1 had nearly completed construction on the equipment building. Work was being finished on the office-museum-laboratory building, the service building, and the manager's residence. Grading and landscaping were completed at the headquarters site, and numerous concrete culverts had been installed on the truck trails. Building materials had been gathered for the construction of the secondary headquarters at Triana, Alabama. Since the start of the project, 700,000 trees and shrubs of various species had been planted on the refuge by the Hartselle camp and other CCC camps. The enrollees had dug 50 pounds of kudzu crowns, which were sent to Noxubee, Mississippi, to be planted. Photographs in the report showed enrollees shelling corn to be sent to the Mattamusket Refuge on the North Carolina coast and examining the remaining cornstalks for food for waterfowl.

The "Narrative Report" for May–July 1941 recorded that with Mr. Atkeson detailed to Noxubee, very little biological work was being done by the CCC enrollees. Good weather allowed uninterrupted work on the refuge headquarters and associated buildings. At the Triana secondary headquarters, work had begun on the service building, cistern, and residence excavations. Fieldwork included gathering seeds, constructing the truck trail, and planting experimental plots and waterfowl food plots. Overall, the CCC activities had been greatly slowed by the lack of enrollees and proper supervision. Additional refuge personnel were to be assigned to assist in the supervision of the CCC fieldwork. It was hoped that company strength would remain at the full quota.

According to the "Narrative Report" for August–October 1941, Mr. Steenis had returned to the refuge and was continuing his research on waterfowl and food plot improvements. He supervised a CCC crew in the collection, drying, cleaning, and planting of *Echinochloa crusgalli* and *Polygonum pennsylvania* seed. Rootstocks of *Eleocharis quadrangulata* and *Scirpus* were also collected and planted. Most of the CCC work during the last three months had been confined to the construction of the bathhouse, the fill across Yellow Gal Slough, collecting and planting seed, and finishing the headquarters buildings. The Hartselle CCC camp had established a side camp at Athens, where they were working at the Elk River Fish Hatchery. It was anticipated that once the CCC enrollees finished the roadside signs and entrance gate, public visitation to the refuge would increase. Local fishermen were already aware of the excellent fishing, and most were strong supporters of the wildlife program.

The annual "Narrative Report" for 1941 reported that the Hartselle CCC camp, Alabama FWS-1, had completed a successful year. The enrollees had completed construction of the manager's residence, service building, office-museum-laboratory building, and equipment building. The entrance gateway and fence, the pasture, and the boathouse were nearly completed by the end of June. Work had begun on the garage–service building, the cistern, and the patrolman's residence at Triana. Road improvements with concrete culverts and wooden bridges were made. Between January 15 and March 15, another 619,440 trees and shrubs had been planted on the refuge by the Hartselle and other TVA CCC camps.

According to the "Narrative Report" for November 1941–January 1942, excellent weather had allowed the work crews to progress uninterrupted. The CCC enrollees continued their construction at the headquarters at Flint Creek Island and the secondary headquarters at Triana. Work had begun on a waterfowl display pool and the patrolman's residence during the three-month period. The enrollees had planted 40,000 trees on the refuge and assisted in the shelling and sacking of corn. Tree seeds were collected. Hardwood seeds sent to the Wilson Dam nursery included 120 pounds of pecans, 200 of walnuts, 240 of tupelo, 65 of hickory, and 5 of red cedar.

The "Narrative Report" for February–April 1942 recorded that the CCC work had been confined to the completion of the secondary headquarters at Triana, the patrolman's residence at the headquarters, and the ponds at the Elk River Fish Hatchery. It was unlikely that the enrollees would complete the work at Triana, as word had been received that the camp was to be disbanded by the end of May 1942. It was hoped the refuge would complete the projects. During the three-month period, the WPA had planted trees and shrubs at the headquarters site. The WPA had been approved to complete the CCC work. Efforts had been made to have the CCC enrollees work on a malaria-control project on a dike adjacent to Decatur as a national defense project, but it would have to be finished with other labor. The CCC enrollees were also to erect a fire tower at Turkey Mountain before the 1943 fire season. The WPA project had been suspended on April 12, 1942, as all local labor was needed at the Huntsville Arsenal. With the loss of the CCC camp and the WPA labor, the fire protection work would have to be done by regular refuge staff.

A "Narrative Report" for May–August 1942 recorded that the CCC work was terminated on June 30, 1942. The headquarters was not finished, but it was in "good operating condition." Refuge staff was finishing the patrolman's residence, the waterfowl display pool, and the roads, courts, walks, and miscellaneous landscaping and grading. The patrolmen were occupying their residences but were also doing the final work on the buildings. It was expected that the work on the buildings would be finished by October 1, and the patrolmen would return to protect the refuge.

According to a "Narrative Report" for January–April 1943, refuge personnel were completing the unfinished CCC and WPA projects.

8
Summary: A Great and Lasting Good Accomplished by the CCC

The Civilian Conservation Corps touched many aspects of the natural resources in the State of Alabama, helping establish state parks, national forests, state and private forests, and checking erosion across the state. Between 1933 and 1942, an average of 30 camps operated in Alabama, with the major work carried out in forest and soil resources (Cohen 1980:147).

According to Perry H. Merrill's *Roosevelt's Forest Army*, based on numbers from 1937, the CCC had given employment to 66,837 men, which included 61,411 junior and veteran enrollees and 5,396 non-enrolled personnel of camp officers and supervisory workers. The total allotment to dependents by the enrollees was over $16 million. The total obligation in Alabama was over $55 million. Merrill also noted that a 50-man side camp from Camp P-70 (a camp for which I could not find any information) was assigned to a state nursery at Autaugaville. Work consisted of constructing four tree cone sheds, an equipment building, underground mains for a sprinkler system, a 200,000-gallon reservoir with an overhead sprinkler system, a five-room office building, and a five-room dwelling. Enrollees erected a fence around the nursery and constructed a system of gravel roads throughout (Merrill 1981:108).

The best summary of the work of the CCC in Alabama was found in the *Moulton Advertiser* of July 16, 1942, printed two weeks after the program had officially ended. The article was titled "A Great and Lasting Good Accomplished by the CCC."

> When the Civilian Conservation Corps closed its books on June 30, it had completed 9-1/4 years of service in conserving the natural and human resources of America. During that period, CCC camps under the jurisdiction of the U.S. Forest Service and State Forester advanced the cause of forest conservation in Alabama by at least a generation, both in the na-

tional forests and on state and privately owned lands. A total of 2,400,000 man-days of work were about equally divided between the national forests and state and private lands.

Highlights of the work accomplished in Alabama included the following items.

The CCC boys, as part of the job of improving the physical facilities of the forests, built 1,800 miles of roads and 490 bridges. They erected 188 buildings for the protection and administration of forest lands including some for public recreation areas. They built 1,430 miles of telephone lines.

Roads and telephone lines are extremely important in controlling forest fires. Other fire protection projects included 61 lookout towers and over 2,200 miles of firebreaks. Fire hazards were reduced along 12,000 miles of road. General fire prevention work occupied 51,000 man-days and fighting fires an additional 33,700 man-days.

Owing to the CCC's improvements in fire protection, it has been possible for the State Division of Forestry to improve fire control on thousands of acres of private timberland where fire protective facilities had been inadequately equipped and organized. On January 1, 1942, over 9,500,000 acres of state and private forest lands in Alabama were under protection.

For sowing in the forest tree nurseries, the CCC in Alabama gathered over 285,000 bushels of pine cones and 62,000 pounds of hardwood seeds. In the Alabama national forests, nearly 20,000 denuded acres were planted to provide future forests. Timber stand improvement work was done on some 114,000 acres, and the inventory of forest resources included estimating timber on over 296,000 acres. Many recreational areas were developed and hunting and fishing greatly improved.

Perhaps the greatest benefit rendered by the CCC in Alabama has been to the boys, largely recruited within the state, who lived and worked in the camps. They learned useful trades and habits of industry and self-reliance and developed strong and healthy bodies. Army officers found ex-CCC boys who entered the armed forces to be in much better than average physical trim, and, as a result of their CCC training in first aid and in such specialized skills as truck and tractor driving and telephone maintenance, able in a short time to handle the mechanized equipment of modern warfare.

When the Alabama CCC boys went home, they would be more useful citizens of their communities. They would be enthusiastic conservationists and could be counted on, through the years to come, to actively aid in protecting and wisely using their state's natural resources.

Of course, because the *Moulton Advertiser*'s article was published only eight months after the attack on Pearl Harbor and nearly three years before the end of World War II, the public could only guess at the contribution that the Civilian Conservation Corps made to the preparation of the young men who would fight the war. Most of the former CCC enrollees I have met and interviewed since 2001 play down their role in the war, although they all agree the time spent in the CCC was the best training they could have had. While proud of their military service, most would rather talk about their time in the CCC and their peacetime contributions to Alabama's resources. That is their legacy, their "great and lasting good."

Appendix A. CCC Camps in Alabama

United States Forest Service

F-1	Moulton	Company 463	May 19, 1933
F-2	Danville	Company 464	May 26, 1933
F-2	Danville	Company 3475	May 1, 1935
F-3	Haleyville	Company 1403	May 28, 1933
F-4	Moulton	Company 258, 463	October 29, 1933
F-5	Double Springs	Company 3476	April 16, 1935
F-6	Heflin	Company 3477-C	July 17, 1935
F-7	Talladega	Company 3478-C	July 17, 1935
F-9	Andalusia	Company 3474-C	February 4, 1936
F-10	Munford	Company 3478-C	June 22, 1939
F-11	Moulton	Company 3476	October 2, 1939
F-12	Piedmont	Company 3477-C	October 1, 1939

Soil Conservation Service

SES/SCS-1[a]	Gainesville	Company 476	May 19, 1934
SES / SCS-2	Dadeville	Company 1405	May 25, 1934
SES / SCS-3	Camp Hill	Company 444	October 18, 1934
SCS-4	Brundidge / Troy	Company 4435-C	August 16, 1935 June 22, 1938
SCS-5	Carrollton	Company 3479	August 26, 1935
SCS-6	Greensboro	Company 3480-C	August 2, 1935
SCS-7	Clanton	Company 3481	September 6, 1935
SCS-8	Alexandria	Company 3482-C	July 19, 1935
SCS-9	Auburn	Company 4447	August 6, 1935
SCS-10	Greenville	Company 4436	August 12, 1935

SCS-11	Linden	Company 4437	August 14, 1935
		Company 2451-V-C	October 3, 1937
(P-58)	Clayton	Company 1432-C	July 1933
SCS-12			April 1935
SCS-13	Ashland	Company 4488	August 23, 1935
SCS-14	Dothan	Company 4447	October 1, 1939
		Company 3477-C	November 16, 1941
SCS-15	Cullman	Company 4472	September 20, 1939
SCS-16	Monroeville	Company 3480-C	October 8, 1939
SCS-17	Hamilton	Company 1405	October 2, 1939
SCS-18	Eutaw	Company 2541-V-C	June 3, 1940
SCS-19	Talladega	Company 3479	June 3, 1940
SCS-20	Evergreen	Company 4436	June 1, 1940
		Company 4434-C	January 16, 1942
SCS-21	Roanoke	Company 4488	April 1, 1940
		Company 3480-C	November 3, 1941
ASCS-1[b]	Dothan		March 1942

a. The Soil Erosion Service (SES) was created on August 25, 1933, in the Department of Interior. It was transferred to the Department of Agriculture on April 27, 1935, creating the Soil Conservation Service (SCS).

b. In March 1942, Camp SCS-14 was closed. Camp ASCS-1 was opened for the 19th Enrollment Period, listed as a National Defense SCS Camp at Napier Field, Dothan, Alabama.

Tennessee Valley Authority

Initial TVA Camps TVA 1–TVA-5	Nitrate Plant No. 2 Sheffield, AL	Companies 251, 283, 285, 286, 2426-V	October 14, 1933
TVA-2,	Nitrate Plant No. 2	Company 285	October 23, 1933
TVA-13	Wilson Dam	Company 5403	Aug. 1935–Jan. 1936
		Company 4499	August 3, 1935
TVA-3	Nitrate Plant 1 & 2	Company 2426-V	October 13, 1933
TVA-P-5	Joe Wheeler Dam		February 7, 1934
TVA-P-3	Wilson Dam		January 11, 1936
TVA-P-4	Nitrate Plant No. 2	Company 251	October 20, 1933
TVA-P-5	Nitrate Plant No. 2	Company 283	October 20, 1933

TVA-6	Athens	Company 286	May 25, 1934
		Company 5401	August 3, 1935
TVA-7	Huntsville	Company 3483	August 21, 1935
		Company 2449-V	September 30, 1938
TVA-8	Guntersville	Company 5432	October 1, 1939
TVA-9 (BS-1)[a]	Hartselle	Company 3403	1935, 1939 – 1942
TVA-10	Scottsboro	Company 5432	August 28, 1935
TVA-11	Moulton	Company 3487	August 3, 1935
TVA-11	Moulton	Company 2449-V	October 10, 1937
TVA-12	Russellville	Company 3488	August 8, 1935
TVA-P-12	Huntsville	Company 5402	August 19, 1935
TVA-P-13[b]	Huntsville	Company 3486	June 19, 1935
TVA-14	Stevenson	Company 5432	August 15, 1940

a. Camp TVA-9 at Hartselle was established in 1935 for 5th Period, reestablished for 14th Period, and switched to Camp BS-1, Biological Survey. Camp BS-1 was switched to FWS-1, Fish and Wildlife Service, for 16th Period.

b. Camp TVA-P-13 at Huntsville switched to SP-16 in 1937 (Monte Sano SP). TVA-2, Company 4499, was switched to TVA-13 at Wilson Dam.

State Parks

SP-1	Hacoda	Company 2421-V	July 18, 1933
SP-2	Oxford	Company 468	April 15, 1934
SP-3	Uriah	Company 230	October 20, 1933
SP-3	Uriah	Company 1432-C	January 15, 1936
SP-4	Weogufka	Company 260	October 20, 1933
SP-4	Weogufka	Company 4498	August 10, 1935
SP-5	Fort Payne	Company 472	November 16, 1933
SP-6	Foley	Company 259	June 3, 1934
SP-6	Foley	Company 1425	July 26, 1935
SP-6	Foley	Company 2436-V	January 19, 1942
SP-7	Munford	Company 465-C	November 13, 1934
SP-7	Munford	Company 468	July 7, 1936
SP-8	Bessemer	Company 487	October 5, 1934
SP-10	Selma	Company 444	October 24, 1934
SP-10	Selma	Company 2420-V	June 2, 1938
SP-11	Citronelle	Company 230	June 17, 1935
SP-11	Citronelle	Company 5412	August 1935

SP-11	Citronelle	Company 4457-C	August 8, 1939
SP-12	Auburn	Company 4448	August 22, 1935
SP-13	Gordon	Company 4449	August 15, 1935
SP-14	Linden	Company 2445-V-C	August 1, 1935
SP-15	Moundville	Company 444	June 1, 1938
SP-16[a]	Huntsville	Company 3486	March 1937
SP-17	Munford	Company 2420-V	June 20, 1939
SP-19	Fort Payne	Company 2436-V	Sept. 10, 1941

a. Previously TVA-P-13, which began on August 5, 1935.

Private Forest Projects

P-54	Brewton	Company 2403	June 28, 1933
P-55	Vredenburgh	Company 479	June 25, 1933
P-57	Glencoe	Company 2423-V-C	July 17, 1933
		Company 444	July 17, 1934
P-58	Clayton	Company 1432-C	June 23, 1933
P-59	Northport	Company 465-C	June 22, 1933
P-60	Chatom	Company 2420-V	July 18, 1933
P-61	Bay Minette	Company 484	June 25, 1933
P-62	Bessemer	Company 487	June 24, 1933
P-63	Jackson	Company 1415-C	June 29, 1933
P-73	York	Company 467	June 2, 1933
P-75	Chapman	Company 4434-C	July 15, 1935
P-76	Vredenburgh	Company 4435-C	September 20, 1938
P-77	Uriah	Company 1485	May 1, 1939
		Company 3477-C	July 11, 1941
P-78	Brewton	Company 4434-C	December 3, 1939
P-79	Robertsdale	Company 1490	July 2, 1940
P-80	Dadeville	Company 5488	July 6, 1940
P-81	Bessemer	Company 3490	August 8, 1940

State Forest Projects

S-51	Oxford	Company 468	June 3, 1933
S-52	Chunchula	Company 1485	June 14, 1933
S-53	Florala	Company 1483	June 15, 1933
S-56	Townley	Company 467	June 2, 1933
S-62	Bessemer	Company 487	December 1933

Army

Army-1	Ft. McClellan	Company 475-C	June 23, 1933
Army-2	Ft. McClellan	Company 475-C	February 3, 1936
Army-1	Ft. McClellan	Company 4407-C	October 25, 1937

Biological Survey

BS-1	Hartselle	Company 3403	October 3, 1939

Appendix B. CCC Camps in Alabama by Enlistment Period

First Period, April 1–September 30, 1933

National Forest	3 Camps
State Forest	5 Camps
Private Forest	6 Camps
Private Erosion	2 Camps
State Park	1 Camp
Army	1 Camp
Total	18 Camps

Second Period, October 1, 1933–March 31, 1934

National Forest	4 Camps
State Forest	5 Camps
Private Forest	7 Camps
Private Erosion	2 Camps
Army	1 Camp
TVA (Forestry)	5 Camps
State Park	4 Camps
Total	28 Camps

Third Period, April 1–September 30, 1934

National Forest	4 Camps
State Forest	3 Camps
Private Forest	7 Camps

Private Erosion	2 Camps
State Park	6 Camps
Army	1 Camp
TVA (Forestry)	2 Camps
TVA (State Park)	3 Camps
Soil Erosion Service	2 Camps
Total	30 Camps

Fourth Period, October 1, 1934–March 31, 1935

National Forest	2 Camps
State Forest	1 Camps
Private Forest	3 Camps
Private Erosion	1 Camps
State Park	8 Camps
Army	1 Camp
TVA (Forestry)	2 Camps
TVA (State Park)	3 Camps
Soil Erosion Service	3 Camps
Total	24 Camps

Fifth Period, April 1–September 30, 1935

National Forest	6 Camps
State Forest	1 Camps
Private Forest	4 Camps
State Park	11 Camps
Army	2 Camp
TVA (Forestry)	8 Camps
TVA (State Park)	4 Camps
Soil Conservation Service	13 Camps
Total	49 Camps

Sixth Period, October 1, 1935–March 31, 1936

National Forest	6 Camps
State Forest	1 Camps

Private Forest	4 Camps
State Park	11 Camps
Army	1 Camp
TVA (Forestry)	6 Camps
TVA (State Park)	3 Camps
Soil Conservation Service	12 Camps
Total	44 Camps

Seventh Period, April 1–September 30, 1936

No record in the Camp Directories for Alabama, National Archives records.

Eighth Period, October 1, 1936–March 31, 1937

National Forest	5 Camps
State Forest	1 Camp
Private Forest	3 Camps
State Park	9 Camps
Army	1 Camp
TVA (Forestry)	5 Camps
TVA (State Park)	3 Camps
Soil Conservation Service	11 Camps
Total	38 Camps

Ninth Period, April 1–September 30, 1937
No record in the Camp Directories for Alabama, National Archives records.

Tenth Period, October 1, 1937–March 31, 1938

	1-1-38	*4-1-38*	*6-1-38*
National Forest	5 Camps	4 Camps	3 Camps
State Forest	1 Camp	1 Camp	1 Camp
Private Forest	3 Camps	3 Camps	2 Camps
State Park	6 Camps	5 Camps	5 Camps
Army	1 Camp	0 Camps	0 Camps
TVA (Forestry)	5 Camps	5 Camps	3 Camps
Soil Conservation Service	10 Camps	10 Camps	9 Camps
Total	31 Camps	28 Camps	23 Camps

Eleventh Period, April 1–September 30, 1938 (Revised)

National Forest	4 Camps
State Forest	1 Camp
Private Forest	2 Camps
State Park	6 Camps
TVA (Forestry)	5 Camps
Soil Conservation Service	10 Camps
Total	28 Camps

Twelfth Period, October 1, 1938–March 31, 1939

National Forest	4 Camps
State Forest	1 Camp
Private Forest	2 Camps
State Park	7 Camps
TVA (Forestry)	4 Camps
Soil Conservation Service	9 Camps
Total	27 Camps

Thirteenth Period, April 1–September 30, 1939

National Forest	4 Camps
Private Forest	3 Camps
State Park	7 Camps
TVA (Forestry)	4 Camps
Soil Conservation Service	9 Camps
Total	27 Camps

Fourteenth Period, October 1, 1939–March 31, 1940

National Forest	4 Camps
Private Forest	3 Camps
State Park	7 Camps
TVA (Forestry)	4 Camps
Soil Conservation Service	9 Camps
Biological Survey	1 Camp
Total	28 Camps

Fifteenth Period, April 1–September 30, 1940

National Forest	4 Camps
Private Forest	6 Camps
State Park	7 Camps
TVA (Forestry)	4 Camps
Soil Conservation Service	9 Camps
Biological Survey	1 Camp
Total	31 Camps

Sixteenth Period, October 1, 1940–March 31, 1941

National Forest	4 Camps
Private Forest	6 Camps
State Park	7 Camps
TVA (Forestry)	4 Camps
Soil Conservation Service	9 Camps
Fish and Wildlife Service	1 Camp
Total	31 Camps

Seventeenth Period, April 1–September 30, 1941

National Forest	3 Camps
Private Forest	6 Camps
State Park	5 Camps
TVA (Forestry)	3 Camps
Soil Conservation Service	9 Camps
Fish and Wildlife Service	1 Camp
Total	27 Camps

Eighteenth Period, October 1, 1941–March 31, 1942

National Forest	3 Camps
Private Forest	4 Camps
State Park	4 Camps
TVA (Forestry)	3 Camps
Soil Conservation Service	7 Camps
Fish and Wildlife Service	1 Camp
Total	22 Camps

Nineteenth Period, April 1–June 30, 1942

National Forest	1 Camp
Private Forest	1 Camp
TVA (Forestry)	1 Camps
Soil Conservation Service	3 Camps
National Defense (TVA/FS)	1 Camp
National Defense (SCS)	1 Camp
Total	8 Camps

Source: *CCC Camp Directory for Alabama*

Appendix C. CCC Camp Newspapers in Alabama

???	Co. 4448	Auburn	Camp SP-12	1936
4435 Flash	Co. 4435	Brundidge	Camp SCS-4	1936–1938
Advocate	Co. 4436	Greenville	Camp SCS-10	1936
Baldwin Bawls	Co. 484	Bay Minette	Camp P-61	1935
Big Bee	Co. 476	Gainesville	Camp SCS-1	1936–1937
Bull Thrower	Co. 5401	Athens	Camp TVA-6	1935–1937
Bullard Bombshell	Co. 1405	Dadeville	Camp SCS-2	1936–1938
Camp Beacon	Co. 472	Fort Payne	Camp SP-5	1935
Camp Clay Broadcast	Co. 3486	Huntsville	Camp SP-16	1937–1938
Camp Clay Crier	Co. 3486	Huntsville	Camp TVA-P-13	1936–1937
Camp Hart Mirror	Co. 1405	Dadeville	Camp SCS-2	1934
Camp Jester	Co. 487	Bessemer	Camp SP-8	1935–1936
Carver Outlook	Co. 3477	Heflin	Camp F-6	1936
Cedar Creek Courier	Co. 5412	Citronelle	Camp SP-11	1937
Chatham Chatter	Co. 2420	Chatom	Camp P-60	1935
Chattahoochee Chatter	Co. 4449	Gordon	Camp SP-13	1936–1937
Cheaha Echoes	Co. 468	Oxford	Camp SP-2	1935
Chewacla Echo	Co. 4448	Auburn	Camp SP-12	1936–1937
Chunchula Siren	Co. 1485	Chunchula	Camp S-52	1935
Clanchiala Bugler	Co. 3481	Clanton	Camp SCS-7	1937
Clarion	Supply	Ft. McClellan	Dist. "D" Supply	1934–1936
Dope	Co. 4437	Linden	Camp SCS-11	1936
Flag Mountain News	4498	Weogufka	Camp SP-4	1935
Gulf Breeze	Co. 1425	Foley	Camp SP-6	1936–1938
John Roger News	Co. 476	Gainesville	Camp SCS-1	1935
Mail Bag	Co. 4436	Greenville	Camp SCS-10	1938
Mess Kit	Co. 4436	Greenville	Camp SCS-10	1936
Messenger	Co. 1432	Clayton	Camp P-58	1935

Monte Sano Broadcast	Co. 3486	Huntsville	Camp SP-16	1938
Monte Sano Broadcast	Co. 5402	Huntsville	Camp TVA-12	1936–1937
New Deal	Co. 3479	Carrollton	Camp SCS-5	1938
Open Pond Breeze	Co. 3474	Andalusia	Camp F-9	1937
Reflector	Co. 260	Weogufka	Camp SP-4	1934–1935
S.C.S. Sentinel	Co. 4436	Greenville	Camp SCS-10	1938
Sanford News	Co. 4447	Auburn	Camp SCS-9	1936–1938
See See See	Co. 251	Wilson Dam	Camp TVA-P-4	1935
Siren	Co. 1485	Chunchula	Camp S-52	1935–1936
Tower	Co. 1432	Uriah	Camp SP-3	1936–1937
Two Spot	Co. 4434	Chapman	Camp P-75	1936–1937
Valley Creek News	Co. 444	Selma	Camp SP-10	1936–1937
William Spratt News	Co. 467	York	Camp P-73	1935–1937
Wilson Dam Spillway	Co. 4499	Wilson Dam	Camp TVA-13	1936

Bibliography

Newspapers

The following newspapers are archived at the Alabama Department of Archives and History, Montgomery, either on microfilm or as original bound newspapers.

Andalusia News, various dates 1937
Andalusia Star, January 1935–July 1942
Ashland Progress, January 1935–December 1936
Birmingham Post, September–December 1937
Cleburne News, May 1935–December 1940
Covington News, various dates 1937–38
Decatur Daily, September 1939–June 1940
Democrat-Reporter, Marengo County, May 1935–July 1942
Dothan Eagle, August 1939–March 1940, October–November 1941
Evergreen Courant, May 1940–April 1942
Florala News, April 1933–December 1934
Florence Herald, September 1933–December 1936
Gadsden Times, March 1933–December 1934
Haleyville Spotlight, January 1937–November 1939
Montgomery Advertiser, April–December 1933, July–September 1934, January–June 1938, January–February, May–July 1942
Moulton Advertiser, January 1933–August 1942
Our Mountain Home, Talladega County, January 1935–August 1942
The Onlooker, Baldwin County, March 1933–June 1942
Piedmont Journal, August 1934–August 1942
Progressive Age, Scottsboro, October 1933–July 1942
Roanoke Leader, January 1940–June 1942
Sheffield Standard, September 1933–December 1936
Shelby County Democrat, March 1933–December 1941
Shelby County Reporter, January 1935–December 1937
Tuscaloosa News, October 1933–June 1935, January 1938–August 1942
Union Banner, Chilton County, January 1935–July 1938

CCC Camp Newspapers

The following CCC Camp Newspapers were on microfiche, obtained from the "CCC Camp Newspaper Guide" at the Center for Research Libraries, University of Chicago (listed by order of company number).

"Reflector," Civilian Conservation Corps Company 260, Camp SP-4, Weogufka, Alabama. 2nd December issue, 1934; 1st February issue, 2nd February issue, 2nd April issue, 1st May issue Memorial Day issue, Fourth of July issue, September 1935.

"Cheaha Echoes," Civilian Conservation Corps Company 468, Camp SP-2, Oxford, Alabama. August 16, 1935.

"Camp Beacon," Civilian Conservation Corps Company 472, Camp SP-5, Fort Payne, Alabama. April 19, May 10, 24, June 7, July 19, August 2, 17, 1935.

"Camp Jester," Civilian Conservation Corps Company 487, Camp SP-8, Bessemer, Alabama. 1st May issue, 2nd May issue (May 15), 1st June issue (June 1), December 1935; May 28, 1936.

"Wabama News, Alabama in Wawona," Civilian Conservation Corps Company 487, Camp YNP-7, Wawona, California. December 18, 25, 1937; January 1, 17, 24, 1938.

"Open Pond Breeze," Civilian Conservation Corps Company 3474, Camp F-9, Andalusia, Alabama. January 25, February, March 1937.

"Carver Outlook," Civilian Conservation Corps Company 3477, Camp F-6, Heflin, Alabama. February 12, March 31, November 23, 1936.

"Camp Clay Crier," Civilian Conservation Corps Company 3486, Camp TVA-13-P, Huntsville, Alabama. March 14, May 9, 23, June 6, 17, July 4, August 15, September 18, October 18, 30, 1936; January 26, 1937.

"Camp Clay Broadcast," Civilian Conservation Corps Company 3486, Camp SP-16, Huntsville, Alabama. August 7, October 15, November 25, December 16, 1937; January 25, 1938.

"Monte Sano Broadcast," Civilian Conservation Corps Company 3486, Camp SP-16, Huntsville, Alabama. February 25, April 20, 1938.

"The Mess Kit," Civilian Conservation Corps Company 4436, Camp SCS-10, Greenville, Alabama. April 15, May 1, June 1, July 1, August 15, September 15, October 15, December 15, 1936; January 15, 1937.

"At the Camp, Activities at the Greenville CCC Camp, A Column Conducted by the Camp Educational Advisor." Civilian Conservation Corps Company 4436. Column appearing in the *Greenville Advocate*, July 10, 17, 24, 31, 1936.

S.C.S. Sentinel, Civilian Conservation Corps Company 4436, Camp SCS-10, Greenville, Alabama. April 30, May 31, June 30, 1938.

"The Mail Bag," Civilian Conservation Corps Company 4436, Camp SCS-10, Greenville, Alabama. August, September, October, November, December 1938.

"The Dope," Civilian Conservation Corps Company 4437, Camp SCS-11, Linden, Alabama. March, April 1936.

"Monte Sano Broadcast," Civilian Conservation Corps Company 5402, Camp TVA-12-P, Huntsville, Alabama. May 20, June 25, July 31, September 22, 1936; February 1937.

Civilian Conservation Corps Company and District Annuals

C.C.C. Company 487, Camp Ala., S-62, Bessemer, 1933–1934. Birmingham: Alabama Engraving Company, 1934.
Memories of District D, Civilian Conservation Corps, 1934. Civilian Conservation Corps. Little Rock: Typography and Presswork by Parke-Harper Company, Engravings by Peerless Engraving Company, 1934.
Memories of District E, Civilian Conservation Corps, 1934. Civilian Conservation Corps. Little Rock: Typography and Presswork by Parke-Harper Company, Engravings by Peerless Engraving Company, 1934.
Memories of District G, Civilian Conservation Corps, 1934. Civilian Conservation Corps. Little Rock: Typography and Presswork by Parke-Harper Company, Engravings by Peerless Engraving Company, 1934.
Official Annual of District E Fourth Corps Area, 1935. Civilian Conservation Corps. Baton Rouge, Louisiana: Presswork and Typography by Ramires-Jones Printing Company, Baton Rouge, Louisiana. Engravings by Shreveport Engraving Company, Shreveport, Louisiana. Published by Direct Advertising Company, 1935.
Official Annual of District D Fourth Corps Area, 1936. Civilian Conservation Corps. Baton Rouge, Louisiana: Presswork and Typography by Ruralist Press, Inc., Atlanta, Georgia. Engravings by Shreveport Engraving Company, Shreveport, Louisiana. Published by Direct Advertising Company, 1936.
Official Annual of District G Fourth Corps Area, 1936. Civilian Conservation Corps. Baton Rouge, Louisiana: Presswork and Typography by Ruralist Press, Inc., Atlanta, Georgia. Engravings by Shreveport Engraving Company, Shreveport, Louisiana. Published by Direct Advertising Company, 1936.
Official Annual, Civilian Conservation Corps, C District CCC, Fourth Corps Area, 1937. Civilian Conservation Corps. Baton Rouge, Louisiana: Published by Direct Advertising Company, 1937.
Official Annual 1937, CCC, District H IV Corps Area. Civilian Conservation Corps. Baton Rouge, Louisiana: Published by Direct Advertising Company, 1937.
Official Annual, Civilian Conservation Corps, District D CCC, Fourth Corps Area, 1938, Civilian Conservation Corps. Baton Rouge, Louisiana: Published by Army and Navy Publishing Company, February 1, 1938.
Fresno District, Civilian Conservation Corps, 9th Corps Area, Headquarters: Fresno California, January 1938. Civilian Conservation Corps. Portions obtained from the Yosemite National Park Research Library
Official Annual, Medford District, Civilian Conservation Corps, 9th Corps Area, 1938. Civilian Conservation Corps. Portions obtained from the Rouge River National Forest, Medford, Oregon.

Miscellaneous CCC Documents

"Special Order No. 82," from the Headquarters of Company 2403, Camp P-54, Brewton, Alabama. June 30, 1934. Copy of order provided by Mr. Gordon Wright, son of Jesse C. Wright, Enrollee, Company 2403.

Archived Sources

Alabama Department of Conservation. 1944. *CCC Administration Files*. Alabama Department of Archives and History. Record Group RC 2, Montgomery.

Civilian Conservation Corps. *Camp Inspection Reports*, Alabama, 1933–1942. National Archives and Records Service, Record Group No. 35, Washington, D.C.

——. *Camp Educational Reports*, Alabama, 1933–1942. National Archives and Records Service, Record Group No. 35, Washington D.C.

——. *CCC Camp Directory*, Alabama, 1933–1942. National Archives and Records Service, Record Group No. 35, Washington, D.C.

——. *Historical Record of CCC Camp Buildings*, Alabama, 1933–1942. National Archives and Records Service, Record Group No. 77, Washington, D.C

——. *National Park Service Narrative Reports*, Alabama, 1933–1942. National Archives and Records Service, Record Group No. 79, Washington D.C.

U.S. Department of Agriculture, Forest Service. "Frank W. Rasor, Forest Supervisor, to Mrs. Marie Owen Bankhead, Alabama Department of Archives and History." Letter dated November 19, 1945. USDA Forest Service Files, Montgomery, Alabama.

U.S. Department of Interior, Fish and Wildlife Service. Quarterly Narrative Reports, August 1939–April 1943. Wheeler Wildlife Refuge, Decatur, Alabama.

Walter B. Jones Photograph Collection. The University of Alabama Museum of Natural History, The University of Alabama, Tuscaloosa.

Papers of Walter B. Jones. Alabama Collection, The Hoole Library, The University of Alabama, Tuscaloosa.

Research Papers and Special Studies

Burleson, David A. 1975. "Alabama's State Park System." Master's thesis, Auburn University, Auburn, Alabama.

Gunnels, Robert D. 1990. "The Civilian Conservation Corps in Alabama." Master's thesis, Auburn University, Auburn, Alabama.

Horn, Jennifer M. 2002. "History and Historical Resources Survey of the Civilian Conservation Corps at Cheaha State Park and Surrounding Talladega National Forest." Master's thesis, Jacksonville State University, Jacksonville, Alabama.

Medlock, O. C. 1985. "Alabama Soil and Water Conservation, The First 50 Years: 1935–1985." USDA Soil Conservation Service, in-house publication

Books and Publications

Alabama Relief Administration. 1935. *Two Years of Federal Relief in Alabama.* Wetumpka: Wetumpka Printing Company.

Baklanoff, Joy D., and Arthur F. Howington. 1989. *The Mounds Awaken: Mound State Monument and the Civilian Conservation Corps.* The University of Alabama State Museum of Natural History, Special Publications No. 3. October.

Cohen, Stan. 1980. *The Tree Army, A Pictorial History of the Civilian Conservation Corps, 1933–1942.* Missoula, Montana: Pictorial Histories Publishing Company.

Ermentrout, Robert Allan. 1982. *The Forgotten Men, The Civilian Conservation Corps.* Smithtown, New York, Exposition Press.

Evison, Herbert. 1939. "Unique Archaeological Museum Completed." *The Regional Review* 2, 5 (May):2–8. Published by the Department of Interior, National Park Service, Region One, Richmond.

Garrison, Ellen. 2001. "Walter B. Jones and Moundville." *Alabama Heritage* (Summer):6–17. Published by The University of Alabama and The University of Alabama at Birmingham.

Hoyt, Ray. 1935. *"We Can Take It": A Short Story of the C.C.C.* New York: American Book Company.

Ickes, Harold L. 1953. *The Secret Diary of Harold L. Ickes, The First Thousand Days, 1933–1936.* New York: Simon and Schuster.

Lacy, Leslie Alexander. 1976. *The Soil Soldiers, The Civilian Conservation Corps in the Great Depression.* Randor, Pennsylvania: Chilton Book Company.

Leuchtenburg, William E. 1963. *Franklin D. Roosevelt and the New Deal.* New York: Harper and Row, Publishers.

Lyon, Edwin A. 1996. *A New Deal for Southeastern Archaeology.* Tuscaloosa: The University of Alabama Press.

McElvaine, Robert S. 1993. *The Great Depression, America, 1929–1941.* New York: Times Books.

Merrill, Perry H. 1981. *Roosevelt's Forest Army, A History of the Civilian Conservation Corps, 1933–1942.* Montpelier, Vermont: Perry H. Merrill.

Resettlement Administration. 1936. *First Annual Report, Resettlement Administration.* Washington: U.S. Government Printing Office.

Schlesinger, Arthur M., Jr. 1958. *The Coming of the New Deal, The Age of Roosevelt.* Boston: Houghton Mifflin Company.

State of Alabama. 1944. *Annual Report, Department of Conservation, State of Alabama. October 1, 1942–September 30, 1943.* Wetumpka, Alabama: Wetumpka Printing Company.

Watkins, T. H. 1993. *The Great Depression, America in the 1930s.* Boston: Little Brown and Company.

———. 1999. *The Hungry Years: A Narrative History of the Great Depression in America.* New York: Henry Holt and Company, 1999.

Works Progress Administration. 1936. *Landlord and Tenant on the Cotton Planta-*

tion. Washington: Works Progress Administration Division of Social Research, Monograph 5. T. J. Woofter, Jr. Coordinator of Rural Research.

Works Progress Administration. 2000. *The WPA Guide to 1930s Alabama*. (Originally published in 1941 as *Alabama: A Guide to the Deep South* by the Alabama State Planning Commission, compiled by workers of the Writers' Program of the Works Project Administration in the State of Alabama, in the American Guide Series.) New Introduction by Harvey H. Jackson III. Tuscaloosa: The University of Alabama Press, 2000.

Websites and Article Sources

Decatur, Morgan County, Alabama, Convention & Visitor Bureau. *Wheeler Wildlife Refuge*. <http://www.decaturcvb.org.> (December 7, 2002).

NACCCA Database. National Association of CCC Alumni. <http://www.cccalumni.org.> (February 23, 2001).

National Park Service. *The Civilian Conservation Corps and the National Park Service, 1933–1942: An Administrative History*. Appendix C. <http://www.nps.gov/history/history/online_books/ccc/cccacl.htm> (April 5, 2003).

Tennessee Valley Authority. <http://www.tva.gov.> (April 12, 2002).

University of Chicago, Center for Research Libraries. <http://wwwcrl.uchicago.edu.> (January 4, 2002).

United States Fish & Wildlife Service. <http://www.fws.gov.> (December 7, 2002).

Index of Names

Allgood, Miles C. (Congressman), 189
Allison, Colonel E. F. (Allison Lumber Company, conservationist), 197
Almon, Edward B. (Representative from Lawrence County): discusses reforestation program with President, 13; asks for CCC camps in Alabama National Forest, 35

Bankhead, Mrs. Marie Owens (Alabama Department of Archives and History), 40
Bankhead, William B. (Representative from Alabama): asks for CCC camps in Alabama National Forest, 13, 35
Bennett, Dr. Hugh H. (Chief of SCS), 63
Bethune, Mary McLeod (Director, NYA's Division of Negro Affairs), 11
Black, Hugo (Senator), 130, 161, 189
Bradfield, Henry (CCC enrollee, saves fellow enrollee), 36
Brandon, William W. (Governor of Alabama), 114
Bunker, Colonel Page S. (Alabama State Forester): submits initial work plans to Washington, 13, 15, 16; private land projects clarified, 17, 102, 161, 173, 181, 193

De Priest, Oscar (Congressman, R-Illinois): asks for amendment to Emergency Conservation Work Act, 13
Dixon, Frank M. (Governor of Alabama), 115
Duncan, Dr. L. N. (President of Alabama Polytechnic Institute, Auburn), 65, 71
Dunn, Miss Loula (Alabama State Welfare Director), 25, 29

Evison, Herbert (National Park Service): describes museum at Moundville, 166

Fechner, Robert (Director of CCC): nominated as Director, 13, 14, 15, 17, 21, 22, 23, 25, 26; death, 27, 36, 95, 96, 114, 119, 131, 162, 164, 167; visits Moundville for dedication of museum, 166; closes Motion Picture Laboratory, 167

Gallagher, Dr. Buell Gordon (President of Talladega College), 54
Grant, George (Congressman), 79, 202
Graves, Bibb (Governor of Alabama), 10, 114; visits Gulf Shores Park, 135, 137
Greene, William (President of American Federation of Labor): comments on CCC, 12–13

Hartman, A. W. (Regional CCC Officer, Atlanta, GA), 33, 34
Hill, O. V. (Talladega County Agent, Extension Service), 76
Hobbs, Sam F. (Congressman), 71
Holt, Thad (Director, Alabama State Relief Administration), 6, 8, 14, 17, 21
Hopkins, Harry (Director, Federal Emergency Relief Administration), 6; director of the Works Progress Administration, 9

Howard, Colonel Milford W. (Former Congressman): makes charges against Project Superintendent Phillips, Camp SP-5, 130

Ickes, Harold L. (Director, Public Works Administration), 7–8

Jones, Walter B. (State Geologist, Director, Alabama State Museum of Natural Science): explores cave in Monte Sano Mountain, 99; supervises beetle project at Camp TVA-P-13, Monte Sano, 101; appointed Director of Department of Conservation, 115, 181; excavates flexed burial at Gulf Shores Park, 137, 139; purchases Moundville Archaeological Site, 160, 161–62; wife Hazel trains enrollees, 161, 163–64, 166

Kenlan, Charles H. (Assistant to CCC Director James J. McEntee), 156, 167
King, General E. L. (Fourth Corps Area Commanding Officer), 19

MacArthur, General Douglas (Chief of Staff of Army): addresses Congress denying Emergency Conservation Work is "draft act," 13
Mallory, James Milton (Regent, Alabama Museum of Natural History): supports full CCC camp at Moundville, 161–62; defends work at Moundville to CCC Director Fechner, 162; suggests Director Fechner should be invited to Moundville Museum Dedication, 164
McEntee, James J. (Assistant to CCC Director Fechner): selected as Director upon Fechner's death, 27, 28, 31, 32, 132, 151, 167, 190
McNutt, Paul V. (Head of Federal Security Agency), 31, 32

Oliver, William B. (Congressman), 160–61, 197

Perkins, Frances (Secretary of Labor): addresses Congress on wages, 12

Razor, Frank W. (Forest Supervisor, NF's in Alabama): letter regarding Hubbard's Plantation House, Camp F-3, 40; visits Talladega National Forest, 53
Roosevelt, Franklin Delano: asks Congress for a civilian conservation corps program, 1; organizational style, 1; New Deal offers hope to nation, 5; Creates the Civil Works Administration, 8; State of Union Message, 1935, 8; Signs Emergency Relief Appropriation Act of 1935, 8; creates Resettlement Administration, 9; Creates Works Progress Administration, 9; meets to discuss Emergency Conservation Work, 12; establishes Emergency Conservation Work, 12–13; appoints CCC Advisory Board, 13; signs Emergency Conservation Work Act, 13; consolidates CCC with the NYA, 31; signs Tennessee Valley Authority Act, 81; visits Wheeler Dam Park, 85, 122, 137

Starnes, Joe (Congressman), 48
Stuart, Mayor R. Y. (Chief of US Forest Service): asks for amendment to Emergency Conservation Work Act, 12; meets with state foresters, 13, 35

Toler, Brooks (Chief of Department of Forestry, Alabama), 29
Tugwell, Rexford (Under Secretary of Agriculture, Director of Resettlement Administration), 9

Wallace, Henry (Secretary of Agriculture): terminates Resettlement Administration, 9
White, F. M. (Clay County Agent, Extension Service), 59, 71
Williams, Aubrey (Director of National Youth Administration), 10, 11
Winch, Mr. (Marengo County Agent, Extension Service), 59

Index of Places

Alabama National Forest, 13, 16, 35, 42, 95, 107

Alabama State Parks: Bromley, 114; Cedar Creek, 115, 151–53, 158; Chattahoochie, 115, 156–57, 158; Cheaha, 114, 115, 117–19, 133, 141–43, 150, 176–79; Chewacla, 114, 115, 153–56, 158; Chickasaw, 115, 157–60; DeSoto, 114, 115, 127–33, 140, 179–180; Fort Toulouse, 114; Gulf, 114, 115, 133–40; The Lagoons, 114; Little River, 115, 119–20, 164; Monte Sano, 114, 115, 169–75; Mound State Monument, 112, 140, 145, 146, 147, 149, 160–69; Muscle Shoals and Wilson Parks (TVA), 115; Oak Mountain, 115, 143–47; Panther Creek, 114. *See also* Geneva State Park; Salt Springs State Park; Talladega County State Park; Valley Creek Regional Park; Weogufka State Park; Wheeler Regional Park

Anniston Army Depot, 77

Black Warrior National Forest, 19, 42, 43, 97

Blue Pond Plantation, Conecuh National Forest, 45, 104

Brushy Creek Recreation Area, Alabama National Forest, 43, 44

Cedar Creek State/Regional Park, 115, 151–53, 158

Chandler Springs, Talladega National Forest, 52, 53, 55, 106, 142, 176

Chattahoochie State/Regional Park, 115, 156–57, 158

Cheaha State Park, 13, 50, 114, 115, 117–19, 133, 141–43, 150, 176–79

Cheatham Knob, Alabama National Forest, 35–37

Chewacla State Park, 114, 115, 153–56, 158

Chickasaw State/Regional Park, 115, 157–60

Conecuh National Forest, 20, 44; Conecuh Purchase Unit, 44, 104, 105

Desoto State Park, 114, 115, 127–33, 140, 179–80

Devil's Den Recreation Area, Talladega National Forest, 54, 55, 56

Flagg Mountain, 13, 122, 124

Fort Barrancas, Florida, 15, 135, 182, 185, 187

Fort Benning, Georgia, 15, 38, 39, 60, 65, 70, 120, 136, 191, 196, 197

Fort Bragg, North Carolina, 15, 83

Fort Dix, New Jersey, Second Corps Area, 40, 41, 82, 87, 88, 121, 123

Fort McClellan, Alabama, 6, 14, 15, 29, 35, 37, 44, 59, 60, 61, 83, 84, 91, 93, 115, 122, 127, 140, 142, 143, 146, 177, 178, 185, 187, 192, 194, 195, 197, 204–7

Fort McPherson, Georgia, 15, 62

Fort Morgan, Alabama: transient camp, 6; side camp from Camp SP-6, 139

Fort Moultrie, South Carolina, 15, 148

Fort Oglethorpe, Georgia, 15, 78, 80, 84, 133

Fort Screven, Georgia, 15

Fourth Corps Area, 15, 23, 24, 25, 29, 34, 69, 177, 200, 204

Geneva State Park, 114, 115, 133–40
Gulf State Park, 114, 115, 133–40
Guntersville Lake, 91

Hubbard Plantation House: used as Camp F-3 headquarters, 38; burns to ground, 39–40

Joe Wheeler Dam, 84, 86, 207
Joe Wheeler Pool Migratory Waterfowl Refuge, 92, 210
Joe Wheeler Reservation, 30

Kinlock Springs, Alabama National Forest, 10, 38, 39

Lake Chinnabee Recreation Area, Talladega National Forest, 57
Little River Regional Park, 114, 115, 119–20, 164

Monte Sano Park, TVA, 89, 90, 98, 100, 103, 104
Monte Sano State Park, 19, 115, 169–75
Motion Picture Laboratory, Department of the Interior, 167
Mound State Monument, 112, 140, 145, 146, 147, 149, 160–69
Moundville Archaeological Park, 160
Mount Olive, Alabama National Forest, 38, 39
Muscle Shoals and Wilson Parks (TVA), 86, 115

Napier Field, Dothan, Alabama, 33, 75
Natural Bridge Picnic Grounds, Alabama National Forest, 43
Nitrate Plant No. 1, 81, 84
Nitrate Plant No. 2, 81–84, 87, 88

Oak Mountain Recreation Demonstration Area, 10, 145, 147, 156
Oak Mountain State Park, 115, 144–47
Open Pond Recreation Area, Conecuh National Forest, 20, 46–47

Panther Creek Regional Park, 115. *See also* Geneva State Park
Pea Vine Falls, Oak Mountain State Park, 146, 147
Plattsburg Barracks, New York, Second Corps Area, 40, 120, 133, 136

St. Stephens State Park, 13, 114
Salt Springs State Park, Clarke County (Proposed), 148
Sipsey River Picnic Grounds, Alabama National Forest, 43
Skyway Motorway, Talladega National Forest, 49, 52, 53, 55, 56, 57
Sumter State Park, 13, 114

Talladega County State Park, 114
Talladega National Forest, 48; Talladega Purchase Unit, 48, 51, 54, 106, 142, 143, 177

Valley Creek Regional Park, 115, 148–50

Weogufka State Park, 13, 111, 115, 120–27
Wheeler Regional Park (Proposed TVA), 115
Wheeler Wildlife Refuge, 207
Wilson Dam, 83, 84, 86, 87, 98, 208
Wilson Dam Nursery, 83

Index of Topics

Advisory Board/Council, CCC, 13, 32, 156
Age limits, CCC, 14, 21; lowered with the Civilian Conservation Corps Act, 1937, 23
Agricultural Adjustment Administration (AAA), 2, 5; found unconstitutional, 7
Alabama, Great Flood of March 1929, 3
Alabama Department of Agriculture, 5
Alabama Department of Conservation: Division of Forestry, 29, 30, 181, 186; Department of Conservation Act signed, 115, 164, 181
Alabama Museum of Natural History: excavates flexed burial at Gulf Shores Park, 137; begins work at Moundville, 160, 165
Alabama Polytechnic Institute (API, Auburn), 65, 153, 155, 188
Alabama Relief Administration, 5–6, 14, 17
Alabama state budget: 1927, 3; 1932, 5
Alabama State Commission of Forestry, 21, 22, 114, 116, 158, 181
Alabama State Department of Welfare, 22, 74
Alabama State Land Act, 114
Alabama State Park Committee, 114
Alabama State Public Works Administration, 7
Alphabet Agencies, 1, 8; overlapping responsibilities, 1
Army Air Corps Advanced Flying School, Napier Field, Dothan, Alabama, 75

Bank closures in Alabama, 3
Bankhead-Jones Farm Tenancy Act of 1937, 9
Biological Survey, 92
Boll Weevil, 4
Bureau of Biological Survey, 207–8

Civilian Conservation Corps Act, 1937, 2, 23, 24
Civilian Conservation Corps (CCC) camps: description, 14
Central Repair Shop, Talladega, 31, 55, 72
Civil Works Administration (CWA), 2, 7, 8
Communistic Propaganda, 190–91
Cotton Prices and Production, Alabama, 4
Cotton Reduction Program, 6
County Agents, Extension Service: Mr. Fant, Chilton County, 63; Mr. O. V. Hill, Talladega County, 76; Mr. C. M. Ling, Houston County, 73, 74; Mr. M. D. Thomason, Dale County, 74; Mr. F. M. White, Clay County, 59, 71; Mr. Winch, Marengo County, 59

Educational Program: established in CCC, 18; Educational Advisors meet in Montgomery, 19, 23, 24, 26
Elk River Fish Hatchery, 89, 212, 213
Emergency Conservation Work Act, 1, 13, 20, 21, 24
Emergency Relief Appropriation Act of 1935, 8, 9

Emergency Unemployment Relief Act, 1
Erosion, severe in Alabama: percentage of accelerated erosion in Alabama, 5, 58

Farm Mortgage Debt and Prices, 4
Farm Security Administration (FSA), 9
Federal Emergency Relief Act, 6
Federal Emergency Relief Administration (FERA), 6, 8, 19
Federal Security Agency, 2, 26, 31
Fish and Wildlife Service, 30, 92, 207, 210

Glencoe Rifle Range, Alabama National Guard, 188
Great Depression, causes of, 3

"Happy Days" (National CCC Newspaper), 132, 138, 171, 175
Health Program for CCC Enrollees, 23

Idle Women in Alabama, camps, 9–10

Juvenile Delinquency problem, national, 20

Marion Fish Hatchery, 6
Menu, Christmas and Thanksgiving meals, 18
Military Commitment of CCC enrollees, 20, 25, 27
Mound Pageant, Moundville, 164–65

National Defense Training, 28, 31, 74, 169, 203, 204, 213
National Industrial Recovery Act, 7
National Park Service, 88, 103, 114, 124, 127, 128, 131, 137, 139, 145, 146, 156, 159, 162, 166, 170
National Reemployment Service, 10, 146
National Youth Administration (NYA), 2, 10, 11, 31, 40, 153, 155

Park, Parkway, and Recreational Study Area Act, 114
Pellegra, 4
Pneumonia, CCC enrollees tested with new vaccine, 28
Polio outbreak/vaccinations, 99
Public Works Administration (PWA), 2, 7

Reconstruction Finance Corporation, 17
Red Cross lifesaving and water safety course, 20, 47
Redwood trees: giant redwood trees planted at Gulf Shores Park, 138
Relief Requirements Dropped for CCC, 23, 27
Resettlement Administration (RA), 2, 8
Rural Electrification Administration (REA), 7
Rural Rehabilitation Administration, 6

Savings program for CCC enrollees, 29
Second Corps Area: enrollees transferred from western states to the South, 18, 40, 87, 120, 123, 125
Soil Conservation Service (SCS), 30, 58, 59
Soil Erosion Service (SES): transferred to Department of Agriculture, becomes Soil Conservation Service, 58
Standard of living in Alabama, 4
State of the Union message, 1935, 8
Steel industry, 4, 11

Tenant farmers, 4, 5, 7, 9, 209
Tennessee Valley Authority Act, 81
Tennessee Valley Authority Forestry Relations Department, 91
Transients, 6

Unemployment: 1932, 3; 1941, 11; 1943, army of jobless disappear, 11; loss of pride, 4

Veterans: assisting in CCC camps as role models, 16; included into CCC, 16; typical Veteran described, 85, 177–78
Veterinarian Corps, 24

World War II: shifting focus from Great Depression to war production, 11; Pearl Harbor and US entry into war, 32
Works Progress Administration (WPA), 2, 8, 9, 52, 146, 172, 173, 207, 208, 209, 210, 211, 213
WPA Recreation Project of Madison County, 170